Methodological Approaches in Kurdish Studies

Kurdish Societies, Politics, and International Relations

Series Editor: Bahar Baser

This series strives to produce high quality academic work on Kurdish society and politics, and the international relations of Kurdish organizations and governments (Kurdistan Region of Iraq) both regionally and globally. The books in this series explore themes of contemporary relevance as well as presenting historical trajectories of the Kurdish populations. The series contributes to the rapidly growing literature on this topic with books that are original and make substantial empirical and theoretical contribution. The series' main focus are the Kurds and the social, cultural, and political environment in which Kurdish issues play out. The subjects that we are interested in include but are not limited to: the history of the Kurds, Kurdish politics and policies within Iraq, Iran, Turkey, and Syria, as well as Kurdish politics and their impact on the international relations of the Middle East. This series also publishes books on the policies of the USA, Europe, and other countries toward Kurdish movements and territories, and interdisciplinary research on Kurdish societies, religions, social movements, and the Kurdish diaspora. Lastly, our aim is to contribute to the academic literature on Kurdish culture, arts, cinema, and literature. This series speaks to audiences outside academia, and is not limited to area-studies topics. All books in this series will be peer-reviewed and demonstrate academic quality and rigor.

Titles Published

Methodological Approaches in Kurdish Studies

Theoretical and Practical Insights from the Field

Edited by
Bahar Baser, Mari Toivanen, Begum Zorlu,
and Yasin Duman

LEXINGTON BOOKS
Lanham • Boulder • New York • London

Published by Lexington Books
An imprint of The Rowman & Littlefield Publishing Group, Inc.
4501 Forbes Boulevard, Suite 200, Lanham, Maryland 20706
www.rowman.com

6 Tinworth Street, London SE11 5AL, United Kingdom

British Library Cataloguing in Publication Information Available

The hardback edition of this book was previously catalogued by the Library of Congress as follows:

Library of Congress Cataloging-in-Publication Data

Names: Baser, Bahar, editor.
Title: Methodological approaches in Kurdish studies : theoretical and practical insights from the field / edited by Bahar Baser, Mari Toivanen, Begum Zorlu, and Yasin Duman.
Description: Lanham, Maryland : Lexington Books, 2018. | Series: Kurdish societies, politics, and international relations | Includes bibliographical references and index.
Identifiers: LCCN 2018040700 (print) | LCCN 2018046270 (ebook) | ISBN 9781498575225 (Electronic) | ISBN 9781498575232 (pbk) | ISBN 9781498575218 (cloth)
Subjects: LCSH: Kurds—Study and teaching. | Ethnology—Fieldwork. | Ethnology—Methodology.
Classification: LCC DS59.K86 (ebook) | LCC DS59.K86 M47 2018 (print) | DDC 305.891/5970072—dc23
LC record available at https://lccn.loc.gov/2018040700

To my grandparents, Naciye and Hafız Muharrem İka

BB

For my research participants

MT

To my parents, Gulê and Ûnis

YD

To my mother

BZ

Contents

Introduction

Methodological Approaches in Kurdish Studies: Politics of Fieldwork, Positionality, and Challenges Ahead

Mari Toivanen and Bahar Baser

This edited volume presents thirteen contributions that reflect upon the practical, ethical, theoretical, and methodological challenges of conducting ethnographic research in settings characterized by authoritarian tendencies, securitization policies, and tightening state control as well as conflictual interethnic relations and deteriorating security situations. They shed light to the intricacies of conducting fieldwork on highly politicized and sensitive topics, addressing both the epistemological and theoretical as well as the practical challenges related to such fieldwork. In this manner, this volume contributes and builds on the existing and rapidly increasing literature on research methods in politically sensitive and unstable contexts (Cohen and Arieli 2011; Romano 2006; Mazurana et al. 2013; Koch 2013; Art 2016; Clark and Cavatorta 2018). For instance, Mazurana et al. (2013) discuss how to adapt research methods to conflict settings and what ethical, methodological, logistical, and security challenges researchers in conflict field contexts face. Similarly, Clark and Cavatorta's (2018) recent edited volume addresses how under institutional constraints and violence scholars conduct research in the Middle East and North Africa, especially in a period of increasing authoritarianism. The contributors of this book also raise such methodological issues as ethics, trust, access, and researcher positionality, and how all those become negotiated in the course of the fieldwork. What differentiates this book from existing literature in the field is that it is the first academic endeavour that deals with methodological tendencies in Kurdish Studies in a comprehensive manner, including outsider and insider researchers' perspectives, and from a variety of disciplines including anthropology, sociology, political science, and history among others.

CONDUCTING "RISKY" FIELDWORK

The fact of completing fieldwork in conflict settings and on highly sensitive topics includes methodologically different dynamics for the researcher to consider, compared to fieldwork in nonconflict settings (Mazurana et al. 2013). This includes considering both the epistemological and theoretical implications as well as the practical and logistical ramifications conducting such "risky" fieldwork entails. Firstly, conducting fieldwork on politically sensitive topics and/or in conflict regions entails potentially physical risks for the researcher as well as the participants. For instance, for researchers, physical risks can be present when travelling to remote areas and to conflict zones, but they can also experience what is called "secondary trauma." This means that researchers might be affected by the narratives of their interviewees and by victims' narratives on violence and war crimes, especially if they are working on topics that entail postwar trauma. Researchers can also be criminalized by certain governments and become targeted by state authorities, as the recent events in Turkey reveal (Baser and Öztürk 2017). The research participants also run several risks in such contexts by agreeing to take part in the research process, which need thorough methodological reflection. The "risk management" is part of methodological design, in form of careful data collection (for instance, whether to record interviews or not) and protection (for instance, through anonymization). Furthermore, the data can change nature with time and become differently politicized depending on the time period: for instance, information provided by the interviewees during less securitized periods can later on in a more authoritarian and securitized context become a source of criminalization and hostility by the state. Also, producing knowledge in such contexts becomes a highly sensitive issue considering the stigmatizing impact it might have on the community and its members, thus raising questions of representation, visibility, and power. As such, the reflections presented in this volume provide insights to these aspects by addressing the following methodological questions:

- What methodological challenges and risks do researchers encounter when studying highly politicized phenomena and when conducting fieldwork in politically unstable circumstances?
- How do researchers navigate the power relations, risks, and the potential control by the authorities and the state?
- How can researchers adapt their research methods and approaches to politically unstable or rapidly changing environments? What associated risks are there for researchers and research participants?
- How do these aspects affect knowledge-production about the studied phenomena? What barriers to knowledge production derive from structural inequalities?

There is, indeed, an increasing focus on both the more epistemological and theoretical implications of such fieldwork, as well as on the practicalities and logistics of completing fieldwork in conflict settings. Challenges and risks are present in fieldwork conducted in conflict settings and on highly politicized topics. However, the complexity of security situations, and the atmospheres of distrust and suspicion can also lead researchers to "think outside the box" and come up with innovative and creative methodologies. In other words, researchers do not stop enquiring when security risks are involved, they just develop tactics and "work-arounds" (Art 2016). As this volume shows, on the one hand, the contributions shed light to more practical and logistical questions of conducting on-site fieldwork in areas that are politically unstable and provide innovative insights into managing the rising challenges and risks, as well as into how to access and navigate in the field. On the other hand, most fieldwork has been conducted in regions where local populations are living under constant environment of insecurity and in the midst of conflict, displacement, and resistance. Research participants often belonged to oppressed minorities and politically marginalized communities, thus raising essential questions about power relations and trust between the researcher and the participants, as well as about representation and the ethical aspects of such ethnographic fieldwork.

THE KURDISH GEOGRAPHY OF FIELDWORK

Another commonality for the contributions is namely the fact that the studied phenomena deal with Kurdish studies and that the research participants are members of different Kurdish communities in the Middle East and in diaspora. We posit that such literatures on geographies of fieldwork and on ethnography can contribute toward the more general methodological literature on conducting research in conflict settings. The Kurdish case constitutes a noteworthy case study in this regard because it is the largest stateless population in the world and it is engaged in resistance movements in four main countries of the Middle East: Iran, Iraq, Syria, and Turkey. Accordingly, contributors' fieldwork experiences are mainly situated in Iraq, Syria, and Turkey. Besides addressing questions pertinent to more general research discussions related to conducting fieldwork in conflict regions and with highly politicized topics, being the first edited volume whose contributions specifically focus on the methodological questions rising from fieldwork research conducted in Kurdish-populated regions and with Kurdish participants, the volume also contributes methodologically to the field of Kurdish studies. Although there is substantial literature on conducting research in conflict zones, "dangerous places," or in regions such as Middle East, Latin America, and Africa in general (Goodhand 2000; Wood 2006; Baird 2008; Clark and

Cavatorta 2018), to this date there exists no specific methodological article, let alone a monograph that is solely dedicated to studying the Kurdish populations and Kurdish-relates issues. Perhaps due to the sensitivity of the topic, researchers often stay aloof of reflecting on their ethnographic experience, and particularly of discussing the failures during fieldwork (Harrowell et. al. 2018), the perceived power relations (due to ethnicity, religion, or gender), and what impact these issues bear upon their work. Therefore, this volume particularly draws from contributors' everyday experiences, observations, and interactions in the field in Kurdish-populated regions to address the following questions:

- How do research positionalities shift and come to be in the politically unstable circumstances of Kurdish regions? To what extent are insider and outsider positionalities based on ethnicity, religion, or ideological affiliation in the region? To what extent are fieldwork experiences and encounters gendered?
- How to account for the ethical aspects before, during, and after fieldwork?
- How to give voice and relate to the every-day experiences of those belonging to marginalized communities and minorities?

This volume includes contributions from scholars from various interdisciplinary backgrounds, ranging from sociology and political science to social psychology and anthropology. The complexity of security situations and the atmospheres of distrust and suspicion have led the contributors to be creative and to adapt their research methods in ways that at times transcend disciplinary boundaries and conventions. Relatedly, the contributions also open the often-considered Pandora's box of discussing the failures in what is often a "messy" research field, and how to adopt one's methods to rapidly changing political circumstances. This necessitates greater reflexivity in existing power relations of the surrounding context and how those affect, not only the interaction situations between the researcher and the participants, but also the overall research process. The contributions unravel this, for instance, by unpacking positionalities beyond ethnicities, and by showing how gendered and other positionalities are constructed in fieldwork interactions. Most importantly, they are doing it in a very open and honest way: each chapter offers narratives from the field which reflect on the failures as much as on the successes, in a way that has never been done before in Kurdish Studies. Therefore, the contents of this book are essential, especially for early career researchers who are about to embark on fieldwork. In the following sections, we will first present the specificities of studying the Kurdish case in different contexts and then move forward to present the chapters that address these questions in more detail.

THE GEOGRAPHICAL AND POLITICAL
CONTEXT: THE KURDISH CASE

Kurdistan Divided

The region of Kurdistan is usually employed to refer to a land area with large Kurdish-speaking populations stretching over Turkey, Iraq, Iran, and Syria, mainly, and with smaller territories in western and central Asia.[1] The land area comprises approximately 518,000 square kilometres, which is a rough equivalent to surface of France. More precisely, the Kurdish populations reside in quite extensive areas of eastern Turkey, northern Iraq, western Iran, and northern Syria, and they form the fourth largest ethnic group in the region after Arabs, Persians, and Turks, consequently constituting rather sizeable ethnic and linguistic minorities within these four states. The estimated number of Kurds varies between 25 and 30 million (McDowall 1996; Hassanpour and Mojab 2005, 214), and the numbers are unequally divided, with Turkey having the largest Kurdish-speaking population, followed by Iran, Iraq, and Syria. In addition, many Kurds have settled outside Kurdistan. For instance, Istanbul hosts approximately 3 million Kurds and therefore can be said to be "the biggest Kurdish city."[2] The Kurdish diaspora, settled mostly in Europe and Northern America, stands around—million individuals today (Institut kurde).

Today Kurds form a rather diverse group in terms of language, religion, and political affiliation. They live both in urban or rural areas, either in the Kurdistan region, outside it in Istanbul, Bagdad, or yet Teheran, or in diaspora communities outside the Middle East (Taucher et al. 2015). To make matters more complex, the Kurds, who live in Syria, Iraq, Iran, and Turkey tend to be at least bilingual, speaking Kurdish and the official language of the country they live in. This is perhaps most noticeable in Turkey, where, because of strict assimilation policies and the prohibition of the Kurdish language until the 1990s, many Kurds nowadays speak mostly Turkish. Such historical context of political, linguistic, and other forms of oppression is still visible today, as it resonates and structures everyday interactions and inter-ethnic relations in the Kurdish regions. It also becomes visible and pertinent in fieldwork experiences, often leading to negotiations over research position-alities and trust, as observed by this volume's contributors of different ethnic and linguistic backgrounds.

What differentiates the Kurdish case from other literatures of geography, is the division of Kurdistan into four main nation-states, and the state of stateless that structures Kurdish politics, identities, and social organization both in Kurdistan and in diaspora. In this regard, it is worth mentioning two major historical developments that have been particularly significant in terms of the division of Kurdish lands. The first one dates back centuries to the Ottoman and Persian empires. Indeed, the borders between Iran, Turkey, and Iraq, where large Kurdish majorities today reside are roughly consistent with the treaty between the Ottoman and Persian empires in 1639, which divided Kurdistan into Ottoman and Iranian zones. The region of Kurdistan was situated between the Ottoman and the Persian empires from the seventeenth century till the early twentieth century, when it, alongside Armenia, was the empires' battlefield until the First World War (Hassanpour and Mojab 2005, 215–216). The second major development took place a century ago. This border that had lain between the two empires became officially fixed only in the early twentieth century. It was the time when modernist Western ideas of "territorial integrity," that is the indivisibility of the nation-states, and the colonial desires swooped over the region. In the wake of the downfall of the Ottoman Empire and in consequence of the treaties signed by colonial powers, Kurdistan was allocated to the political spaces of Turkey, Iraq, Iran, and Syria. This also meant that the subjects of premodern states, including the Kurds, had remained more or less attached to the land and tribal affiliations (*ibid.*), before ideas of a Kurdish state and "homeland" started to emerge in the early twentieth century. This division of Kurdish lands was in a sense "cemented" by a series of treaties in the early twentieth century that set the nation-states' boundaries in the Middle East for the decades to come (Ali 1997).

Therefore, the "Kurdish issue," has from the very beginning of the twentieth century been a cross-border issue, and it remains so to this date. The cross-border character of the "Kurdish issue" and the formation of Kurdish identities both in Kurdistan and in diaspora continue to be informed by the "state of statelessness" of Kurdistan. This also presents particular conditions to conduct fieldwork in the Kurdish regions that expand over different national and often conflict-ridden settings. Furthermore, Kurdish minorities have experienced minority policies varying from assimilation to genocidal measures in their respective host countries since the early twentieth century. At times, there have been outbursts of violent conflict due to the suppression of the Kurdish ethnic identity and the refusal to grant the Kurdish minorities political, cultural, and linguistic rights.

In Turkey, the conflict between the Kurdistan Worker's Party (PKK) and the Turkish state has lasted for almost four decades. The conflict developed from a low-intensity war to a full-fledged one in the 1990s. According to the Uppsala Conflict Data Program, it has resulted to almost 30,000 deaths and numerous forced disappearances. The 1990s were definitely the bloodiest ones of the conflict, until the PKK struck a unilateral cease-fire in 1999. The first decade of the millennium witnessed a relatively peaceful period in Kurdish-Turkish relations, especially compared to the previous decade.

Then, the conflict intensified again, and the imposition of curfews on Kurdish cities, the state-inflected violence and arbitrary arrests of Kurds, and court sentences under the premises of the anti-terrorism legislation have become frequent from 2014 onward. Although between 2009 and 2015, the political environment in Turkey was relatively less hostile toward Kurdish political mobilization due to the ongoing peace process, the situation has quickly deteriorated due to the authoritarian shift in Turkey (Baser and Öztürk 2017). The current situation stands in stark contrast to the beginning of the decade, since the country was experiencing a rather open political atmosphere for peace negotiations until the conflict resumed in 2015. The conflict has also caused significant Kurdish migration from Turkey to Europe over the years. The PKK is considered to be a "terrorist" organization in Turkey and in 2002, as a result of diplomatic pressure from Turkey, the PKK was added to the US' and EU's list of terrorist organizations. This situation has affected the diaspora Kurds as well and at times curtailed their mobilization patterns. They have been criminalized in many countries and the "terrorist stigma" has become an ordinary part of life, especially when the high politics between their host countries and Turkey have been at play.

The Kurdish Region in Iraq (KRI) has also suffered under various Iraqi regimes, especially during the Saddam Hussein era. Until after the 1991 Gulf War, a Kurdish nation-state never seemed feasible. However, third party interventions in the Middle East's internal and international conflicts made it possible for the Iraqi Kurdish Regional Government (KRG) to flourish. Kurds in Iraq have had a semi-autonomous region ruled by the Kurdish Regional Government since 1992, but it was particularly after the 2003 US-led invasion of Iraq that Iraqi Kurds had renewed hopes for Kurdish autonomy and subsequent independence. Iraqi Kurds have been successful in formulating self-rule in Northern Iraq and moved toward establishing a de facto state. For instance, ever since 1991, the Kurds in Iraq have had administrative control of their area's language education and today the language is used widely across the administration, education, and in other sectors of society. Therefore, the Iraqi Kurdish society looks drastically different from that in the 1990s. Since 2003, the region has witnessed an unprecedented societal stability and economic wealth, partially in form of foreign investments. Overall, compared to the rest of Iraq, the Kurdistan Region of Iraq (KRI) has been politically stable and relatively prosperous, although disputes between the main political parties continue to simmer. Indeed, in spring 2014, the war being waged in Syria was starting to show spillover effects on Iraq, particularly with the recent takeover of Iraqi cities by IS. This situation shook the societal stability of the de facto Kurdish state in northern Iraq, but also provided the KRG with an opportunity to push forward claims for independence. The KRG held a referendum to assess support for independence in

September 2017 which caused uproar among the political circles in central Iraq and received a harsh reaction from the Iraqi Army and the central government. KRG's decision also did not receive a worldwide support for its right of self-determination.

The Syrian Kurds have been referred to as the "forgotten Kurds" as they have received little attention from the media and researchers (Tejel 2009), particularly compared to Kurds from Iraq and Turkey. However, two major events have played in favour of the Syrian Kurds, which has also made them a more visible actor in the ongoing conflict in Syria. The first one was the retreat of the Syrian regime from the Kurdish areas, which left the area under the control of the Democratic Union Party (PYD). The second one was the emergence of the IS, which to Kurds' fortune, became the common enemy for them and the international coalition (Schott 2017). Since the withdrawal of the Syrian government forces in 2012, the PYD quickly filled the power vacuum and declared three Kurdish cantons located in the region of Rojava, Efrîn, Cezîre, and Kobanî, autonomous. An autonomous region called Rojava was established (Küçük and Özselçuk 2016; Leezenberg 2016). Following the PKK leader Öcalan's ideals, Kurdish political movement in Rojava established a system called democratic autonomy which challenged the traditional central and nation-state systems (Leezenberg 2016). The model emphasized bottom-up democracy, active citizenship participation, and the equal representation between men and women. This also applied to the military organization (YPG/YPJ), including women-led battalion units that received considerable international attention in the 2010s (Baser and Toivanen 2016). The Kurdish troops engaged in armed battle against IS in the outskirts of the de facto autonomous region of Rojava in Northern Syria between 2013 and 2017. The Kurdish troops are affiliated with the PKK, although this relationship is often contested since the latter features on EU's and US' list of terrorist organizations.

This edited volume does not, unfortunately so, include contributions from scholars, who would have conducted fieldwork related to the Kurdish case in Iran. Suffice to say that what differentiated Iran from Iraq and Turkey with regard to the states' minority relations to Kurds was that, in the beginning, the Kurds were treated as a tribal community and an integral part of the Iranian state and as a result, the Kurdish nationalism took different forms in Iran compared to Iraq and Turkey, for instance (Natali 2005, 118–120). The Kurdish question is a highly politicized one in Iran, as well, as shown by the cases of arbitrary imprisonment of Kurdish activists and executions of individuals deemed politically active in Kurdish organizations, along with suppression of female Kurdish activists on the basis of both ethnicity and gender (Amnesty International 2008). In terms of ethnic and linguistic rights, recent years' human rights abuses of Kurds in Iran amount to discrimination in employment, housing, and education on the basis of ethnicity (Kurdish) and/or religion (Sunni Islam) and a ban on Kurdish-language education.

All these contexts posed different challenges to researchers depending on each one's political climate, leaders, and as well as the nature of the organic Kurdish movements themselves. Studying Kurdish communities originating from Turkey has become a highly difficult task since the foundation of the Turkish republic in 1923. Kurds have been prosecuted in a variety of ways under different governments and the political turmoil in Turkey, which has included coups d'états and coup attempts throughout the years, has affected academic freedom on matters related to studying Kurds. Most academics stayed on the safe side and approached these issues from a security studies perspective, usually supressing Kurds' own voices and reaffirming the state's official policy. Those, who tried to approach it from a different perspective such as from a social movements approach or postcolonial studies have suffered serious consequences. For instance, the case of Ismail Beşikçi[3] is a highly known example in this regard. Even in relatively calm political periods in Turkey, studying the Kurdish Question has always remained a taboo in the country. When the peace petition signed by more than two thousand academics became public, it clearly revealed that criticizing government's policies toward the Kurdish population represented crossing the red line in Turkey. Many of them were and continue to be criminalized and put on trial for terrorism charges (Tekdemir et al. 2018). Researching the Kurdish Question in Turkey has had direct consequences for Kurdish academics and for those who have tried to speak on behalf of Kurdish rights and populations. Foreign researchers have also not been immune to repressive policies. Many of them have been detained, arrested, or deported for studying the Kurds, especially in South East Turkey. However, ethnographic research on Kurdish communities has also carried a huge risk: protection of interviewees. From an ethics perspective, anonymizing interviews has not been sufficient means to protect the interviewees as voice recordings or research notes have been confiscated or the researchers might have been monitored without their knowledge. Moreover, temporality is another important factor. What might be safe to say today, might not be so tomorrow. Therefore, as this book shows that conducting ethnographic study on the Kurds can entail many risks that a researcher should take into account, starting from the planning phase all the way up to the completion of the fieldwork, and even beyond that.

Conducting research in Iraqi Kurdistan has entailed other types of risks for researchers compared to their colleagues in Turkey. For instance, during Saddam era, access has been a significant problem. Since 2003, however, Iraqi Kurdistan almost became a *Mecca* for researchers who were working on the Middle East. Relative stability in the region—differently from the rest of Iraq—has made it easier to conduct ethnographic research in different districts. During the war with IS, however, it became to be a dangerous place for those who do fieldwork in regions considered as conflict zones. Academics, who are working on the KRG, have usually received a warm welcome by state officials as well as the locals as they are raising the profile of the region. When it comes to Rojava, however, access has become a major problem for many researchers who have lacked the right networks to reach the right people. Moreover, for researchers who are from Turkey, it has become an additional risk of being labelled as PKK-supporters. For foreigners also, it might mean a short-term detention at the airport when they come back to their homeland. For instance, many European states are monitoring mobility in Middle Eastern borders to detect foreign combatants. Keeping different contexts and different challenges in mind, we have invited contributions that have covered different parts of the Kurdish homeland. The fieldwork for the contributions included in this volume has been conducted in Turkey, Syria, Iraq, and in diaspora.

"Studying the Kurds"?

The Kurdish case also makes visible how producing research knowledge reflects the historically unequal power relations, including colonialist and imperialist tendencies, and to what extent knowledge production and research continues to be shaped and structured according to a nation-state-centered logic (Wimmer and Glick Schiller 2002). For researchers in this field, in particular, this means becoming conscious of how the past and present power relations have affected and continue to affect knowledge production processes related to Kurdish regions and populations. This raises questions, for instance, on how knowledge has selectively been employed by those in power to justify governance and maintain power hierarchies, and to support earlier imperial and later national interests in regions inhabited by Kurds. The state-led oppression and marginalization has not only taken physical and occupational forms, but also intellectual ones. The denial to produce written histories, to receive teaching in one's mother language, to document local forms of knowledge, and to create an independent body of research literature in addition to having been objected to colonizing and orientalizing discourses are only some examples of the intellectual ramifications of state-led repression in the Kurdish regions and on Kurdish populations (see Zeydanlıoğlu 2008).

Therefore, the emergence of a vibrant field of Kurdish studies as an independent field during recent decades is an interesting development in terms of knowledge production on the region and its populations. For instance, there are currently numerous conferences organized specifically on Kurdish politics and social phenomena all around the world and larger conferences such as the ISA (International Studies Association) and MESA (Middle East Studies Association) have panels dedicated to Kurdish-related issues. In addition to that, an indexed, international academic journal, *Kurdish Studies*, was founded some five years ago. Moreover, there is a highly effective mailing list hosting more than 1,000 academics, who work on the Kurdish issues. Called the Kurdish Studies Network, it is led by a Kurdish scholar, Welat Zeydanlıoğlu, who is based in Sweden.

Outside the academic realm, there is an increasing attention to the Kurdish-related matters as the Kurdish populations reside at the heart of the Middle East and at the heart of the geopolitical power struggles that are currently shaping the region. Academics, journalists, civil society organizations, think-tanks, and policy makers constantly produce reports and new research knowledge on Kurdish societies and populations. Although a very welcome development indeed, it seems, however, that the focus is more often than not on what the research outcomes tell us about policy-relevant issues, security-threats, peace prospects, and intricacies of ethnic and religious conflicts. Instead, it seems to be more seldomly questioned how this knowledge is being produced, under what conditions does the knowledge production take place and what are the challenges for both researchers and participants who take part in this process. Also, considering the highly political nature of the Kurdish question, the politicization of research topics and goals deserves more discussion.

As early career/mid-career researchers who have joined numerous conferences and panels and reviewed numerous articles in this field, the debates on the knowledge production on Kurdish studies have not, unfortunately so, received the attention it deserves. We have written an article published in *Ethnic and Racial Studies* (Baser and Toivanen 2018) to start a discussion on this topic. In our experience, what is commonly problematized is an old-fashioned discussion of the insider/outsider dilemma which actually takes its roots from the fundamental question of "Can the Subaltern Speak?" (Spivak 1988). In other words, there have been clashes around the two dilemmas: "speaking as Kurds" or "speaking on behalf of the Kurds as non-Kurds." These discussions have usually remained superficial, failed to unpack the power dynamics and imposed the necessity of being fit in a categorization. Kurdish academics have seldom questioned the ability or sometimes the right of non-Kurdish academics' research on the Kurdish issues. On the other hand, non-Kurdish academics might accuse Kurdish academics for producing biased research. After witnessing these colloquial discussions that were not carried to an academic platform in a published form, we decided to compile this book as a first step. This book aims to fill this gap on how ethnographic knowledge is produced on Kurdish regions and populations by offering contributions from both early career as well as more established researchers to create a platform for discussion on ethnographic research and intricacies of knowledge production on the related topics. Therefore, this volume addresses questions that are more particular to the Kurdish case, including: how do the power relations come about between the researchers and the Kurdish research participants in the context of collective experiences of oppression and marginalization? How to address highly politicized topics in the light of the historical context of the Kurdish question as well as the current sensitive geopolitical situation of Kurds in the region? Ethnographic reflections by researchers in Kurdish studies are, therefore, highly necessary. Along these lines, the contributors have stressed the necessity to adopt a reflexive framework to approach such methodological questions in rapidly shifting political circumstances as well as to pay attention to the historical and contemporary intricacies surrounding the Kurdish case.

REFLECTING ON FIELDWORK EXPERIENCES

One major theme of discussion in methodological research literature has been the insider/outsider positionalities, which has inspired an abundant body of methodological literature (see Nowicka and Cieslik 2014). For instance, an insider researcher is assumed to have "perceived closeness" and a certain level of familiarity and shared attributes with the studied (ethnic) community and its members (Voloder 2014, 3). A long-standing assumption has been that insiders might have better access to the community and may be more able to gain in-depth insights and inside information inaccessible to an outsider. However, it has also been suggested that the relative social proximity or shared ethnicity may even increase the awareness of possible social divisions, such as class that exist between the researcher and the participants (Sultana 2007; Shinozaki 2012). On the other hand, the outsider researcher has been traditionally celebrated as the "neutral" and "objective" academic, who is less likely to be emotionally invested with his/her research participants (Voloder 2014, 3). More critical approaches denounce such views as lauding outsiders, often "white" elites, who claim to be objective (Voloder 2014, 4). Moreover, Kusow (2003) emphasizes that outsider researchers are perceived to be less likely to understand the cultural complexities and the insights that might arise from this difference, although authors such as Bucerius (2013, 691) argue that researchers do not have to be insiders in order to access relevant information—sometimes they can be the "outsider trusted with 'inside knowledge.'"

We have wished to move beyond the traditional approach to insider/outsider positionalities and to approach such positionalities from the perspective of power. Power and privilege are crucial aspects of the research process, and often present in social interaction situations between the researchers and research participants. One way to make the existing power relations visible is to examine different positionalities that are inextricably intertwined with the surrounding power relations in the given context (see Breen 2007, 163; Ryan 2015). For instance, Amelina and Faist (2012, 1716) suggest that a self-reflexive approach "discloses a situational power hierarchy between the researcher and the researched." It is, therefore, of upmost importance that researchers adopt a reflexive approach to understand the dynamics that underpin a research process and social interaction situations in the research field (Guillermet 2008; Nowiska and Cieslik 2014). Reflexive approach allows understanding the particular socio-spatial context that the researcher and research participants mutually co-constitute and that is very much relational (Carling, Erdal, and Ezzati 2013).

The contributions of this volume show that an analysis of different positionalities requires a reflective analysis of the surrounding power relations. Coming from various ethnic, national, and linguistic backgrounds, they illustrate, for instance, that researcher's assumed ethnicity and other social categories gain their meaning in relation to those of the research participants, yet they can shift several times within an interview, or even from one moment to another. Researcher positionality needs to be understood along the lines of a spectrum with its own spatial and temporal constellations that may shift between different research fields, in the course of the fieldwork or even within a particular research setting, such as an interview (Baser and Toivanen 2017). This is also showcased by the contributors, who provide examples of particular moments during fieldwork, where their positionalities have suddenly shifted.

Reflexivity is also significant in terms of the ethical considerations related to any research, but particularly to one, dealing with communities that have experienced long-standing and often continuing marginalization and oppression. This does not merely entail listening people on their own terms, but also considerations of researchers' responsibility as to how to communicate research findings and how to conduct independent research in dire circumstances. Underlining all the contributions is the founding question of how to accord epistemic privilege to communities that have been marginalized, oppressed, and conflict-affected (see Mazurana et al. 2013, 6–7). In other words, how to make their voices heard and how to take account also the fact that the experiences of powerlessness and oppression can simultaneously become sites of agency and resistance to long-standing victimization (Hooks 1990). Therefore, the contributions included in this volume not only open up a space for discussions on intricacies of conducting fieldwork in Kurdish studies from a reflexive point of view but also on the workings of power in knowledge production related to the Kurdish question—and beyond. Also, as the Kurdish studies grow as an independent research field, there will be a vast demand for genuine discussions on critical and independent social scientific research. Each chapter in this book provides a venue for such future discussions, presenting fieldwork experiences from different national and political contexts in the Middle East, carefully reflected upon by contributors from a variety of disciplinary, ethnic, linguistic, and national backgrounds.

THE CONTRIBUTIONS

This edited volume has been divided into four thematic sections. The first one, titled *Research fields on the move: on space and knowledge*, presents contributions that discuss more theoretically, epistemologically, and ontologically orientated questions on knowledge production related to the Kurdish regions and populations. *Vera Eccarius-Kelly* discusses eloquently the merits of conducting critical ethnography and how it can allow scholars to move beyond practices of replication and affirmation of historically and politically normalized power structures. She suggests that this allows scholars to point out the perpetuation of inequalities and injustices, an exercise that can advance the existence of emancipatory knowledge, reduce practices of denigration, and thus lead to more social justice in society. She importantly argues that it is the task of the critical ethnographer to listen and then participate in a dialogue that encourages emancipatory knowledge which will then allow identifying, naming, and rejecting state-endorsed histories and internalized stereotypes on Kurds. The second contribution in this section is by *Joost Jongerden*, who interestingly asks what the daily life activities that he has observed in the Kurdish region mean from a methodological perspective. Indeed, he observed that people and their practices were not fixed on one particular location, such as urban or rural, nor on movement (in the sense of migration), but also on infrastructure and associated activities. Based on this, he argues that social scientists need to think beyond predefined categories to open up new horizons of investigation, and to acquire a vocabulary that does not essentialize their worlds, but one that introduces more open and dynamic concepts to capture how people organize their lives through a range of multi-spatial practices.

The third contribution in this section is offered by *Jowan Mahmod*, who has studied discourses related to Kurdish identity in online and offline data—and in the diaspora context. She raises such methodologically pertinent topics such as anonymity, representation, ethics, and researcher positionality and how they became relevant in the collection of both online and offline data. She shows how the questions of ethics and confidentiality play out differently in an online setting compared to face-to-face social interactions, particularly when discussing topics that are highly sensitive and taboo. On the other hand, she raises the issue of representation by asking which stories are being privileged and presented and which are silenced and left out, particularly in terms of the political and nationalist discourses in online sites. She eloquently identified the ethical challenges this presented to representation, but also to her own positionality as an "insider" that was assumed to have a politically favourable stance similar to the participants of the online discussions. The fourth contribution is by *Marc Sinan Winrow*, who discusses questions involved in engaging in historical archival research on Kurds. He aptly shows how archives on Kurdish populations and history should not merely be treated as repositories of information, but also as spaces expressive of and produced by power relations. He particularly focuses on how the Kurds have been constructed and represented in different imperial and national archives, thus making visible the inseparable connections between colonial and imperial power, history-writing, and representation. Along this reasoning, he argues for a global historical approach that would shed light to the historical entanglements of between more local, national, and transnational histories.

The second section, titled *Fieldwork in troubled terrains*, presents insights from contributors, who discuss their observations when conducting research in "troubled terrains" and what practical questions they have come across during their fieldwork experiences in conflict settings. The first contribution is by *Marlene Schäfers*, who shows through her observations how the immense polarization that dominates politics and society in Northern Kurdistan (in Turkey) shapes the texture of everyday social life. This naturally also presents challenges for field researchers in the region. Drawing from Anthropology, she approaches boundaries as socially constructed markers of division, central for the making of identities and for the constitution of social and political communities, and shows how such boundaries are also subject to continuous renegotiation, including between the researcher and the research participants. She poignantly provides examples of social situations in which she was expected to make explicit her loyalties and to choose one object of allegiance over another, and how she experienced such pulls of allegiance when navigating the research field. She suggests that paying attention to such patterns of dominance is of upmost importance to grasp how political subjects are shaped in contexts of protracted conflict and enduring violence, but also to deal with the practicalities of fieldwork in such contexts.

The second chapter in this section is offered by *Demet Arpacık*, who aims to understand and explain the position of a researcher who works with marginalized subaltern communities that have experienced long-standing political domination and pressure by the state. The author draws from her experiences with the Kurdish community members in Istanbul, and discusses her fieldwork experiences from the perspective of researcher positionality. How do we position ourselves and how are we positioned by community members, particularly if we are positioned to belong to the dominating majority? On the other hand, the author discusses the challenges to conduct such research in a politically sensitive context and the difficulties of situating oneself against the political domination of the state, media, law, and other structures of power. Discussing the fact of conducting fieldwork in "dangerous" research settings, with risks prevailing both in the fieldwork setting as well as arising from the surrounding political and judicial contexts, she also suggests that it is imperative to consider the concept of "danger" as a methodological tool for fieldwork.

The third section focuses on the insider/outsider dilemma and the practicalities involved in navigating and negotiating one's positionality during the fieldwork. The chapters show that the surrounding sociopolitical circumstances and the conflictual settings present particular challenges for researchers in terms of positionalities. The first contribution in this section is by *Francis O'Connor and Semih Celik*, who relay their experiences when conducting fieldwork in Northern Kurdistan in 2012, during the relatively bloody month in the ongoing conflict between the Turkish armed forces and Kurdistan Workers' Party (PKK). In the context of the state's clampdown on Kurdish civil society and the destruction of the Kurdish cities, the authors rely their experiences with participants, who had been directly and indirectly affected by the conflict. Authors show how they negotiated access and aimed to gain their participants' trust. Conducting fieldwork in the authoritarian context also meant that particular measures had to be taken to ensure the participants' security and that the knowledge of the eventual presence of state surveillance bodies in the region also led to feelings of paranoia among the authors. They also discuss their "dual" positionality as outsiders, one of Turkish background and another of Irish ethnicity, and show how the dynamics of "dual" outsiderness played in interaction situations, shaped by the physical and socio-spatial environment surrounding them. The authors conclude that the "dual outsiderness" created a subjective space through which knowledge could be collaboratively produced, thus transforming the feeling of outsiderness and paranoia into sources of insights and revelation.

The second contribution in this section is by *Marlies Casier*, who opens the challenges in researching the Kurdish organisation, PKK that is listed as a terrorist organization both by Turkey as well as by the European Union and the United States. Based on her fieldwork in Europe as well as in Turkey, she reflects on the challenges of conducting ethnographic research about an organization that, due to criminalization, seems to be "nowhere," whilst practically being "everywhere." She pays particular focus on the challenges she experienced as an "outsider," and how the surrounding political climate in which the research subjects were criminalized led to taking particular precautions. The third contribution is by *Yeşim Mutlu*, whose study on the social consequences of internal displacement experienced by youth and women during the 1980s and 1990s in the Kurdish regions in Turkey led her to conduct interviews in Diyarbakır and Istanbul. Drawing from the tradition of critical ethnography, she discusses the interplay of ascribed identities that she experienced during her fieldwork. Having to negotiate her positionality as a "Turkish" female researcher, she accounts how also her social standing as an academic, her social relations to Kurdish friends and other factors played into how she became positioned in the field as "Turkish, but good." She also provides interesting insights into secondary trauma and discusses how she became isolated in her own social setting due to the choice of research topic.

The last contribution in this section is by *Yasemin Gülsüm Acar and Özden Melis Uluğ*, who discuss their positionalities as Turkish outsiders when conducting fieldwork with Kurdish participants in Turkey. The authors draw from the theorization of social identity to illustrate how their positionalities were constructed beyond singular identities as Turkish versus Kurdish, and intersectionally based on attributes such as gender, age, education, and social class. They call for researchers in social psychology to acknowledge their privileges and to reflect upon those when conducting research on highly sensitive topics and with marginalized communities.

The fourth and final section, titled *Essays on field experiences*, includes reflections on field notes from Syrian Kurdistan and Iraqi Kurdistan. The first contribution belongs to *Lana Askari*, where she reflects on her research experience in the Kurdistan Region of Iraq. As a returnee from the diaspora, her account entails reflections on both insider and outsider positionalities which she distinctively explains in her chapter. Askari also takes a gender lens while she examines her ethnographic approach to the field, finding that it had an immense impact on how the locals reacted to her and her research in general. In her chapter, she argues that rather than getting fixated in insider/outsider discussions, fieldwork should be crafted through shifting daily interactions and identities. The second contribution by *Thomas Schmidinger* reflects on his ethnographic fieldwork in Iraqi Kurdistan and Syrian Kurdistan, including Rojava. The chapter lays out the complexities of conducting fieldwork in a contested and politicized territory. He draws attention to the fact that a researcher must carefully design ethnographic work before entering a conflict zone. It is a brutally and honestly written chapter, in which the author reveals the passionate nature of himself as an academic and the resilience as a researcher who learns to manoeuvre difficult situations when necessary.

NOTES

1. We employ the terms "Iraqi," "Syrian," and "Turkish Kurdistan," whereas also geographical indicators of Southern (Iraq), Western (Syria), Eastern (Iran), and Northern (Turkey) Kurdistan are in use.

2. See http://www.institutkurde.org/en/kurdorama/.

3. Ismail Beşikçi spent more than a dozen years of his life in prison due to his studies on Kurdish communities. See: https://en.wikipedia.org/wiki/%C4%B0smail_Be%C5%9Fik%C3%A7i.

BIBLIOGRAPHY

Ali, O. 1997. "The kurds and the Lausanne peace negotiations, 1922–1923." *Middle Eastern Studies* 33, no. 3: 521–534.

Amelina, Anna and Thomas Faist. 2012. "De-naturalizing the national in research methodologies: Key concepts of transnational studies in migration." *Ethnic and Racial Studies* 35, no. 10: 1707–1724.

Amnesty International. 2008. *Human rights abuses against the Kurdish minority.* London: Amnesty International Publications.

Art, David. 2016. "Archivists and adventurers: Research strategies for authoritarian regimes of the past and present." *Social Science Quarterly* 97, no. 4: 974–990.

Baird, Adam. 2018. "Dancing with danger: Ethnographic safety, male bravado and gang research in Colombia." *Qualitative Research* 18, no. 3: 342–360.

Baser, Bahar and Erdi Özturk. 2017. *Authoritarian politics in Turkey: Elections, resistance and the AKP.* London: I.B. Tauris.

Baser, Bahar and Mari Toivanen. 2016. "Gender in the representations of an armed conflict. Female Kurdish combatants in French and British media." *Middle East Journal of Culture and Communication* 9: 294–314.

Baser, Bahar and Mari Toivanen. 2018. "Politicized and depoliticized ethnicities, power relations and temporality: Insights to outsider research from comparative and transnational fieldwork." *Ethnic and racial studies* 41, no. 11: 2067–2084.

Breen, Lauren J. 2007. "The Researcher 'in the middle': Negotiating the insider/outsider dichotomy." *Australian Community Psychologist* 19, no. 1: 167–174.

Bucerius, Sandra Meike. 2013. "Becoming a 'Trusted Outsider': Gender, ethnicity, and inequality in ethnographic research." *Journal of Contemporary Ethnography* 42, no. 6: 690–721.

Carling, Jørgen, Marta Bivand Erdal, and Rojan Ezzati. 2014. "Beyond the insider–outsider divide in migration research." *Migration Studies* 2, no. 1: 36–54.

Clark, Janine A. and Francesco Cavatorta. 2018. *Political science research in the middle east and north Africa: Methodological and ethical challenges.* Oxford: Oxford University Press.

Cohen, Nissim and Tamar Arieli. 2011. "Field research in conflict environments: Methodological challenges and snowball sampling." *Journal of Peace Research* 48, no. 4: 423–435.

Goodhand, Jonathan. 2000. "Research in conflict zones: Ethics and accountability." *Forced Migration Review* 8, no. 4: 12–16.

Guillermet, Elise. 2008. "Reflexivity – A tool for the anthropologist." *Antropoweb.*

Harrowell, Elly, Thom Davies and Tom Disney. 2018. "Making space for failure in geographic research." *The Professional Geographer* 70, no. 2: 230–238.

Hassanpour, Amir and Shahrzad Mojab. 2005. "Kurdish diaspora." In *Encyclopedia of diasporas. Part I. Immigrant and refugee cultures around the world,* edited by Melvin Ember, Carol L. Ember and Ian Skoggard, 214–224. Berlin: Springer.

Hooks, Bel. 1990. *Yearning: Race, gender and cultural politics.* Boston: South End Press.

Institut kurde de Paris (Kurdish Institute of Paris). "The Kurdish population." https://www.institutkurde.org/en/info/the-kurdish-population-1232551004. Last visited July 22, 2018.

Koch, Natalie. 2013. "Introduction–Field methods in 'closed contexts': Undertaking research in authoritarian states and places." *Area* 45, no. 4: 390–395.

Küçük, Bülent and Ceren Özselçuk. 2016. "The Rojava experience: Possibilities and challenges of building a democratic life." *South Atlantic Quarterly* 115, no. 1: 184–196.

Kusow, Abdi M. 2003. "Beyond indigenous authenticity: Reflections on the insider/outsider debate in immigration research." *Symbolic Interaction* 26, no. 4: 591–599.

Leezenberg, Michiel. 2016. "The ambiguities of democratic autonomy: The Kurdish movement in Turkey and Rojava." *Southeast European and Black Sea Studies* 16, no. 4: 671–690.

Mazurana, Dyan, Jacobsen, Karen, Gale and Lacey Andrews. 2013. *Research methods in conflict settings: A view from below.* Cambridge: Cambridge University Press.

McDowall, David. 1996. *A modern history of the Kurds.* New York: I.B. Tauris.

Natali, Denise. 2005. *The Kurds and the state: Evolving national identity in Iraq, Turkey and Iran.* New York: Syracuse University Press.

Nowicka, Magdalena and Anna Cieslik. 2014. "Beyond methodological nationalism in insider research with migrants." *Migration Studies* 2, no. 1: 1–15.

Romano, David. 2006. "Conducting research in the middle east's conflict zones." *Political Science Politics* 39, no. 3: 439–441.

Ryan, Louise. 2015. "'Inside' and 'Outside' of what or where? Researching migration through multi-positionalities." *Forum: Qualitative Social Research* 16, no. 2.

Shinozaki, Kyoko. 2012. "Transnational dynamics in researching migrants: Self-reflexivity and boundary-drawing in fieldwork." *Ethnic and Racial Studies* 35, no. 10: 1810–1827.

Spivak, Gayatri Chakravatory. 1988. "Can the subaltern speak?" In *Can the subaltern speak? Reflections on the history of an idea,* edited by Rosalind Morris, 21–78. New York: Columbia University Press.

Sultana, Farhana. 2007. "Reflexivity, positionality and participatory ethics: Negotiating fieldwork dilemmas in international research." *ACME: An International E-Journal for Critical Geographies* 6, no. 3: 374–385.

Taucher, Wolfgang, Mathias Vogl and Peter Webinger. 2015. *The Kurds: History, religion, language and politics.* Austrian Federal Ministry of the Interior.

Tejel, Jordi. 2009. *Syria's Kurds: History, politics and society.* New York: Routledge.

Tekdemir, Omer, Mari Toivanen and Bahar Baser. 2018. "Peace profile: Academics for peace in Turkey." *Peace Review* 30, no. 1: 103–111.

Voloder, Lejla. 2014. "Introduction: Insiderness in migration and mobility research: Conceptual considerations." In *Insider research on migration and mobility: International perspectives on researcher positioning,* edited by Lejla Voloder and Liudmila Kirpitchenko, 1–20. Farnham: Ashgate.

Wimmer, Andreas and Nina Glick Schiller. 2002. "Methodological nationalism and beyond: Nationstate building, migration and the social sciences." *Global Networks* 2, no. 4: 301–334.

Wood, Elisabeth John. 2006. "The ethical challenges of field research in conflict zones." *Qualitative Sociology* 29, no. 3: 373–386.

Zeydanlıoğlu, Welat. 2008. "The white Turkish man's burden: Orientalism, kemalism and the Kurds in Turkey." In *Neo-colonial mentalities in contemporary Europe,* edited by Guido Rings and Anne Ife, 155–174. Newcastle upon Tyne, UK: Cambridge Scholars Publishing.

Part I

RESEARCH FIELDS ON THE MOVE: ON SPACE AND KNOWLEDGE

Chapter 1

Critical Ethnography

Emancipatory Knowledge and Alternative Dialogues

Vera Eccarius-Kelly

The email's unsettling subject line read *"you viper,"* comparing me to a venomous snake because I had translated an online article critical of the treatment of ethnic communities in Turkey from German to English. Opponents of Kurdish identity and self-determination have long relied on hyperbolic, nationalistic, and deeply patriarchal language to intimidate their ideological nemeses. A reader clearly intended to portray me as devious, deceitful, and duplicitous. In the actual body of the message I was labeled a *"birthing agent of evil."* In March 2016, Turkish president Erdoğan also compared Kurds to snakes after European governments criticized Turkey's militarized and violent approach to silencing organized Kurdish protests and dissent. *Hürriyet Daily News* (2016) reported that Erdoğan had warned "countries which directly or indirectly lend support to terror organizations: you are nursing a viper in your bosom. That viper you have been nourishing can bite you at any time."

Mobilized Kurds and their perceived allies in academia and beyond are frequently labeled as traitors and supporters of terrorism. It was noteworthy that the Turkish president also relied on gendered notions to highlight the depth of supposed Kurdish trickery and deceit. Since my students had just begun a systematic examination of xenophobic, chauvinist, and jingoistic expressions for the purpose of creating absolutes in terms of race, ethnicity, gender, religion, and so forth, I decided to display the email message on classroom monitors. Dissecting the multilayered verbal insults, the undergraduate students were aghast but also curious about the language that was chosen to threaten me.[1] Some students asked "How are you producing an evil idea when you translate a policy criticism? Why is gender a factor here? Can academic work give life to wicked offspring?"

Most Kurdish Studies researchers encounter particular sensitivities as they trespass (in)visible boundaries in pursuit of a research project. Fluctuating levels of authoritarianism often shape the types of research questions as they become "unauthorized" in connection to Kurdish ethnic identity, sociopolitical mobilization, and self-determination. Research in Kurdish Studies can seem like a minefield when scholars carry out projects in regions of Kurdistan and even beyond. As projects encounter boundaries of profoundly politicized environments, a constant and critical rethinking of appropriate methodologies becomes essential. Scholars consider the potential long-term implications of particular types of research and engage in reflections related to their own assumptions and biases.

It is hardly surprising that modern Kurdish Studies traverses a wide range of academic areas including the study of languages, literatures, and linguistics; projects related to peace and conflict studies; ethno-nationalism, migration, and diasporas; and intersectional approaches to the study of gender, race, human rights, and the environment. Kurdish Studies clearly overlaps with traditional and long-established fields such as anthropology, linguistics, history, sociology, and political science. Over the past decade, research related to ethnicity, nationalism, migration, and diasporas demonstrated an increasing openness to scholars with a focus on interdisciplinary and boundary spanning approaches to social inquiry (Forsberg, Birnir, and Davenport 2017, 1–2). A growing body of work has been published by researchers who emphasize linkages across predictable academic and national boundaries. Interdisciplinarity, transnational approaches, and the pursuit of a wider range of methodologies now shape the future of the field in spite of troubling restrictions involving research in all regions of Kurdistan.

This chapter explores how scholars can engage in new ethnographic perspectives to overcome boundaries and silences in their research. The use of critical ethnography, a methodology that emerged out of critical theory, allows scholars to go beyond practices of replication and affirmation of historically and politically normalized power structures. According to Cannella and Lincoln (2011), this approach can be applied by social scientists and anthropologists with an interest in exploring nontraditional, interdisciplinary, and emerging research ideas. As a critical ethnographer, one is obligated to abandon a rigid commitment to neutrality and instead point out the perpetuation of inequalities and injustices by challenging the status quo. Involvement in critical ethnography means that researchers have specific political goals in mind to enhance discourses that could lead to more social justice in society, to advance the existence of emancipatory knowledge, and to reduce practices of denigration (Madison 2012; Carspecken 1996).

Critical ethnographers reflect not only on how political activism may help to overcome patterns of repression, but they also engage in an analysis of their own positionality along the way. A process of self-reflection allows researchers to explore their own positions of privilege and power instead of focusing exclusively on a critique of institutional controls or the state of the national status quo. According to Noblit, Flores, and Murrillo (2004, 3): "Critical ethnographers must explicitly consider how their own acts of studying and representing people are acts of domination even as critical ethnographers reveal the same in what they study."

Dispossessed, expelled, and migrating populations have long confronted inscribed scholarly knowledge by demonstrating that neat categories of global or regional concerns in contrast to local issues do not hold true (Mezzadra and Neilson 2012). But despite a growing emphasis on transnational or interdisciplinary methodological framing in the social sciences, Kurds (just as Palestinians, Kashmiris and Berbers, for example) are frequently represented as a people driven by the immutability of ethno-nationalist desires. The broader literature of political science, including the fields of security studies and international relations, tend to privilege static interpretations of ethnicity, group identity, and culture. State-centric studies can repeat processes of ethnic ordering to affirm categories of indexed minority groups for political purposes (Yeğen 2009 and Somer 2005). The legacy of scholarly knowledge acquisition is that fields of study are still entangled with colonial/ imperial power structures and privilege a sense of uniformity and homogeneity in research. In fact, scholarly interpretations of objectivity and neutrality have been used to "Other" Kurds and Kurdish Studies researchers by reinforcing silences rather than examining the increasing overlap between ethnic, socio-linguistic, and/or religious identities—although excellent ethnographic studies exist (Özyürek 2006).

Increasingly diverse studies have emerged that explore expressions of Kurdishness in specific geographic settings, yet it continues to be challenging for scholars to weave larger contextual accounts that integrate the influence of porous borders on the Kurdish sense of self. Kurds, of course, have undergone traumatic experiences over multiple historical periods and continue to be shaped by migratory processes related to their marginalization and expulsion. In that context it is essential to dissect the ways in which powerful regional states systematically denied Kurds an experience with independence. The absence of a Kurdish state made it extremely difficult to produce distinct knowledge as Kurds were deprived of opportunities to write their histories, prohibited from contextualizing communal memories and customs, and prevented from emphasizing the values of sociocultural practices and communal behaviors in their society. Over decades Arab, Turkish, and Iranian state institutions intensified their long-standing patterns of colonizing Kurds and orientalizing Kurdish discursive manifestations. In such an environment of both physical and intellectual occupation, hostile state institutions including security forces as well as state-controlled media continued to produce essentialized and profoundly detrimental knowledge about Kurds. In addition, educational practices served to renounce, repudiate, and deny the existence of a separate Kurdish ethnicity. Among the common tactics employed by regional state institutions were the repression of Kurdish languages and customary practices through assimilation policies that focused on constant efforts to publicly denigrate and humiliate Kurdishness (Çelik, Bilali, and Iqbal 2016).

Iraqi Kurdistan can be considered a recent and partial exception to this experience. Since the early 1990s the Kurdistan region has operated as a proto-state as Kurds controlled their own security forces and media outlets, managed regional educational policies, and enforced separate governing institutions. Yet, such progress was only achieved by Kurds in Iraq after Saddam Hussein's genocide against them. Today, the Kurdistan region is far from sovereign despite its innovative use of para-diplomacy for over a decade. Following the 2017 Kurdistan Independence Referendum, Baghdad reasserted its control over wide swaths of territory which once again presents a particularly complex challenge for future aspirations related to Kurdish independence.

Kurds in the European, North American, and Australian diasporas have been more successful in reimagining their identities in less constrained political environments. Articulating their communal traumas from expulsion and genocide, many engage in mobilization activities that result in the formation of transnational networks to support their brethren in the various homeland regions. Kurds in the diaspora transformed Kurdish communities in the homeland regions, and vice versa, by continuing to challenge representations of rigid, monolithic, or permanent identities. Scholars can integrate such processes into an understanding of a more activist analysis of Kurdish socialization to grapple with identity formation and expressions of Kurdishness (Gurlay 2007).

Ethnographic narratives contribute to a more complex scholarly understanding of the construction and fluidity of a variety of identities. Members of Kurdish communities actively participate in shaping versions of Kurdishness through shared familial memories, music, storytelling, or symbolic (re)productions of identities. It is the work of the critical ethnographer to first listen and then partake in a dialogue that encourages emancipatory knowledge. Critical ethnographers are expected to engage in an examination of the lived experiences of Kurds so that shared knowledge can contribute to envisioning alternatives to repressive socioeconomic and political realities. The purpose of critical ethnography is to partake in anti-colonial thinking by rejecting notions of established scholarly neutrality and objectivity. The reimagining of Kurdishness through shared communal dialogues encourages changes in the ways in which Kurds acquire and produce knowledge about themselves and their communities. The experience of identifying, naming, and rejecting state-endorsed histories and internalized stereotypes make it possible to imagine the Kurdish self in a new and unrestrained way.

FROM SECURITIZATION THEORY TO CRITICAL ETHNOGRAPHY

Securitization theory grapples with the impact of political speech acts[2] while critical ethnography engages in a dialogue of dissent to imagine societal change. Bringing together what appear to be disparate ways of "theorizing" and "doing" can contribute to new avenues in Kurdish Studies research. Securitization theory engages in a systematic study of how threats are realized in politics by relying on discourse analysis, case study approaches, and on ethnographic work (Balzacq 2011). Critical ethnography, while different from conventional ethnographic approaches, relies on participant observations and various interviewing methodologies. Together the two approaches encourage multiple layers of analysis to enhance a scholar's ability to analyze and envision the fundamentals of a new sociopolitical environment.

Securitization theory (Copenhagen School) offers a quite distinct way of evaluating and seeing (Buzan, Wæver, and de Wilde 1998).[3] As a theoretical approach it focuses on analyzing the use of extreme speech for the purpose of constructing a particular politicized issue as a national threat. The question to resolve based on this school of thought is not whether a threat is objectively measurable or merely based on subjective perception. Instead, the Copenhagen School focuses on the ways in which a specific issue is purposefully framed and politicized by powerful players to construct a particular national threat.[4] In that sense, securitization theory identifies very specific rhetorical tools that serve power structures in linking a political issue to historical connotations of invasion, loss of control, war, and extreme threat. According to Wæver (2009), three elements appear in speech acts for the purpose of engaging in extreme forms of politicization: (1) the identification of an existential (imminent) threat, (2) the use of arguments in favor of applying exceptional countermeasures to deal with the threat, and (3) the justification for breaking with established legal norms and social rules to counter the existential threat. The result of relying on securitization processes tends to be that the selected speech elevates an issue to such an extreme level of threat (and urgency) that it becomes remarkably challenging to break away from the established pattern. Buzan, Wæver, and de Wilde (2009) have argued that securitization theory provides a tool to scrutinize under what conditions specific ethnic, religious, or racial groups are "securitized" to enhance power structures that deny individuals, groups, or communities a free, equal, or peaceful existence.

In contrast to analyzing speech acts, critical ethnography engages in a radical critique that rejects repressive structures and processes of subjugation. Yet, the most significant step a critical ethnographer can take is to share in dialogue about a different type of society. As such Thomas (1993, 18) argued that critical ethnographers are inherently political in their work, which distinguishes them from conventional ethnographic researchers. While all ethnography aims to elicit cultural meanings and points of view through the use of participant observation and interviews, critical ethnographers integrate an analysis of the sociohistorical environments that directly shape the lives of participants. They purposefully position themselves within communities and aim to meaningfully contribute to thinking about a better (more free, just, or equal) society. This process of thinking, of course, is radical at its core as it critiques inherent barriers that curtail alternative ways of imagining. Critical ethnography pursues a way of "seeing" that may be most familiar in the context of Marxist and feminist analysis and critical race theory (O'Neill 2010).[5] In combination, the speech act analysis of securitization theory and the imaginative aspect of critical ethnography present a formidable approach to rethinking variations of Kurdistan and unfamiliar expressions of Kurdish identity.

It is well documented that various states have relied on political securitization strategies to classify Kurds as a fundamental threat to the cohesion and existence of modern nation-states (Çelik 2015 and Entessar 2014). In recent years, the AKP-led (Justice and Development Party) government in Turkey has claimed that the Kurdish threat is so grave that regular liberal democratic consultative processes can no longer be considered sustainable in the country (Geri 2016 and Kadioğlu 2013). Extreme versions of politicization tactics such as relentlessly linking Kurds to terrorist activities and claiming that all Kurdish political organizing is inherently violent in motivation have permanently transformed the state's relationship with the ethnic group (Bilgin 2011). Under such conditions, fairly benign governance issues related to state-ethnic group relations are so politicized that they fall outside the bounds of regular democratic processes.[6] Violence against Kurds is entirely normalized in the country as searches, detentions, and physical assaults have become routine. Any criticism of state-sponsored aggression (ranging from bureaucratic repression to the direct use of violence) or of the use of emergency measures to subdue Kurdish protests are framed as spreading terrorist propaganda or as treason.

The dreadful abuse and mistreatment of sociologist Ismail Beşikçi is among the best known international examples of how Turkey relied on trumped up charges to erase scholarly knowledge related to the lived experiences of

Kurds. Beşikçi spent nearly two decades in jail as a political prisoner for so-called communist and terrorist propaganda related to his scholarly work. He has continued to openly criticize the Turkish state's repressive policies toward Kurdish communities. Among his best-known works is *International Colony Kurdistan*, which was originally published in 1991 by the Gomidas Institute in London (reprinted in 2015). Beşikçi has been prosecuted repeatedly for supposedly engaging in terrorist propaganda. In 2017 an arrest warrant was issued in Ankara accusing the eighty-year-old revered scholar of membership in the PKK.

A more recent example of the long-standing practice in Turkey to securitize its political environment provides further context. According to Başer, Akgönül, and Öztürk (2017), the Turkish state activated counterterrorism policies to intimidate, silence, detain, and imprison the peace petition signatories called "Academics for Peace." The message to the general public was simple: dissent is terrorism. Elger et al. (2017) proposed that one does not even have to be a citizen living in Turkey to be accused of hostile, treacherous, and terrorist activities under these measures. The Turkish state has demonstrated that it aims to securitize the transnational Kurdish realm as well.

According to German police phone taps and surveillance activities, an Erdoğan confidant and Justice and Development Party (AKP) member by the name of Metin Kulunk provided financial support to a nationalist Turkish gang that operates in Germany (Winter 2017). This gang is known as *Osmanen Germania* (Ottoman Germans). Dozens of *Osmanen Germania* chapters pretended to be "boxing clubs," yet functioned as violent gangs of thugs by enforcing loyalty to the Erdoğan regime among ethnic Turkish (Kurdish and Armenian)-Germans and immigrants. Leaders of the club chapters received specific instructions to engage in orchestrated attacks on dissenters (Winter 2017). Similarly, the Kurdish-German professional soccer player Deniz Naki reportedly was shot at in Germany following criticism of the Turkish government's military invasion into the Kurdish region of Afrin, Syria (Naber 2018). Naki's former soccer club had refused to carry a banner onto the pitch that read "Our Hearts and Prayers are with our Soldiers." Naki's online remarks about his solidarity with Kurdish people may have motivated the attempted assassination in Germany.

PRACTICAL TOOLS FOR AN ETHNOGRAPHER

A key question that emerges for Kurdish Studies researchers with an interest in ethnographic methodologies is how to pursue meaningful projects when such dire circumstances emerge. Depending on one's research focus new interviews with political activists are extremely challenging to carry out or even dangerous for the participants. Similarly, relying on interview data that was collected long ago can potentially create problems for participants. Publications from less securitized periods could suddenly become scrutinized by hostile states for detailed information about Kurdish activists, their gathering spaces, or organizing techniques. In various parts of Kurdistan, as well as in the diaspora, it is essential to protect Kurdish interview participants by anonymizing the collected data and making sure not to disclose town or village-level information.

To put these observations into a more concrete context, an anonymous journal reviewer once suggested that my sources (the interview participants) should be identified to make their assertions "provable" and to place them into a more convincing "scientific context." In the securitized environments experienced in nearly all areas of Kurdistan, such a choice could have detrimental effects on interview participants and their family members. In another example, an anonymous reviewer proposed that I was biased against [country X] and that "for the safety of colleagues, it may be advisable to remove the biased assessment of [country X]."[7] This appeared to have been an effort to reduce the level of criticism by claiming that it otherwise would hurt progress in terms of ethnic relations in the country. Even more directly, one reviewer edited my word choices to neutralize my language (or to "make my assessment more scientific") by removing the descriptor "barbaric" related to Saddam Hussein's al-Anfal campaigns. The substitute adjective recommended to me was to use the term "stern" instead of "barbaric."[8] Sometimes reviewers reflect specific ideological positions and their recommendations are not acceptable.

Over the years, I have chosen to take handwritten notes in multiple languages when I pursue interviews, and rely on codes that are not readily intelligible by others. I do not record participants' names or other markers that may lead to easy identification of participants in the future; I also avoid obvious repetitive patterns in terms of the timing or locations of interview meetings during periods of high securitization.[9] I have added Skype interviews, but will only rely on the technology when participants suggest communicating that way. There is certainly a growing fear that social media apps are monitored (or perceived to be monitored) in a number of countries.

A central role in critical ethnographic methodology is to pursue an alternative approach to thinking about or imagining positions of justice and equality. In an abstract way, radical alternatives seem appealing, but in the lived experience they can be quite distressing. In one particular interview with an ethno-nationalist Kurd living in the diaspora, I learned that he had been thinking about returning to a particular part of Kurdistan during a period of increasing securitization. I was alarmed because I considered him a friend, so I challenged him by asking why he would endanger his own safety and potentially disrupt his family's well-being. He responded to me in staccato sentences, which indicated his annoyance with me but also expressed frustration about restrictions to his ability to travel freely despite the fact that he held a valid (Western) passport.

> My mother died when I was a little boy. My older sister was like my mother. She fed me, cared for me, loved me. Then she went off into the mountains to fight. She was captured and horrible things were done to her. She was killed. People found her dead body. I want to go to her grave. Villagers know where she is buried. She was like my mother and I need to go to the place where she is buried. I want to go and see her grave. Do you get that I need to go there? I have papers.

He ended up not going to Kurdistan that year and I gained insights into how to ask questions without imposing my own views. The way I framed my question fundamentally challenged his thoughts and motivations. I clearly suggested that he failed to consider his family's needs (which, of course, I had no information about). I neglected to think about my own positionality as a researcher and made obvious assumptions and value judgments about rational behavior in a securitized environment.

Similarly, I learned to resist speaking for Kurds at various conferences. I have been asked by Turkish scholars to explain to them "what Kurds want" or what "Kurdishness" represents. My answer today is to pose counter-positions such as "I'm not sure who you refer to when you speak of the Kurds," or "I recommend that you engage in dialogue with a wider variety of community members in your country to learn about the diversity of perspectives."

In essence, Wilkinson (2013) argued that positionality (also referred to as reflexivity in the literature) requires ethnographers to examine themselves within a broader analysis of their world view based on personal experiences, backgrounds, assumptions, values, and biases. Interviews (if structured, semi-structured, or unstructured) tend to be shaped by the ethnographer's views and assumptions. Efforts to identify one's own positionality disrupt the potential for biased portrayals of issues and aim to prevent personal experiences from overtaking or fully controlling a study. Ethnographers use many different ways to self-reflect; they can integrate personal vignettes (as above) into a study, write about specific reflections related to interactions between participants and scholars, and integrate particular points into the concluding sections of a project. Madison (2012, 7–8) proposed that positionality is used as a technique to consistently reflect on and disclose potential assumptions that are made by scholars.

PURSUING CRITICAL ETHNOGRAPHY
IN KURDISH STUDIES

Ethnographic methodologies evoke thoughts of extensive anthropological field work among native communities. Predominantly relying on participant observation, such projects recorded societal norms and values in distinctly bounded communities (Mead 1928). In the late eighteenth century both Catholic and Protestant missionaries carried out Kurdish ethnographies, followed by military officers, diplomats, and colonial administrators in the service of the British, French and Russian imperial authorities (van Bruinessen 2014, 25–27). Their goals included the acquisition of specific cultural language and tribal knowledge with the intent to advance strategic regional and colonial interests.

Wolcott (2008) suggested that modern ethnographic methods are less rigidly defined and more widely accepted at the intersection of the social sciences and the humanities. Ethnographers grapple with the meanings of lived culture, the impact of collective memory, and motivations for particular sociopolitical engagements, among many other areas. They provide in-depth analysis by exploring how communities are shaped by transnational migration, gender dynamics, the impact of globalization and the stresses of climate change. Most importantly, as King's work on Iraqi Kurdish society shows (2014), ethnographic projects embrace a holistic approach to communities by examining a multifaceted portrayal of daily life.

Semi-structured or unstructured interviews and participant observation are the preferred methods as ethnographic researchers seek out individual participants to provide them with insightful information. While such researchers rarely spend months or years within specific communities, they often invest significant amounts of energy to build trusting relationships based on social interactions. Often relying on the snowball method, ethnographers identify participants who introduce them to their friends and acquaintances. Sometimes researchers develop connections within specific social circles or gain access to sociopolitical networks to carry out repeated projects.[10] Rather than offering a detached and impersonal examination of cultures, ethnographic methodology accepts the development of relationships between researchers and participants. Yet, remnants of colonial power structures can still be discovered in the ways in which ethnographers at times control their participants, direct conversations, or elicit information that would not organically emerge.

For example, in the late 1990s I was part of a project that recorded the oral histories and testimonies of Kurdish asylum applicants who were in the process of resettlement in Minnesota and the Dakotas. While most of the social scientists involved with the project relied on the agreed upon sequence of questions, some pursued additional unvetted questions in the areas of their scholarly interest. Perhaps the scholars lacked sensitivity or knowledge about the predicament of the Kurdish refugees, but by asking questions related to security issues they dramatically shifted the power dynamics. It appeared that some Kurdish participants became worried or seemed perplexed by the unexpected inquiry about their encounters with the PKK. It was common knowledge among the Kurds that their asylum status could be compromised if they were perceived to have connections to the PKK. Many of the Kurdish asylum seekers likely encountered the PKK while escaping Saddam Hussein's regime or the internecine violence in Iraqi Kurdistan as they crossed the border into Turkey. Eliciting such information from vulnerable individuals, however, represented an attempt by the scholars to directly shape and control the flow of the narratives. By shifting the focus of the testimony to an agenda that would not organically emerge under the circumstances, the researchers essentially disadvantaged and disempowered the Kurdish participants.

Finally, when research is published, scholars sometimes reimpose a sense of distance between themselves and their participants to affirm long established academic hierarchies. Cultural geographers Crang and Cook (2007, 7–16) suggest that some researchers rely on detached or impersonal language to sound more authoritative, and that others prefer to couch their ideas in academic terminology to convince reviewers that a project was deserving of respect and publication. This may be a challenge that is frequently encountered by younger researchers who believe that abiding by scholarly conventions is the only way to become recognized in their fields.

When I first explored possibilities related to an ethnographic project on the absence of Kurds in exhibits or museums, I wanted to learn more about critical ethnography to avoid past mistakes. I discovered that the Metropolitan Museum of Art (MET) in NYC had received textile donations from the estate of Frederick Davis Greene. As an influential missionary with the American Board in Van (affiliated with the Evangelical Alliance), he was deeply concerned about the treatment of Christian communities under Abdul Hamid's reign (Salt 1993, 132). The Greene Estate had donated clothing items and textiles to the museum and curators decided to identify the items as: *Armenian [Kurdish]*.[11] In 1896 Greene published *The Rule of the Turk*, in which he suggested that "Armenian and Nestorian villagers are much better off as serfs of the powerful masters of these strongholds than as the victims of Kurdish plunder and of Ottoman taxation and oppression which they are now (49)." Greene (1896, 52) then stated that "the Kurds are a race of fine possibilities, far superior to the North American Indian, to whom they are often ignorantly compared. Under a just, intelligent, and firm government much might be expected of them."

Greene's judgment about Kurds (and Native Americans) represented the typical authoritatively stated missionary commentary that classified tribal people in ethnographic writings. What had bothered me (more) was that the curatorial team at the MET provided no substantive information about Greene's role in Van and simply identified the textiles as *Armenian [Kurdish]* without any additional sociohistorical context. What exactly did that mean? Was it impossible to tell whether these textiles were made and worn by Armenians or Kurds? Was it beyond reasonable to expect that the interwoven histories of these two communities could be pulled apart? Was this a sign of cultural denial (Sarewitz 2013)?[12] My 2013 notes show early reflections on the discovery of the items and the questions they raised for me.

> Greene's disturbing commentary is steeped in deeply racist and orientalist understandings, and he categorized groups that did not share his faith or urbane self-perceptions accordingly. It would be a challenge to curate an exhibit that could adequately address the multilayered experiences of diverse communities with the Ottoman Empire along with a satisfactory contextualization of the role of missionaries. As front-line representatives and information gatherers, missionaries conveyed detailed characterizations about regional communities to the West. Would it not make sense to make mention of Greene's political and religious agendas on the MET's website, so that visitors to the virtual museum could better understand how textiles became labeled as Armenian first and only in parenthesis as Kurdish?

As I initiated interviews with Kurds in the diaspora about the omission of Kurds in exhibits, I inquired if existing locations or buildings would be of interest to Kurds for an imaginary museum project. I abandoned that idea fairly quickly, but I recorded one of the more powerful personal accounts as a participant explained to me how it felt to go near the former Diyarbakır Prison in Turkey. As I listened I grasped the essential meaning of emancipatory knowledge acquisition through critical ethnography. The Kurdish participant was engaging in imagining an alternative society, a place where he would have the influence to free his family's history.

> Diyarbakır Prison represents deep human suffering to Kurds. People experienced unimaginable tortures in that place and now there is a lot of talk about making it into a museum. Is it possible to turn such a terrifying place into a museum? I had not been to Diyarbakır in many years, but this time I decided to go and look for myself. As a structure this prison is menacing and the stories told by my family made the place even scarier. I went to check the gates to see if I could find information about it or even take a look inside. I didn't see a guard and that was surprising to me. My heart was pounding when I walked closer to the gate because I was nervous to go near it. In the past people had entered through the gate and never returned to their families. My palms were sweaty and I was not sure what to expect, but everything was locked up. I took photos instead, but then I was thinking about not being able to go inside and it made me

very angry. It felt like part of my family history has been imprisoned in there as well. (Eccarius-Kelly 2015, 183.)

An interest in exploring methodologies that construct interactions and relationships in more egalitarian and anti-colonial ways demands a fundamental focus on pursuing justice and on being openly political. Despite that realization, I also understood that my training in political science and international relations pushed me to make a claim to rationality and objectivity. It took some time to discover how to integrate aspects of ethnography into my projects. Engaging in critical ethnography, however, meant that I needed to go much further as it required an exploration of new ways of thinking about notions of objectivity and positionality. I struggled to let go of habits related to ordering, categorizing, and abstracting.

While ethno-nationalism led me originally to meet members of the Kurdish diaspora, I tended to examine systems of sociocultural and political repression through the eyes of a political scientist. A radical ethics had not been an area of focus in my academic experience. As part of my studies I learned about expressions of nationalism in the aftermath of the genocide by the Baathist regime during al-Anfal/Halabja. I knew of a growing body of work that examined the existing knowledge on genocide, trauma, and memory among Kurds (Fischer-Tahir 2012). Several Turkish military coups (1960, 1971, and 1980) and the rise of guerrilla warfare by the PKK during the 1980s and 1990s marked periods that significantly contributed to my growing interest in theories related to internal colonialism, rural sociology, and ideologies of resistance (Jongerden and Akkaya 2013).

Most recently the rise of the Islamic State and the battle for Kobani, the Kurdistan Referendum, and Turkey's renewed emphasis on a military solution to Kurdish self-determination by attacking Afrin measurably reshaped Kurdish Studies. The Syrian civil war and the refugee crisis further complicated efforts to determine the size and composition of various Kurdish diaspora communities. Thousands of Kurdish refugees fled without papers; some relied on human smugglers; and many have been forced to remain in the shadows as undocumented laborers across the continent. More than twenty-five years ago, van Bruinessen (1992, 66) noted that between a quarter and a third of all Kurds effectively lived outside of the territorial region of Kurdistan; he suggested that only a small minority might ever be able to return to the homeland. An estimated 1.5 to 2 million Kurds now live throughout Europe with about 1 million Kurds dispersed in Germany (Eccarius-Kelly 2011, 203). In response to these realities, Kurdish Studies had to embrace a host of new intersectional methodologies related to migration, identity, and political mobilization. What does that mean for someone interested in critical ethnography?

Making a meaningful contribution as a scholar could involve highlighting Kurdish narratives that have not been fully embraced or searching for a deeper understanding of the fluidity of what it means to be Kurdish today. Most recently, I interviewed ethnic Kurdish artists, writers, and documentarians in the diaspora to explore what they might envision to be included in a Kurdish exhibit. The participants had complete freedom of imagination to shape displays and express particular preferences without concern for political realities. The types of imaginary spaces and displays artists and writers discussed showed how Kurds in the diaspora grapple with ideas that might help them narrate their own heritage and culture. After referencing folkloric expressions of culture, one writer added "we have written literature, too, and a lot of poetry, and a tradition of exceptional contemporary novels in all Kurdish languages." Another artist emphasized dengbêj songs[13] to learn about the past and to appreciate connections to the natural environment (Eccarius-Kelly 2018). Perhaps the most significant contribution scholars with an interest in critical ethnographic methods can make is to allow their participants to use their imagination to create alternative ways of seeing.

CONCLUDING THOUGHTS

It is essential that critical ethnographers are radical in the sense of promoting the re-writing of lived experiences to open imaginary spaces. Instead of a commitment to objectivity and neutrality, scholars need to favor the pursuit of justice through a participatory role in the exchange of information and an engagement with alternative dialogues. They must reject the practice of securitizing and essentializing Kurdishness. Critical ethnographic methodology represents a deeply political agenda as it encourages a process of hearing and seeing alternatives. In essence, the experience of participating in such a dialogue needs to free participants to reimagine their own histories and retell their lived experiences. As critical ethnographers collect testimonies and interviews through dialogues, Kurdish participants engage in the production of their own emancipatory knowledge as they articulate aspirations and thoughts related to the ways in which Kurdish communities can live in a more just and equitable society.

NOTES

1. It is possible that my students would respond differently today since President Trump relies on similar rhetoric to attack his ideological opponents.

2. In linguistics and the philosophy of language, a speech act refers to an utterance that is performative in its communication.

3. I have chosen to rely on the Copenhagen School rather than the Paris School of Security Studies for this chapter. The Copenhagen School focuses on an analysis of speech acts, while the Paris School examines actual practices of state securitization. The Paris School's main thinker, Didier Bigo, identified new ways in which external and internal security agencies operate. According to Didier, external security forces (such as the secret service) now frequently search inside a nation's borders to scrutinize refugees, asylum applicants, and immigrant communities for connections to external enemies. In contrast, internal security forces (such as the police and border guards) are often quite outward looking as they aim to identify potential terrorist activities linked to transnational diasporas communities, for example. Since this chapter predominantly explores examples of speech act that are used to weaken Kurdish identity or silence their discursive manifestations, the Copenhagen School is the preferred choice.

4. Here one could easily reference the frequent remarks made by President Trump related to Mexican immigrants as "rapists and criminals."

5. Critical theory provides the theoretical framework for critical race theory, which examines society at the intersection of law, race and power structures.

6. Turkey is no longer classified as a state that aspires to democracy, but rather as an illiberal or authoritarian state. Freedom House most recently gave Turkey an aggregate score of 38/100, reflecting a dramatic decline in the levels of freedom. The country "received a downward trend arrow due to the security and political repercussions of an attempted coup in July [2016], which led the government to declare a state of emergency and carry out mass arrests and firings of civil servants, academics, journalists, opposition figures, and other perceived enemies." For additional information, see https://freedomhouse.org/report/freedom-world/2017/turkey

7. I paraphrased the reviewers' criticisms here. As my colleagues in the field of Kurdish Studies know, I accept constructive criticism and tend to be open to suggestions for change. Several of my projects improved significantly because reviewers' offered thoughtful advice and recommendations over the years. I object to suggestions that appear to focus on whitewashing, obfuscating, or omitting criticisms because a reviewer may have a political agenda that is different from mine.

8. In essence, barbaric means cruel and extremely brutal; I would similarly define Hitler's genocide targeting Jews and Roma as barbaric. Perhaps the reviewer assumed I was making a judgment about Saddam Hussein as an Arab leader (which was not my intention). However, to suggest to me to substitute the word stern for barbaric seemed to indicate a different agenda. Stern simply references rigid, strict, and uncompromising behavior, which seemed wholly inappropriate in this context.

9. I lost a significant portion of my interview notes in Chiapas, Mexico, after being detained and interrogated by the Mexican military in the so-called rebel-occupied territories in 1995. Thankfully, I had obscured my interview notes by mixing German, English, and Spanish and I had taken the precaution to assign random names to the guerrilla members I interacted with. However, the military was able to confirm the general region I spent time in and may have identified specific villages. Overall, it was a frightening experience for everyone involved.

10. Ethnographic projects are very distinct from survey focused research, which relies on standardized questionnaires to control for specific aspects in a study. In

contrast to the snowball method, specific participants are selected for surveys and then asked to reply to the same questions (often using a Likert scale, which is a five or seven-point scale to express how much participants agree or disagree with a particular statement). Such surveys allow researchers to engage in very specific comparisons.

11. The Greene Estate items are not displayed in the MET but are available as images through the online database.

12. Daniel Sarewitz's piece on the exhibit of the Enola Gay at the Smithsonian Air and Space Museum offers excellent contextual reading related to choices made by curators. He criticizes the fact that every detail is described about the plane with the exception that it delivered the nuclear weapons to kill hundreds of thousands of people.

13. In Kurdish cultural tradition, epic vocal pieces are performed by individual reciters or storytellers who preserve historic accounts, legends, and the collective memory of the Kurdish people. The singers are often unaccompanied by musical instruments.

BIBLIOGRAPHY

Balzacq, Thierry, ed. 2011. *Securitization Theory: How Security Problems Emerge and Dissolve*. London: Routledge.

Başer, Bahar, Samim Akgönül and Ahmet Erdi Öztürk. 2017. ""Academics for Peace" in Turkey: A Case of Criminalising Dissent and Critical Thought via Counterterrorism Policy." *Critical Studies on Terrorism* 10, no. 2: 274–296. https://doi.org/1 0.1080/17539153.2017.1326559

Bilgin, Pinar. 2011. "The Politics of Studying Securitization? The Copenhagen School in Turkey." *Security Dialogue* 42, no. 4–5: 399–412.

Beşikçi, Ismail. 2015. *International Colony Kurdistan*. London: Gomidas Institute.

van Bruinessen, Martin. 2015. "Kurdish Studies in Western and Central Europe." In *Wiener Jahrbuch für Kurdische Studien*, edited by Maria Six-Hohenbalken, 18–96. Vienna: Wiener Verlag für Sozialforschung.

———. 1992. "Kurdish Society, Ethnicity, Nationalism and Refugee Problems." In *The Kurds: A Contemporary Overview*, edited by Philip Kreyenbroek and Stefan Sperl, 26–52. New York: Routledge.

Buzan, Barry, Ole Wæver, and Jaap de Wilde. 1998. *Security: A New Framework for Analysis*. Boulder: Lynne Rienner Publishers.

Cannella, Gail S. and Yvonna S. Lincoln. 2011. "Ethics, Research Regulations, and Critical Social Science." In *The Sage Handbook of Qualitative Research*, edited by Norman K. Denzin and Yvonna S. Lincoln, 81–89. Thousand Oaks: Sage Publications.

Carspecken, Phil Frances. 1996. *Critical Ethnography in Educational Research: A Theoretical and Practical Guide*. New York: Routledge Press.

Çelik, Ayse B., Rezarta Bilali, and Yeshim Iqbal. 2017. "Patterns of 'Othering' in Turkey: A Study of Ethnic, Ideological, and Sectarian Polarisation." *South European Society and Politics* 22, no. 2: 217–238. https://doi.org/10.1080/13608 746.2016.1250382

Çelik, Ayşe Betül. 2015. "The Kurdish Issue and Levels of Ontological Security." In *Conflict Resolution and Ontological Security*, edited by Bahar Rumelili, 52–70. Abingdon: Routledge.

Crang, Mike and Ian Cook. 2007. *Doing Ethnographies*. Thousand Oaks: Sage Publications.

Eccarius-Kelly, Vera. 2018. "Cleansing the Galleries: A Museum in the Imagination of Kurdish Diaspora Artists and Activists." In *Essays on Kurdish Narratology and Folklore: Oral Tradition, History, and Nationalism*, edited by Alireza Korangy, forthcoming. Frankfurt: Harrassowitz Verlag.

———. 2015. "The Imaginary Kurdish Museum: Ordinary Kurds, Narrative Nationalisms and Collective Memory." *Kurdish Studies* 3, no. 2: 172–191.

———. 2011. *The Militant Kurds: A Dual Strategy for Freedom*. Westport: Praeger International.

Elger, Katrin, Maximilian Popp, Christian Reiermann and Michael Sauga. 2017. "Nazis, Spies and Terrorists: Can the German-Turkish Relationship Be Saved?" *Spiegel Online*, August 10, 2017.

Entessar, Nader. 2014. "Between a Rock and a Hard Place: The Kurdish Dilemma in Iran." In *Conflict, Democratization, and the Kurds in the Middle East,* edited by David Romano and Mehmet Gurses, 211–224. New York: Palgrave Macmillan.

Fischer-Tahir, Andrea. 2012. "Gendered Memories and Masculinities: Kurdish Peshmerga on the Anfal Campaign in Iraq." *Journal of Middle East Women's Studies* 8, no. 1: 92-114. https://doi.org/10.2979/jmiddeastwomstud.8.1.92

Forsberg, Erika, Johanna Kristin Birnir, and Christian Davenport. 2017. "Introduction: State of the Field of Ethnic Politics and Conflict." *Ethnopolitics* 16, no. 1: 1-4. https://doi.org/10.1080/17449057.2016.1235873

Geri, Maurizio. 2016. "From a History of Exclusion to the Securitization of the Kurdish Issue: A Step of Democratic Regression in Turkey." *Muslim World Journal of Human Rights* 13, no. 1: 25–43. https://doi.org/10.1515/mwjhr-2016-0006

Greene, Frederick D. 1896. *The Rule of the Turks*. New York: Putnam.

Gurlay, William. 2017. "Oppression, Solidarity, Resistance: The Forging of Kurdish Identity in Turkey." *Ethnopolitics* 17, no. 2: 130–146. https://doi.org/10.1080/174 49057.2017.1339425

Hürriyet Daily News. 2016. "Turkey's Erdoğan says Europe 'nursing a viper in its bosom' by direct, indirect support of 'terror.'" March 18, 2016.

Jongerden, Joost and Ahmet Hamdi Akkaya. 2013. "Democratic Confederalism as a Kurdish Spring: The PKK and the Quest for Radical Democracy." In *The Kurdish Spring: Geopolitical Changes and the Kurds*, edited by Mohammed Ahmed and Michael Gunter, 163–185. Costa Mesa: Mazda Publishers.

Kadıoğlu, Ayse. 2013. "Necessity and the State of Exception: The Turkish State's Permanent War with Its Kurdish Citizens." In *Turkey between Nationalism and Globalization*, edited by Riva Kastoryano, 142–161. Abingdon: Routledge.

King, Diane E. 2014. *Kurdistan on the Global Stage: Kinship, Land, and Community in Iraq*. New Brunswick: Rutgers University Press.

Madison, Soyini D. 2012. *Critical Ethnography*. Thousand Oaks: Sage Publications.

Mead, Margaret. 1928. *Coming of Age in Samoa*. New York: William Morrow & Company.

Mezzadra, Sandro and Brett Neilson. 2012. "Between Inclusion and Exclusion: On the Topology of Global Space and Borders." *Theory, Culture & Society* 29, no. 4–5: 58–75.

Naber, Ibrahim. 2018. "Ein feiger Versuch, mich in Deutschland zu ermorden." *Die Welt*, January 31, 2018.

Noblit, George W., Susana Y. Flores, Jr. Murillo Enrique G. 2004. *Postcritical Ethnography*. University of Michigan: Hampton Press.

O'Neill, Shane. 2010. "Struggles Against Injustice: Contemporary Critical Theory and Political Violence." *Journal of Global Ethics* 6, no. 2: 127–139.

Özyürek, Esra. 2006. *The Politics of Public Memory in Turkey*. Syracuse: Syracuse University Press.

Salt, Jeremy. 1993. *Imperialism and the Ottoman Armenians 1878–1896*. London: Frank Cass.

Sarewitz, Daniel. 2013. "Museums, Part 2: Objectivity and Denial." *As We Now Think* (blog), January 13, 2013.

Somer, Murat. 2005. "Failures of the Discourse of Ethnicity: Turkey, Kurds, and the Emerging Iraq." *Security Dialogue* 36, no. 1: 109–128.

Thomas, Jim. 1993. *Doing Critical Ethnography*. Newbury Park: Sage Publications.

Wæver, Ole. 2009. "What Exactly Makes a Continuous Existential Threat Existential – and How is it Discontinued?" In *Existential Threats and Civil-Security Relations*, edited by Oren Barak and Gabriel Sheffer, 19–36. Plymouth: Lexington Books.

Winter, Chase. 2017. "Turkish AKP Politician Linked to Osmanen Germania Boxing Gang in Germany." *Deutsche Welle*. December 14, 2017.

Wilkinson, Cai. 2013. "Ethnographic Methods." In *Critical Approaches to Security: An Introduction to Theories and Methods*, edited by Laura J. Shepherd, 129–145. New York: Routledge.

Wolcott, Harry F. 2008. *Ethnography: A Way of Seeing*. Lanham: Altamira Press.

Yeğen, Mesut. 2009. "Prospective-Turks" or "Pseudo-Citizens": Kurds in Turkey." *Middle East Journal* 63, no. 4 (Autumn): 597–615. Project MUSE.

Chapter 2

Living Structures

Methodological Considerations on People and Place

Joost Jongerden

SETTING THE SCENE

Reaching a height of 1,938 meters, Mount Karacadağ is a basalt-rich massif in the southeastern part of Turkey. It runs between Diyarbakir to the northeast, a city on the bank of the Tigris with a population of close to a million, and Urfa to the southwest, near to the Euphrates, with over half a million people. The higher parts of this volcano shield mountain are used for summer pasture, with mobile sheep-herding encampments. Since the dairy factories do not collect the milk when the farming families move out to the high meadows, the women process it, unpasteurized, into cheese. The soft, white (feta) cheese is pressed, chopped into blocks, and left to rest in salted water. Most is sold to traders or at open markets in nearby towns and cities, where it competes with the factory cheese sold in supermarket chains, like Carrefour.

In the lower parts of the mountain, rice is grown, although yields are low in the stony fields. From a *dönüm*, an old Ottoman measurement equal to the amount of land that could be ploughed by a team of oxen in a day (but today fixed at 1,000 m^2 or 0.1 hectares), the yield of the land varieties in Karacadağ is about 400–500 kg,[1] while that of improved varieties cultivated can approach 700–800 kilograms nowadays. In spite of their low yield, the land varieties with their middle-size grains and late maturity are highly appreciated. They are resistant to the drought and cold, even though they are susceptible to lodging (Alp et al. 2010).[2] In the Kurdistan region, the black-streaked white rice is praised for its aroma and taste, with city-dwellers willing to pay a relatively high price for it. While a kilo of ordinary rice costs slightly less than one euro, local consumers are willing to pay double that for the Karacadağ rice, which is easy to distinguish due to its colour and size.

Many landowners have the rice produced on their land under sharecropping arrangements, in which a tenant cultivates for a share of the yield or return. Among both landowning and sharecropper households in the villages, moreover, there may be one or more members who earn an additional income through seasonal work. Some do seasonal work in agriculture, both inside and outside the region, such as harvesting cotton (in Urfa, Çukurova), hazelnuts (to the north, in the Black Sea Coastal region), or tomatoes (in Manisa, far to the west, on the Aegean). Not only are people mobile, traveling to the agricultural centers of employment, since the work also moves to the labor, such that the bags of the vegetable *kereng* (*acanthus*) traders bring to the villages. The traders collect the *kereng* after it is cleaned and used to export it to Syria before the war.

During October to May, when labor is not needed at the farm, some of the young men also work for cash in Istanbul and other metropolitan areas in the west or south of Turkey, where they mostly earn a living in the informal sector. Many of the young men from one of the villages I visited in 2012 work in waste recycling. They walk down the streets collecting tins, paper and cardboard, plastic and glass bottles and the like, which they sell to middlemen and recycle centres. The money these young men earn in the city goes to the family back home and toward savings for a future marriage. The family, meanwhile, sends yogurt, cheese, and other processed foods from the village to support their sons in the city.

Not all men work in precarious jobs, of course. In one village, a man and his brother explain how they went to Istanbul decades ago and established a business in Istanbul producing clothes for the east-European market. The brothers earn a good income now and live there most of the time, but if you ask "Where are you from?" they will respond " Karacadağ," not Istanbul. In the village they grow wheat, but not for the money, they say. They grow wheat to mark the land. It shows the land is not what they call "ownerless," and by growing the wheat they say, "This land is ours; stay away!" One day, when they retire, they say they will settle in the village, and in anticipation of this return and to show their belonging to the village, they have constructed new houses, financed by their city earnings.

Moving our focus from the mountains to the plains, one of the main changes we see in the landscape over the last few years is the expansion of the city and construction of villas further into the countryside. Some of these villas are built on bulges in fields, giving the impression of small castles overlooking the land, where wheat, lentils, and watermelons are grown. These are the new "mansions" of large landowners. Half of the year or more, the buildings remain unoccupied, since the landlords also tend to have houses in nearby cities and/or one of the main cities in the western part of the country, in Istanbul or Ankara, mainly. They leave the daily work to "their villagers," whose cattle are allowed to graze on the land in return for a part of the produce. These large landowners come to the village at sowing and harvest times, to check on the work, and for anniversaries and other celebrations, such as the main religious holidays and the weddings of their sons, which are held locally even when the son has been away for many years.

In addition to the deeply rooted sense of home, this returning for marriage may be explained as an expression of patrilocality, in which the wife moves to or near the domicile of her husband's parents. It takes a contemporary twist though: although holding the wedding ceremony in the village establishes that as the locality of the new couple, this may itself be partly a symbolic construction, as they, too, may only actually live there for a few months of the year. Education functions as another strong urban pull on young people, as it promises an income and possibly a good one—often a family will send the younger children off to city schools/universities, with the older ones taking on home-farm duties—and girls have a special motivation to follow this route if they desire to escape the pressures of elders and traditional (patriarchal) social relations.

While the old landlords did not have an additional occupation and their livelihoods were derived from the land, their sons and daugthers, mostly do have another job, which may even supply their principal income. Some are professionals, they are doctors or have a job in the booming construction sector, as lawyers, independent building contractors, or architects. One architect-building contractor recalls how he had a huge rock brought from his village to the gated community he constructed in the city of Diyarbakır, symbolically locating the village in the city.

Marking the Karacadağ land more broadly, there are not only the mountain and its plains, with villages and the two cities, but also roads. Often taken for granted or just the subject of complaints about their pockmarked condition, the roads are an important "actant" in the landscape. They connect people and places, and compress distances between the different socio-spatial settings in which life organizes. Widened in recent years, and with extra lanes added, cars pass by with dizzying speed, while heavily loaded trucks seem to have difficulty with every single slope. Years ago, the trucker-farmer was a common phenomenon, small-holders independently eking out a second income through delivery services. The trucker-farmer would organize journey routes to stop by his land as necessary, but otherwise only spend time in the village during the planting and harvesting seasons.

Today, many people on the road are the relatively well-off urbanites commuting to work or traveling between gated communities in the city and holiday villages by the sea or in the hills. Sometimes unengaged in agriculture and protected at home by armed security and camera surveillance, these people tend to be quite disconnected from the rural environments they pass through and stay in. For those moving between poor villages and rundown urban areas for reasons of subsistence and family ties, of course, the situation is rather different. Minibuses also carry their village occupants to shops and markets and the children to schools (there has been a massive closure of rural schools since 2000, and the children are now bussed daily to the district town or city from around 90 percent of the villages). Talks between the Kurdistan Workers Party (PKK) and Turkey had brought calm to the war-prone region, until President Erdoğan initiated another round of deadly conflict in the summer of 2015. Now, the roads around Mount Karacadağ are again carrying military convoys and dotted by checkpoints, which are targeted by an occasional car-bomb.

THE PROBLEM

So, what do these descriptions of daily life activities all mean from a methodological perspective? What does the production of cheese and cultivation of rice, the seasonal migration into precarious jobs, issues around gender and education, the multiple living places and the car-bomb all tell us from a methodological perspective? Basically, and this is the central problem addressed, what could be easily preconceived as a spatial identity—the Mount Karacadağ agricultural countryside—has been characterized in terms of various human practices, with our interest focused on extended networks of activities and processes of becoming. While the starting point was a concern with the rurality and the lives of people in spaces defined as rural, the activities people engage with make clear that no preconceived identity can be assumed. Our description did, in fact, take us from the rural to the urban (with the selling of cheese and linkage of roads), as well as to the mountain meadows (the summer encampments) and a further away "beyond" (export of products to Syria), and it pointed toward various socio-economic- and gender-specific activities. Mount Karacadağ is not only a basalt-rich massif, it is also constituted through multiple (sets of) unfolding practices and interactions and their relations with many "elsewheres."

What most transpires from the description of daily activities, therefore, is the intermingling or connectivities of village and city, rural and urban, and the observation that of people calling the village their "home" are not living in the village, or not all the time. That is, the *spatial approach* taken here facilitates a certain dissolution wherein conventionalized conceptualizations may give way to an alternative reading that arguably better reveals patterns of the social world people contsruct and live in. These developments take various forms, such as the phenomena of semi-absentee urban rural farmers following an agro-social calendar that combines village return to work the land with family visits for important events. Villagers, meanwhile, maintain their small-holdings through a multitude of family-based, age (life-stage) related arrangements, with income derived from agricultural produce supported by or (increasingly) just supplementing that derived from work elsewhere (or from pensions, an important financial input/transfer nowadays). Family farming labor is typically organized around this by casual employment opportunities, which take family members away from the village, and the return movements, which bring them back again to work on the farm (Öztürk, Hilton, and Jongerden 2012; Öztürk, Jongerden, and Hilton 2018). From here, we can draw various conclusions.

First and foremost, we see how people's lives are linked to broader geographical, socioeconomic, and political domains, such as the (non-)collection of milk, the price of rice, and the development of the construction sector—or the discontinuation of peace talks and resumption of armed conflict and a military "solution." Here, it is not the place, the city, or the village that establishes the setting of life, but the wider networks of practices that people are part of. These are always changing, moreover, constantly resetting the spaces—or *spatialities*—of our lives, at varying rates, in many ways and for innumerable reasons over and through time. This presents a dynamic picture, one involving *movement*, both the major migrations of seasons and years across hundreds and thousands of kilometers and the daily and weekly local trips spanning "home" and "outside." Conceptually, we may say, the notion of place and time are closely related, and also that the conceptualization of place is connected but not opposed to space, which enables a dynamic understanding of the rural, or any other spatial identity.

Second, we see how people move among socio-spatial settings, from the village in a mountainous area, where the rhythm of life is no longer determined by agricultural activities, to the city, where the leftovers of consumption provide a living for village boys. Since the prices of agricultural products tend to fluctuate and in the long-term decrease (the terms of trade decline), there has been a relative reduction of farmers' incomes (Öztürk 2012). Smallholders have responded to the increasing pressure on agriculture not only by heightened involvement in the market, through more intensive/productive farming arrangements and practices, but also by income (livelihood) differentiation, or *pluriactivity*. Families organize for the continued maintenance of the smallholding through off-farm and out-of-village income supplementation and replacement—including, even, through the informal waste collection sector.

Third, the examples from people's daily lives introducing the dimension of movement and focus on mobility emphasizes the decision-making framework within which people change their location (the physical positioning of bodies, residence, etc.). Crucially, people are *agents*, not merely buffeted by the winds of change around them—and they are *social* actors, moreover, making decisions not (just) as atomized individuals but (also) as (members of) larger social structures, such as extended families. Interestingly, this means that we should not only look at those who move, but also at the non-movers (Sirkeci 2013).

As indicated, a critical factor in this decision-making is the (cultural) reproduction of the household, which in rural areas is organized around the land. Smallholders and small enterprise farming families make decisions about who will stay and who will leave and why and how long for according to a wide variety of social and economic considerations. Pluriactivity and external (including self-) employment, retirement revenues, and other social security benefits and transfers have made the difference, enabling households to maintain and reproduce their smallholdings.

From the above, we may conclude that boundaries—relations of interiority—do not define social life. Instead of assuming a bounded setting for this, therefore, we propose the concept of *activity space*, as introduced by the political geographer Doreen Massey. Massey (1995) defined activity space as "the spatial network of links and activities, of spatial connections and of locations, within which a particular agent operates." This is a heuristic device rather than a robust theoretical concept, employed "to help us into a particular way of thinking about the spatial organization of society." It goes beyond the "common sense" assumption, that is, which links people to place. Again, place and space are not a binary, but dimensions of the spatial, both *extending* and *grounding* investigation:

> [P]laces, in fact, are always constructed out of articulations of social relations [. . .] which are not only internal to that locale but which link them to elsewhere. Their "local uniqueness" is always already a product of wider contacts; the local is always already a product in part of "global" forces, where global in this context refers not necessarily to the planetary scale, but to the geographical beyond, the world beyond the place itself. (Massey 1995, 183)

The concept of activity space sensitises us to the spatial extension of practice, such as the way in which arable land, infrastructure, and markets for the production, distribution, and consumption of rice are interrelated, or how the walking of streets in Istanbul is connected to the maintenance of life in villages. It affords an appreciation of three broad processes. First, it directs us to *extension* in the relationships of people from where they live (the grounding, which is where movement, and time, enter); then, it incorporates the many ways in which the people and places are *interrelated*, with a variegated weaving together of resources and relations at a particular locus; and finally, it reveals *entwinement*, how such practices come together in multitudinous, complex ways to form a whole, the spatial unit, as it were, under consideration (such as Mount Karacadağ). House construction or wedding ceremonies in a particular place, for example, are co-produced by the activities and the mobilization of resources from "elsewhere" invested in that place. This makes "the city" and "the village," and "the urban" and "the rural" relational and temporal identities, which are dynamic and always under construction, understood through the practices and processes by which they are produced (Massey 2004, 6). Indeed, the city and the village, the rural and the urban are not given categories, but always need to be explained.

THE RURAL AND THE VILLAGE

The concept of the rural, one may say, evolved by distinguishing it from the urban, which, through its marriage to industry, became the dominant element of capitalism (Mormont 1990, 41). The urban, that is, was identified as a positive, from which the rural followed as its negative, the two being co-defined through a structurally nonequivalent relationship in which the rural was inferior (Wallace-Hadrill 1991). As socio-spatial identities, rural and urban were then ascribed discrete characteristics that could be understood by (as the meaning of) the purportedly equal categories—like "agricultural," "green," and "low population density" signifying and constituting "rural" and "industrial," "grey" and "high population density" for urban. The construction of such rural-urban dualities is powerful because of their simplicity (Sayer 1989, 302). However, not only does the emphasis on differences between entities repress the difference within entities (Sayer 1991, 286), but such understandings are also not descriptive but performative. The (historical) idea that the urban and not the rural is the seat of industry, and that the rural and not the urban is the seat of agriculture, have produced the urban as the seat of industry and the rural as the seat of agriculture.

Although rural sociology took the village to be synonymous with the idea of agricultural community, the connection was a historical coincidence wherein urbanization coincided with industrialization. It was not that village industry could not compete with the city, quite the reverse; village cottage-industries, such as weaving in England, Flanders, and India were so resilient that the looms of village-weavers had to be demolished before urban producers could find sufficient markets for their products, and the urban appropriation of production needed to be sanctioned with armed expeditions into (against) villages. Historically, the effects of the enclosure movement stripped villages of their common land and caused peasants to flock to the cities; then, the industrial revolution of the 18th and 19th centuries, sustained by the steam-machine and protected by the state, brought about a deindustrialization of villages, producing the urban as the centre of industrial production and the rural as the site of agriculture (Köymen 1937; Jongerden 2007, 201–202).

In Turkey, the modern history of rural space was founded on the settling of (nearly all of) Anatolia's seminomadic peoples and tribal groupings, various enforced mass population migrations, and the development of a fairly weak but highly centralised and hierarchical political system that directed the modernisation of agriculture. It was in this context that the village became paramount, as the legal specification of rural settlement units by the state for the purposes of administration (quintessentially defined by the Village Act of 1924, one of the first pieces of legislation enacted in the new Republic following the collapse of the Ottoman Empire).

From the 1950s, industrialization and urbanization developed quickly in the Republic and there was a relative decline in the rural population. Then, as neoliberal policies were enacted, from the 1980s generally and in agriculture especially during the 2000s, the absolute numbers of the rural population decreased. Roughly, from the 1950s to 2000s, the traditional rural-urban population ratio inverted, going from three quarters in villages (and hamlets) to three quarters in cities (and large towns). This indicates urban migration, a profound phenomenon currently transforming countries worldwide. Indeed, Turkey has witnessed the movement of vast numbers of people to the major cities, particularly Istanbul, which alone now houses around a quarter of the national population (Öztürk, Jongerden, and Hilton 2018).

While official (state) statistics show a significant net migration from rural to urban areas, however, they also show this as reversed, with net movements in the *opposite* direction, from city/town to town/city during the periods 1975–1980 and 1995–2000.[3] The statistics also reveal an overall increase in urban-rural migration for 1980–2000, along with an overall decrease in rural-to-rural migration and increase in urban-to-urban migration for 1975–2000, with the latter accounting for about half of all migration during that period (Öztürk 2012, 141).[4]

In the Mount Karacadağ area, in the provinces of Diyarbakir and Sanliurfa, which it spans, the most recent state (*TÜİK*/TURKSTAT) figures for which there is a consistent counting system and during which there was a cessation of hostilities in the PKK-Turkey conflict (so, post 2008 and until 2015) show significant and consistent out-migration from both provinces and for every year. Most of those people went from villages, towns and the two provincial capitals to major cities (so rural-urban and urban-urban flows). However, the in-migration figures were also large—roughly three-quarters of the outward figures, in fact.[5] Clearly, the in-migration is more difficult to explain. Just as the out-migration was to cities, most of the incomers also went to the urban centers, the two provincial capitals, from rural areas and smaller towns and cities elsewhere in the region—but, as in the national figures, there was also a "back-flow" to the villages.

The received wisdom is that people move from the countryside to cities, since the labour demand in agriculture is reducing and job opportunities in the city increasing. Urban-to-urban movement and the decline in rural-to-rural movements may also be largely explained along similar lines; families uproot and people move for employment reasons from towns to cities and from provincial cities to major metropolises, while the mobile rural population tends to move to towns and cities rather than between villages. The high and increasing number of people moving to villages—even, apparently, out-weighing the opposite movement in particular recent periods—requires some consideration, however.

There are several reasons for people to migrate from the city to the countryside. First, people who have been living and working in urban areas (or abroad) return to their village after they retire. This has especially applied to state employees, who, until recently, could retire at a relatively young age, in their early forties even (after 20–25 years of work). Second, people tend to return to their village after living in an urban area for their children's education. Educational opportunities are concentrated in urban areas, and a proportion of the adult village population moves to the city for a decade or two to sustain their children at high school and college, after which they return. Third, there is a category of people who cannot survive in the city, and go back home. This may occur in particular during times of economic downturn and especially among those who are not personally equipped for the city struggle, who cannot sustain a living and/or who lose their paid jobs or other income source (as craftsman, small entrepreneurs, etc.) including precarious employment (as day laborers and street vendors).

Fourth, and especially in the Mediterranean and Aegean region, but also in a region like Dersim, we see a more prosperous category of people moving to new holiday homes and summer villages. A significant section of the population now live in cities in winter and in such villages in summer. Fifth, some people migrate out of city centers to live in nearby green spaces. This essentially comprises the development of professional, commuter-belt communities, suburban villages known in Turkey as '*banliyö*' (from '*banlieu*'). Sixth, there are those who migrate seasonally because living conditions in the village are harsh. During the winters, they live in urban comfort, with relatives or in their own flat, and during the summers they go back home, typically in the spring to plant vegetables in their gardens. Seventh, in the Kurdistan region people deal with forced urbanization as a result of over 3000 villages emptied and destroyed by the Turkish military in response to a PKK-led insurgency during the 1990s (Jongerden 2017).

Interestingly also, rural nonagricultural employment rose from 2.7 million in 1999 to 4.6 million in 2006, before dropping back to 2.9 million in 2010 as a result of the reclassification of villages near cities effectively halving, or so, (village) population counted as "rural" (see note 4). Thus, even in total numbers, there was an increase in rural work outside of farming, an increase that was really quite sharp in relative terms. In the southeast region of Turkey, where Mount Karacadağ is situated, approaching a half of all employees in rural areas are now nonagricultural jobs. Here, we need to distinguish between two phenomena: the rising importance of non-farming income for farmer-households, on the one hand, and the increase in the non-farming rural population on the other. In addition, and complicating matters still further, there has been a growth in urban agriculture: about a quarter of a million agricultural enterprises are now registered in urban areas, where almost 700,000 urban inhabitants are recorded as employed in agriculture (around 10 percent of the total numbers of agricultural enterprises and workers). In the Southeast, around a quarter of all urban employment is in the agricultural sector.

Taking all this as a whole, we begin to shift from simple, albeit powerful generalization (depopulation and impoverishment of the agrarian countryside) to a far more nuanced and complex picture. The weakening relationship between rural settlement and agriculture means that the equation of these, the assumed spatial product of modernity, becomes increasingly untenable. Importantly, from a methodological perspective, this implies that we cannot just talk about urban and rural as discrete and seperate entities.

CONCLUSIONS: METHODOLOGICAL PROPOSITIONS

Originally motivated by tensions in dealing with observed phenomena, this piece has indicated a methodological *approach*, characterized in terms of living structures, and activity space, which brings into focus the ways in which people organize their lives through a range of multi-spatial practices and conceptualizes people and their practices as both grounded in places and in terms of its relations with elsewhere. Thus, we argue, this thinking beyond predefined spatial categories opens new horizons of investigation. For an understanding of the daily lives of people, we need a vocabulary that does not essentialize the spatial setting of people's worlds, in terms of rural and urban or village and city, but introduces more open concepts, and rather than notions of fixity we need dynamic ones. For this, we introduce the concepts of *activity-space*, as coined by Doreen Massey, and *living structures*.

The rooting of people through the idea of sedentary settlement and singular residence should be replaced by an understanding of grounded *living structures*. In order to get at the meaning of this, we may start from the idea of "migration" and state that the sedentary idea of residential relocation implicit in this idea of migration has to be challenged for at least two reasons. First, migration as a bounded and discrete event does not convey movement as inscribed in daily life. Such movement does not (just) consist of single transfers from "origin" to "destination," transfers of permanent residence, but includes (also) multiple origins and destinations variously combined and blurred together in multi-place living structures. Second, the periods of residence cannot easily be distinguished as "temporary" and "permanent" migration—as shown, for example, by the postretirement "returns" of "permanent migrants," and extended stays of "temporary migrants."

Nowadays, we observe, people are increasingly spending their time split between two or three places located in both rural and urban settings, while rural-based households and family complexes are more and more oriented to living structures that include multiple places, in the village (and hamlets), in the local town and the nearest city, and in the distant metropolis(es) and foreign countries. We may refer to this as a *heterolocal* understanding, to get at the different socio-spatial realities in which people live, at the movements of those who integrate innumerable *hybrid residence/employment combinations*. For the scholar, this brings the challenge of conceiving of social reality not in terms of distinct spatial units that can be understood by looking at their internal dynamics but as constituted relationally. There is no "unit of analysis," apart from that which we construct for practical reasons. Thus we propose the concept of living structures, referring by "structures" to the *arrangements/patterns of spatio-temporality through which people live*, and by "living" to the *human dynamics* of this, the (organically emergent) *changing (re)construction*.

The types of human movement involved in living patterns need to be integrated into our concepts of household and settlement. The examples discussed reveal living patterns ranging from the level of individuals to that of households (and communities) that comprise an array of space/place combinations with assorted styles of movement constructed by a range of temporal references, from the mobility forms of daily commuting through seasonal sojourn to life-stage migration. The effect is of a blurring of the rural/urban binary and a transition to an understanding in which rural/urban are no longer considered as discrete categories, to be explained in terms of relations of inferiority. What transpires is a *relational understanding* in which the city and the village, rural and urban, continually *co-produce and redefine* each other through a myriad of *dynamic practices* (living structures).

The terms "village," "city," "urban," and "rural" do not represent preexisting entities. Urban theorists in the 1970s had already problematized the implicit reification of these concepts and argued that we should instead look at the production of spatial forms in contemporary society. This does not mean that we have to do away with them as concepts; rather, they are not to be defined by internal characteristics but explained as *social productions of spatial forms* (Gilbert 1982, 615–667). Relatedly, Levebvre (1991, 89–90) criticized the "ideologically dominant tendency" that "divides space up into parts and parcels," arguing that

> instead of uncovering the social relationships (including class relationships) that are latent in spaces, instead of concentrating our attention on the production of space and the social relationships inherent to it [. . .] we fall into the trap of treating space as space "in itself," as space as such. We come to think in terms of spatiality, and so *fetishize* space (in a way reminiscent of the old fetishism of commodities, where the trap lay in exchange, and the error was to consider "things" in isolation, as "things in themselves").

We need to do away with the idea prevalent in much of the social science literature that the world we inhabit is one of discontinuous units, effecting a "discrete spatial partitioning of territory" (Malkki 2008 [1992], 277). In the end, any spatial form is an "arena of claims and counter-claims, agreements and coalitions that are always temporary and fragile" (Amin 2004, 39), the product of interrelations, is a sphere of multiplicty and always under construction (Massey 2005, 9), as is the case for Karacadağ.

NOTES

1. Data collected by Joost Jongerden in 2012 from Karacadağ villages.
2. Lodging: the bending over of stems near the ground (making them difficult to harvest and reducing yields).
3. Although not in the southeast of Turkey which was heavily affected by the conflict with a forced evacuation of villages (Jongerden 2007).
4. The state agency (*TÜİK* or TURKSTAT) stopped presenting migration figures in easily accessible "rural" and "urban" categories during the 2000s (moving to a province-based presentation), when it also changed the status of a major proportion of village districts (re-categorizing "rural" settlements/areas as "urban") and the counting method; more recent figures are thus unavailable for direct comparison.
5. Some 2–3 percent of the total provincial populations out-migrated annually (around 45,000–55,000 people from Diyarbakir and 30,000–40,000 people from Sanliurfa), but net annual outflow was under 1 percent (c. 0.5% for Sanliurfa and 0.8% Diyarbakir); coupled with relatively high birth-rates, therefore, the total provincial populations rose during this period (from 1.6 to 1.9 million for Sanliurfa, 1.5 to 1.7 million Diyarbakir).

BIBLIOGRAPHY

Alp, Aydin, Simten Yesilmen, Aydin Vural, and H. Sahan Guran. 2010. "Determination of Some Agronomical Characteristics and Ochratoxin-A Level of Karacadag Rice (Oryza sativa L.) in Diyarbakir Ecological Conditions, Turkey." *African Journal of Agricultural Research* 4: 1965–72.

Amin, Ash. 2004. "Regions Unbound: Towards a New Politics of Place." *Geografiska Annaler* 86: 33–44.

Gilbert, Jess. 1982. "Rural Theory: The grounding of Rural Sociology." *Rural Sociology* 47: 609–33.

Jongerden, Joost. 2007. *The Settlement Issue in Turkey and the Kurds: An Analysis of Spatial Policies, Modernity and War.* Leiden & Boston: Brill.

Köymen, Nusret Kemal. 1937. *Village, the Unit of Societal Organization.* Wisconsin: Wisconsin University.

Malkki, Liisa. 2008 [1992]. "National Geographic: The Rooting of Peoples and the Territorialization of National Identity Among Scholars and Refugees." in *The Cultural geography Reader,* edited by Timothy S. Oakes and Patricia L. Price, 24–44. London: Routledge.

Massey, Doreen. 1995. "Places and Their Pasts." *History Workshop Journal* 39: 182–92.

———. 2004. "Geographies of Responsibility." *Geografiska Annaler* 86: 5–18.

Mormont, Marc. 1990. "Who Is Rural? or, How To Be Rural." in *Rural Restructuring, Global Porcessess and their Responses,* edited by Terry Marsden, Philip Lowe and Sarah Whatmore, 21–44. London: David Fulton Publishers.

Öztürk, Murat. 2012. *Agriculture, Peasantry and Poverty in Turkey in the Neo-Liberal Age.* Wageningen: Wageningen Academic Publishers.

Öztürk, Murat, Andy Hilton, and Joost Jongerden. 2012. "Migration as Movement and Multiplace Life: Some Recent Developments in Rural Living Structures in Turkey." *Population, Space and Place* 20: 370–88.

Öztürk, Murat, Joost Jongerden, and Andy Hilton. 2015. "Commodification and the Social Commons: Smallholder Autonomy and Rural–Urban Kinship Communalism in Turkey." *Agrarian South: Journal of Political Economy* 3: 337–67.

———. 2018. "The (re)production of the New Peasantry in Turkey." *Rural Studies* 61: 244–54.

Sayer, A. 1989. "Dualistic Thinking and Rhetoric in Geography." *Area* 21: 301–05.

———. 1991. "Behind the Locality Debate: Deconstructing Geography's Dualisms." *Environment and Planning A: Economy and Space* 23: 283–308.

Sirkeci, Ibrahim. 2013. *Transnational Markets and Transnational Consumers.* Heidelberg Springer.

Wallace-Hadrill, Andrew. 1991. "Introduction." In *City and Country in the Ancient World,* edited by John Rich and Andrew Wallace-Hadrill, xi–xviii. London: Routledge.

Chapter 3

Online-Offline Research on Diasporic Identities

Methodological Benefits, Challenges, and Critical Insights

Jowan Mahmod

New communication technologies are becoming ever more deeply embedded into people's professional and personal lives. Our social realities are increasingly constructed in the online environment, and the online-offline boundaries have become more and more blurred, as have public and private spheres. Whether people are engaged in conversations, game playing, using email, or showing photos and images online, they are constructing identity (Rybas and Gajjala 2007). This means that culture is no longer bound by territory or physical location, and as a result of these new cultural and social interactions, new identity maps are created, underpinned by an altered sense of community (Mahmod 2016). Conducting research online, or both online and offline (multisited), can therefore advance our understanding of identity, diaspora, and transnationalism considerably.

While there has been a growing canon of literature on internet research, the continuous and rapid advances in communication devices make it difficult to find the "right" way to approach online ethnographic study. Ethnographic study usually involves observing and describing a group of people in their natural setting, from one or more perspectives (Vaan Maanen 2011). By immersing themselves into the community, researchers try to understand subjects within a culture, on individual and collective levels, in order to understand and describe what is going on (Rybas and Gajjala 2007).

The purpose of this chapter is to discuss some of the possible reasons for, and benefits of, undertaking research that combines online and offline data within diaspora and identity studies. The arguments and examples are drawn from my PhD thesis[1] which addressed identity-making among young diasporic Kurds in the United Kingdom and Sweden through online ethnography and offline interviews. The chapter, retrospectively, provides an account of the methodological considerations and challenges I faced while carrying out the research on a transnational online community created by diasporic Kurds. I will focus on particular themes that may influence research design and empirical findings, as well as my own role as a researcher. These include the multisited research approach which covers anonymity and authenticity, sensitive content, and online profanity. My experiences of the multisited approach revealed that anonymity, for example, has intrinsic links to authentic self-presentation, and that profanity can be understood as a strategy of self-identification through inclusion—and by definition exclusion.

From this, I move on to discuss the insider/outsider dichotomy and the implications of a partial insider position to the researcher. While I am a researcher first and foremost when conducting a study, I am also a Swedish Sorani-speaking Kurd settled in the United Kingdom while carrying out a PhD project. In the processes of writing, these multiple voices are silenced and omitted wherever possible, or at best just implied. The different layers of my personal identity carry with them the task of demystifying the role of researcher and the multiple voices that construct this role. This reflexivity—the act of disclosing my own position in a study and the necessity of understanding, explaining, and justifying that position—requires a clear self-awareness of my own views and how these might influence the research process, from data gathering to the interpretation of the findings (Greenbank 2003). With this comes the important question of how we collect data; which stories we include, and which are being left out. The chapter concludes by addressing questions of ethics and confidentiality, especially in an online setting.

MULTISITED METHODOLOGY: WHY DO ONLINE-OFFLINE RESEARCH?

New Fields—New Identity Formations

To paraphrase Karim H. Karim (2006) when describing multiculturalism, identity is like the elephant in the old Sufi tale; six blind men who touched individual parts of the animal described it respectively as a wall, a snake, a spear, a tree trunk, a rope, and a fan. The concept of identity may be as ambiguous as it is important. It either says too much or too little, although it plays a central role in everyday life (Brubaker and Cooper 2000). The most important aspect in terms of this chapter is that identities are neither fixed, essentialist, nor permanent; identities are formed and transformed continuously through interactions between people (Hall 1987).

My own research is centered on how identities are created and recreated rather than what they entail or accepting them as fait accompli (accomplished entity), thus, the online ethnographic study proved a fruitful and valuable way of exploring such matters. This awareness became particularly apparent in a discussion thread in one of the forums of the online community that I studied, in which a participant who had settled in Sweden reflected upon how identity changes with space, time, and company. The writer raised a thought-provoking discussion that may echo some of the central questions with which scholars of diaspora and cultural studies have been grappling over the years, but is particularly remarkable in this context, given the political and historical accounts of the Kurds and the existential threat they have endured to their identity.

> Where are you from? If you hear that question in a normal situation, it is common that you answer that you are a Kurd. The answer is obviously influenced by various factors. Factors such as that you belong to a minority in a multicultural society, you belong to an oppressed group [. . .]. What happens if you ask yourself that question? Can you see yourself as only an individual without any categories?[2]

This quote summarizes some of the key dilemmas and interplays observed in research projects on identity and community, and how identities are the products of interaction between the self and others; "you" and "I" become "we" and "they" (Gajjala 2008). Online, these boundaries are less clear, especially when the "they" are not present and the "we" break up into many different subgroups. Such notions have become clear to the members of this online community after years of discussing and exchanging views. As one respondent told me, "Online, it wasn't 'which country do you come from,' but 'which city?'" Kurds growing up in a diaspora community can now discuss issues that concern themselves, and not the "other." By interrogating the imagined identity (Anderson 1983), they explore the social construction of time and space, a new kind of endeavour one could say, which challenges essentialist ideas of identity and belonging. Online discourse shows a different mapping of identity that diverges from offline accounts and from earlier statements and conclusions made about identity, such as the idea that online and transnational activities strengthen and mobilize diasporas.

It is true that the main reason why young Kurds become members of online communities is to discuss common interests and to unite in important matters related to nation-building projects. Digital technologies are a significant and powerful enabler of disruption, and represent a new form of power for individuals and "small players" who until recently stood little chance of success. This is particularly important in the context oppressed groups, "victim diaspora" (Cohen 2001), and their construction and self-representation. This power of new technologies is made evident by the way they are often censored by some authorities. But the newly networked technologies have also provided means to tackle internal matters. And similar to many earlier researchers, I have been confronted with the complexity and the contradictory nature of identities in general, and among the Kurdish diasporas in particular. Linguistic, religious, national, social, cultural diversity, and territorial division among Kurds have certainly not made studying them less complicated.[3] Having said that, in this age of globalization, multiculturalism, immigration, cosmopolitanism, transnationalism, and hybrid identities, I believe that Kurds can say much about questions of ethnicity and identity, not despite their complexity but thanks to it. Adding to this, the Kurdish diaspora belongs to one of the most active and visible diasporas in Europe and has frequently been used to illustrate diasporic engagement to change policy-making (Baser 2011).

New communication technologies have provided a whole gamut of new possibilities for the diaspora to represent itself and to influence political processes. Transnational practices including social and cultural relations across state borders (Glick-Schiller et al. 1992) are especially characteristic for diasporic Kurds, not only to link back to the homeland but also to the various diasporic communities in Europe and beyond. However, these transnational and online exchanges have, perhaps unexpectedly, opened up areas for new discourses and ways to question, negotiate, and redefine identities to better suit the realities of diasporic life.

Online experiences of discussing these sometimes highly sensitive and taboo topics are considerably different from the face-to-face social experiences, and consequently the experience of ethnographically studying them is significantly different. Rather than comparing the online and offline settings, it is useful to explore how these sites are intersecting and experiences are interweaving, that has meaning for the production of identity (Rybas and Gajjala 2007).

Online-Offline Discrepancies: Anonymity, Authenticity, and Profanity

One of the strengths of undertaking online ethnography is the possibility for the researcher to observe interactions without changing the dynamics during the process of participant observation. While it is never fully possible to measure the impact of the researcher, changes in the character of the discussion can be observed, particularly if the researcher has become familiar with the online community before the actual participant-observation takes place. Given my experience as a former group member, I can confirm this from my knowledge of the jargon of the discussions. The great benefit of this kind of research is that the utterances of the participants build the context, rather than the aims of the researcher. I could follow struggles over identity and how participants understood and reacted to various articulations within the online context. This way of capturing the interactions disclosed political, social, economic, and religious issues that were connected to the concepts of identity and belonging. This, Emily Ignacio (2012) explains, offers the researcher the opportunity to see how theories and established concepts within our field can be destabilized and rearticulated. In a similar vein, I witnessed countless discussions about gender, language, cultural values, and norms that challenged the established notions and ideas about what a "real Kurd" is.

One of the most popular and well-articulated discussions online was related to gender, sexuality, and the nature of femininity and masculinity. This contradicts face-to-face interview statements by most respondents, who declared themselves uninterested in taking part in such discussion threads, defining them as "useless." Despite this, all interviewees recognized that they were the most frequently addressed topics, defining areas in which young people of both genders were "testing boundaries." This is especially true for female participants, as topics that are considered taboo can be contested online with more ease and comfort. These spaces have become particularly important for women to ventilate their opinions. It became evident that anonymity and privacy are decisive factors in deciding what kind of topics becomes entrenched online when only discussed reluctantly during interviews. Is it the case that these topics are not important for the respondents, or could there be other reasons? The multisited approach allows for such explorations, and allowed me to discover that respondents who expressed a lack of interest or condemned the banality of the topic did in fact participate in online discussions. Perhaps a better answer to the question can be related back to the explanation that comparative online anonymity opens the door to contesting confines, norms, and traditions that are more apparent in the real world. The most important point emerging from the contradictions between offline and online discussions—and the fact that such sensitive topics evoked massive responses online whilst apparently being uncomfortable topics to discuss face-to-face—centers on the discrepancies between methodologies when collecting material. The use of different methodologies, for instance multisited online-offline research, can mutually contextualize each other (Orgad 2009), although it can also tell us how significantly different the results of producing empirical material can appear. The analysis of online and offline information and how to make collaborative sense of it is anything but straightforward. But such divergences raise questions about what individuals can do online that they cannot do offline. The discrepancies between what people say about their online experiences and what they actually do online are noticeable, making it necessary to reflect upon self-censorship during interviews once respondents have abandoned their anonymity.

Furthermore, of importance for the key questions was not only what they talked about, but *how* they talked about certain topics. The tone of language, whether expressed through love or profanity, could reveal much about their relation to the key themes. Many scholars of internet culture and cyberspace have considered online flaming (online fights) and trolling (deliberately provocative messages posted with an intention of upsetting or distract) as violent and hostile behaviors. Discussions about insults and trolling speak of these as negative and disturbing conversations online and explain this by referring to the structure of the internet and anonymity features that make people loosen tongues. The acts of so-called trolls are aimed at deliberately changing the discussion or provocation through offensive language, according to some scholars (Kuntsman 2009).

In the analysis of my own empirical data, two different kinds of insults could be distinguished. The first type has a clear, deliberate intention to disturb the discussions, but they were often not long-lasting and the participation was shallow. The other category of insults, that I find important to elaborate in relation to the identity discourse, differs from trolling—they are an integral part of the discussion itself and can often be seen in substantial threads. To make a distinction between these different categories and to know what makes the force of an utterance effective to injure, those utterances need to be contextualized. I propose to study the links between these expressions and the interrelated social and cultural links to cultural identity formations. I relate it to issues of self-identification, strategies of inclusion—and by implication, exclusion.

In connection to discussions about authenticity of Kurdish identity, the vocabulary containing insults have worked as strategies to "correct" certain behaviours that are new, or not considered to be enough Kurdish, feminine, or religious in some cases. It is for such reasons that it is important not to explain flames as a feature of new technologies, or as plain rudeness, enabled by the online anonymity. This becomes especially insightful in a comparison between the different forums. These fierce discussions indicate how these issues have an underlying meaning in the contestations of identity and belonging. Even today, insults are considered trolling in many cases. Conversation analysis must be treated with caution as the full context must be made, including those utterances that may be seen as lying outside the context (Ignacio 2012) and not by our own theoretical conventions. Such explorations lead me to the question about how to collect authentic data.

HOW DO WE DISTINGUISH MEANINGFUL DATA?

The different and conflicting accounts in the online community raise questions of representation; whose stories are being privileged and presented, and whose stories are being left out? How do we collect data? Which aspects are important, which are excluded? Kamala Visweswaran (1997) asks what drives our justifications and how we arrive at what we call the "truth" about subjectivities. Many studies about Kurds have stressed the nation-building agenda, patriotism, victimhood, and suffering—deservedly so, as this forms an overwhelming part of their narratives (e.g., Chaliand 1994). But while the existential question of Kurdish identity remains an important topic in my study and in online discussions, there are many other voices that call for attention which contest established concepts of Kurdishness. Frequency and density of discussion themes are an important factor in the selection and data gathering (Geertz 1973). In my project, the number of voices presenting alternative images was too many to ignore. From a methodological and epistemological perspective, these were some of the most challenging questions that I had to deal with in my task as a researcher.

Another conundrum I became aware of during interpreting empirical data was the quiet voices, or the voices that were missing. Why, for instance, was the "honor-killing" debate such a frequently discussed topic in Swedish forums while being barely mentioned among UK-based Kurds? This absence became a more important factor for exploration during their interviews, where I could ask questions about it and make myself more aware of the differences between Kurdish diasporas in the different locations. Diasporas do not create their community in isolation. Each diaspora is strongly affected by its environment, often via policies and citizenship regulations (Waldinger and Fitzgerald 2003). This is particularly true for third- and fourth-generation diasporic Kurds, who may not have the same relationship with the homeland as the first and second generations. Therefore, when we speak of one diaspora, context becomes a critical concept. Theoretical and methodological issues are at stake in terms of what reality-status a researcher gives to his or her material.

The activities of diasporic Kurds in Sweden differ from those of Kurdish diasporas in other places. For example, gender policies and discourses in Sweden have had a great impact on the Kurdish diaspora, whether it concerns the responses to "honor-killing" debates or discussions about gender equality and gender injustices within their own culture. Swedish Kurds are often described by other participants in the online community—as well as during interviews—as being more liberal and open-minded about questions of gender and sexuality, which may reflect Sweden's strong attitudes to gender equality and women's rights as a strong marker of Swedish state identity (De los Reyes 2002). Needless to say, such statements are not representative of the entire diaspora, but the insights serve as a keyhole to the possibilities the internet and the variety of communities and networking sites engender. Having said that, the selection of data and the analysis of it entail more than a simple reference to research aims and theoretical frameworks, and also involves the position of the researcher, especially if this involves the insider-outsider dilemma.

THE INSIDER-OUTSIDER DIALECTIC

In ethnographic studies, the aim of the researcher is to make the unfamiliar familiar, firstly to themselves and then by communication to others. For a researcher with both an insider and outsider role, this becomes more complex, as it means that the familiar must become unfamiliar first. In other words, the outsider researcher has to "go native" to understand the local culture, a researcher with an insider role has to do the reverse (Labaree 2002). The strength of the insider becomes the weakness of the outsider, and vice versa (Merriam et al. 2001).

So, what makes a researcher an insider and outsider at the same time, and what methodological challenges does this throw up? The insider/outsider researcher is both part of a community yet outside it. My research was on the Kurdish community, of which I am a member. Hence, I am an insider. I had also once been a member of the online community I was studying. I was an insider in that sense as well. But the different geographical locations I researched, and different online forums made me an outsider at the same time due to limited familiarity with those locations and the composition of diasporic groups there. This dual positionality made my assumed ethnicity shift from being relevant in one instance to less relevant in another (Baser and Toivanen 2018).

The benefits of being a researcher with an insider status are usually said to make for richer accounts that reflect the realities of the group or culture being studied due to prior knowledge and easier access to the site and the respondents (Paechter 2012). This kind of access also extends to a truer perspective of participants as the researcher's insider status promises greater intimacy and openness (Hodkinson 2005), and like others my insider role helped me access the field and find respondents more easily. Having said that, there are recurring blind spots that I had to overcome as a researcher, such as maintaining a critical distance from the material and dealing with informants who expected solidarity for their cause, and knowing when information is significant. It is, for instance, not uncommon for an insider researcher to take information for granted and leave things unsaid, which an outsider may explore more fully (Breen 2007).

Making the Evident Less Evident

My first encounter with the insider dilemma took place at the early stages of the research. The research design included interviews as the main method of data collection. The online community served, at this point, only as a platform from which to recruit respondents for the interviews. The transnational nature of the community made it easier to identify and recruit diasporic Kurds from the different geographic locations I had chosen for the research.[4] I knew that the transnational community had attracted a great number of diasporic Kurds and had been engaging them deeply over the years in discussions of identity, culture, politics, and religion, producing thousands of threads and online texts. However, the value of such sites for research purposes had bypassed me. Why did I not see the significance of this community for the gathering of new material for the kind of research questions that I was interested in? Especially, considering that online ethnography of this kind had not previously been conducted on Kurdish diaspora. The answer to this is two-fold. As a former member of the community, I had become accustomed to the topics and failed to see how the discussions and the character of the community could offer new material of any value for the kind of research questions I had raised. I would later be repeatedly reminded of this through the reactions of the community members when I first announced my presence and my research project, which could be summed up as "What can you possibly find on a site like this that would be interesting for your research?" My familiarity with the online community had prevented me from seeing it as a source of valuable and hitherto untapped empirical data. One of my objectives was to enter the social life of diasporic Kurds in order to examine the processes of exchange in which cultural and political values and meanings where redefined and produced. As such, the crucial task was to gather information that was not mere details but represented vital keystones in the construction of the narrative. But before I could make them visible to the reader, I myself firstly had to recognize them. The challenge was to make the invisible visible, or the evident less evident.

Another explanation for this is that early internet studies and online ethnographies treated the internet and its virtual space as being separate from real life. Members of the cyberspace community were said to experiment with their identities in ways in which anonymity was a key factor. This in turn cast doubts on both the authenticity of online members and the material collected from online sources. However, the high volume of continuous, diverse, and intense discussions suggest that this is too simplistic a viewpoint.

As explained above, contrary to these statements and my own preconceptions, anonymity proved extremely important for sincerer and serious discussions that may have been too sensitive to discuss, let alone contest, face-to-face. Furthermore, despite the presumed polarity between offline and online discussion due to the invisibility of aural and visual keys, logging onto the online community does not necessarily mean that members shrug off a lifetime of experience and practice acquired through the socioeconomic and cultural frameworks that they occupy (Rybas and Gajjala 2007).

Going back to the dilemma of insider-ness, this becomes even more complex when the researcher is assumed to be in favor of a political stance and is considered to support the interests of marginalized minority groups. Martyn Hammersley (2003) pointed out that studying and understanding a group and its collective sense of injustice within that context does not by design mean supporting it, as this precondition would reduce the range of people that could be studied and diminish the validity of the results. However, while respondents expected me to know a great deal about the topic, as a researcher I was initially careful about raising or showing support for critical issues that the diasporic Kurds had battled against for so many years. Such solidarity can infiltrate supposedly objective research through certain articulations that may then influence the direction of the research ideologically or politically, rather than empirically. Such a position would have consequences for the whole research project, from the selection of material to the arguments and implications of the findings. This issue became more apparent to me during the analytical process of my research and the representation of the empirical data, for which I had overwhelmingly presented a collection of utterances that had a uniting effect and where emphasis was on nationalistic sentiments. If many voices were competing for attention during the data gathering process, there were certainly no fewer voices trying to be heard during the process of analysis.

Guarding the Research Against Biases of the Researcher

The anthropologist Johannes Fabian (1983) asserts that although the purpose of research to some extent is to provide a reaction or a response to other statements produced by other subjectivities, writing may be scientific but it is also "inherently autobiographic." A recurring issue within academic research is objectivity and the importance of remaining objective in order to create, or at least give the impression of (Ratner 2002) results that are free from subjective thoughts and values. However, when researchers explain their choice of research topic and their aims, one has to start by recognizing the role the researcher's subjectivity plays here in choosing the subject in the first place.

Fabian (1983) describes it aptly when he asks whether the presented sight is more objective than sound, smell, or taste. Rather than interpreting objectivity as a way of entering a value-free state of mind, it may instead be used to orient the researcher and keep him or her true to the nature of the research and the empirical data. The researcher must guard the material against their own position and worldview, which is colored by their values, beliefs, political allegiances, religious faith, and so on (Wellington et al. 2005).

What is important is to uphold an awareness of the political nature and implications of our actions, even if they are carried out in the name of research. The choice of topic, methods, and media are all factors which are positioned within our own roles and related in one way or another to this political world. For example, one could consider it antithetical for a Kurd— who is a member of a victim diaspora that has for almost a century attempted to maintain its identity and protect it against systematic assimilation and violence—to attempt to deconstruct the Kurdish identity. But such kind of thinking runs the risks of reproducing an essentialist approach.

Although my research used participants' own statements and words to present quotes that best illustrated my interpretations and arguments, the analysis of the words was still mine; thus, "I am still author, [the] authority" (Ignacio 2005, xxii). As an authority, then, while deciding that my research was not a manifesto for the Kurdish nation-state project, a rereading of theories and earlier literature helped me to recognize invaluable insights into the material and how they were moulded into new theoretical silhouettes by everyday reality. My insider status became obvious when what I was looking for clashed with what I found. Such revelations of the imagining of identities and what could be called "the unselfconscious exercise of abstract thought" (Buchanan 2010), which might infiltrate the research, became possible through continuous discussion with people outside the research. It was important to create distance to the research material in different ways, whether through exchanges with colleagues or the rereading of the interdisciplinary literature, including postmodern and post-structural (feminist) studies. This allowed the empirical findings to speak for the research, rather than my own preconceptions, and thereby strengthening the overall critical position of the research.

Looking back at the research process, my position was not that of a social constructionist at the beginning. But the empirical data and the analytical work came to define me as such. In ethnographic studies, perhaps an equally important goal of the research process is self-reflexivity and what we learn about the self, particularly how we change our own notions about key themes. Against this background, while the aspiration of research is rooted in the intention of contributing new insights and modifying theories, the result of reflection and self-analysis is that such interrogation influences and changes us as researchers.

ETHICAL CONSIDERATIONS

The traditional forms of data gathering used in my project required both the consent of the respondents and assurances from me regarding their confidentiality and anonymity. When it comes to multisited, interdisciplinary, and cross-national studies, this may not be so straightforward, and each case will need to be assessed on its own merits. A researcher can deposit quantities of text online that may be represented in forms that do not necessarily represent traditional published formats. As such, they are more open to borrowing and alteration, and must be fully cited with access date and site reference to ensure that they represent a snapshot of the participants' words. Not only are online texts usually public, they remain at all times easily accessible therefore ready for referencing.

In contrast to earlier online ethnographic studies, and despite gaining permission, I decided not to present the participants' online usernames. This decision was based on the sensitive character of the topics under discussion. Some of these participants have been members for years and their online names may therefore not be anonymous to other participants. The nature of anonymity has changed in the online environment as it is not always about protecting personal details, but also their way of being viewed by others. While the online names of interview participants may be unknown to readers outside of the online community—although this cannot be guaranteed—these online usernames may be easily recognizable to other interview participants.

Although members have an online username, I felt that it would be too easy to disclose their identities by referring to it in my thesis, particularly as some of my interviewees revealed contradictory opinions, accounts, and statements when interviewed face-to-face than they presented online. As far as the interviewees were concerned, I followed the same principle of gaining consent before interviews took place, and I used pseudonyms to ensure anonymity. The most important point that emerged from this, which relates to one of the earlier questions about online and offline settings, is that I had to consider the reasons why people go online, and what they can do and speak about there that they cannot discuss in the offline environment. Ethical questions relating to the online setting are therefore not just a matter of refraining from disclosing personal details, but maintaining the full and complete protection of participants and respecting their privacy and confidentiality when discussing important matters that might jeopardize their position. How to disseminate findings is therefore also of ethical concern. Online ethics represents a complication of offline discussions, as two separate and sometimes conflicting environments have to be accounted for.

CONCLUSIONS

The rapid changes within the communication technologies have nearly made online-offline boundaries collapse, which has had significant implications for identity. This means that we need to pay attention to how the online environment and different communication forms are taking part in people's cultural identity formation, and how this is providing individuals the opportunity to reconstruct their identity. This is especially the case for diasporic communities, such as Kurds, for which the communication technologies have become vital.

The new discourse in the online space has interrupted the Kurdish participants' everyday life implicating essential changes that diverge from the on-the-ground experiences in the context of identity and belonging. From an epistemological perspective, such an inquiry will have meaning for how we produce empirical material and what we present as the realities of the people studied. The examples and insights presented here raise a number of important questions in relation to online-offline methodologies. How does the collection of data occur? Which stories are presented, and which are left out? How do we evaluate and make sense of people's utterances if these change with time, space, and company? While such questions are linked back to the research design, part of the reflection ought to also lie within a reflexive methodology as researchers are part of the cultural and political world they study, and whose positioning both within and outside the field should be carefully deliberated. In the teeth of collecting, interpreting, and presenting the data, we must guard the status of the empirical data against our own preconceptions by interrogating our own role as researchers.

Considering the rapid changes within the communication technologies, we cannot rely on the past and established theories, concerning for instance anonymity, authenticity, and online language including profanity. The internet provides an exclusive space for research on identity in that it offers anonymity in a discursive setting, allowing individuals to authentically discuss sensitive topics without being posed to the risks of the offline environment. This has been important for the Kurdish participants in the research when discussing and contesting sensitive topics that are political or related to question of gender and sexuality. Such understanding demands careful consideration of ethics and confidentiality, even when participants are supposedly protected by anonymity online.

NOTES

1. The Ph.D., within Media and Communications, was conducted between 2008 and 2012 at Goldsmiths, University of London, United Kingdom. The research is interdisciplinary and included a one-year long online ethnography in an online transnational community (Viva Kurdistan), and interviews with the members of the online community.

2. The quote belongs to a thread titled "Where are you from" posted in the Swedish forum (2010-07-20).

3. For a thorough account of the history and the political identity of the Kurds and Kurdish diaspora, see for instance the works by Hassanpour (1992) and McDowall (2004).

4. The transnational community consisted of eight forums representing different countries: Swedish, Norwegian, Danish, British, German, Dutch, French, and the Kurdish. The main focus of my research was the Swedish and British forums, with the Kurdish forum as a point of comparison and the age range of members was from eighteen to thirty years.

BIBLIOGRAPHY

Anderson, Benedict. 1983. *Imagined Communities: Reflections on the Origin and Spread of Nationalism*. London: Verso.

Baser, Bahar. 2011. *Kurdish Diaspora Political Activism in Europe with a Particular Focus on Great Britain: Diaspora Dialogues for Development and Peace Project*. Berlin: Berghof Peace Support.

Baser, Bahar, and Mari Toivanen. 2018. "Politicized and depoliticized ethnicities, power relations and temporality: Insights to outsider research from comparative and transnational fieldwork." *Ethnic and Racial Studies* 41, no. 11: 2067–2084. doi: 10.1080/01419870.2017.1348530.

Breen, J. Lauren. 2007. "The researcher 'in the middle': Negotiating the insider/outsider dichotomy." *Australian Community Psychologist* 19, no. 1:163–174.

Brubaker, Rogers, and Frederick Cooper. 2000. "Beyond Identity." *Theory and Society* 29: 1–47.

Buchanan, Ian. 2010. *Dictionary of Critical Theory*. Oxford: Oxford University Press.

Chaliand, Gérard. 1994. *The Kurdish Tragedy*. London: Zed Books.

Cohen, Robin. 2001. *Global Diasporas: An Introduction*. London: Routledge.

De los Reyes, Paulina. 2002. "Den svenska jämställdhetens etniska gränser – om patriarkala enklaver och kulturella frizoner." In *Det slutna folkhemmet: om etniska klyftor och blågul självbild*, edited by Ingemar Lindberg and Magnus Dahlstedt, 172–187. Stockholm: Agora.

Fabian, Johannes. 1983. *Time and the Other: How Anthropology Makes Its Object*. New York: Columbia University Press.

Gajjala, Radhika. 2008. "South Asian Technospaces and 'Indian' Digital Diasporas?" In *South-Asian Technospaces,* edited by Radhika Gajjala and Venkataramana Gajjala, 37–48. New York: Peter Lang, Digital Formation Series.

Geertz, Clifford. 1973. *Thick Description: Towards an Interpretive Theory of Culture; Selected Essays*. New York: Basic Books.

Glick-Schiller, Basch Linda Nina, and Cristina Blanc-Szanton. 1992. *Towards a Transnational Perspective on Migration: Race, Class, Ethnicity, and Nationalism Reconsidered*. New York: New York Academy of Sciences.

Greenbank, Paul. 2003. "The role of values in educational research: the case for reflexivity." *British Educational Research Journal* 26, no. 6:791–801.

Hall, Stuart. 1998. "Introduction: Who needs identity?" In *Questions of Cultural Identity*, edited by Stuart Hall and Paul du Day, 1–17. London: Sage.

Hammersley, Martyn. 2003. "Conversation analysis and discourse analysis: methods or paradigms?" *Discourses and Society* 14 (November): 751–781.

Hassanpour, Amir. 1992. *Nationalism and Language in Kurdistan 1918–1985*. San Francisco: Mellen Research University Press.

Hodkinson, Paul. 2005. "'Insider research' in the study of youth cultures." *Journal of Youth Studies* 8, no. 2: 131–149.

Ignacio, Emily. 2005. *Building Diaspora: Filipino Cultural Community Formation on the Internet*. New Brunswick, NJ: Rutgers University Press.

Ignacio, N. Emily. 2012. "Online Methods and Analyzing Knowledge-Production: A Cautionary Tale." *Qualitative Inquiry* 18: 237–246.

Karim, H. Karim. 2006. "Nation and diaspora: Rethinking multiculturalism in a transnational context." *International Journal of Media and Cultural Politics* 2, no. 3: 267–282.

Kuntsman, Adi. 2009. *Figurations of Violence and Belonging: Queerness, Migranthood and Nationalism in Cyberspace and Beyond*. London: Peter Lang.

Labaree, V. Robert. 2002. "The risk of 'going observationalist': Negotiating the hidden dilemmas of being an insider participant observer." *Qualitative Research* 2, no. 1: 97–122.

Mahmod, Jowan. 2016. *Kurdish Diaspora Online: From Imagined Community to Managing Communities*. New York: Palgrave Macmillan.

McDowall, David. 2004. *A Modern History of the Kurds*. London: I.B. Tauris.

Merriam, B. Sharan, Juanita Johnson-Bailey, Ming-Yeh Lee, Youngwha Kee, Gabo Ntseane, and Mazanah Muhamad. 2001. "Power and positionality: Negotiating insider/outsider status within and across cultures." *International Journal of Lifelong Education* 20, no. 5: 405–416.

Paechter, Carrie. 2013. "Researching sensitive issues online: Implications of a hybrid insider/outsider position in a retrospective ethnographic study." *Qualitative Research* 13, no. 1: 71–86.

Ratner, Carl. 2002. "Subjectivity and objectivity in qualitative methodology." *Qualitative Social Research* 3, no. 3.

Rybas, Natalia, and Radhika Gajjala. 2007. "Developing cyberethnographic research methods for understanding digitally mediated identities." *Forum: Qualitative Social Research* 8, no. 3.

Shani, Orgad. 2009. "How can researchers make sense of the issues involved in collecting and interpreting online and offline data?" In *Internet Inquiry: Conversations about Method*, edited by Annette N. Markham and Baym K. Nancy, 33–53. Los Angeles: Sage.

Van Maanen, John. 2011. *Tales of the Field: On Writing Ethnography*. Chicago and London: The University of Chicago Press.

Visweswaran, Kamala. 1997. *Fictions of Feminist Ethnography*. Minnesota: University of Minnesota Press.

Wellington, Jerry, Ann-Marie Bathmaker, Cheryl Hunt, Gary McCulloch, and Pat Sikes. 2005. *Succeeding with your Doctorate*. London: Sage.

Chapter 4

Tracing Global History through the Kurds in the Imperial and National Archives and Beyond

Marc Sinan Winrow

In the present day, the Kurdish people are dispersed throughout different states, including Turkey, Syria, Iran, Iraq, and parts of the former USSR. In each of these different states, the Kurds have been represented in the archives of numerous nation-states and empires and that the power relations the Kurds found themselves in played a role in leading to the practice of archiving and/or destroying information. For instance, following the Sheikh Said rebellion of 1925 in Turkey's Kurdish region, the nascent Turkish Republic prepared reports on reforms they sought to implement in the region, which "required that the public officials tasked with implementation be outsiders (Belge 2011, 102)." Such a move meant that the new republic did not document much about the Kurdish regions, having also side-lined local notables who once had close relations with the previous Ottoman state. As a result, Belge (2011, 102–103) notes that "as late as the 1980s, criminal sentences in cases of murder of women by their families were lowered due to the age of the accused in nearly a quarter of the cases in Urfa," since local citizens were able to exploit gaps in the official registers, stemming from the state's neglect in compiling information about its citizens. In Soviet Kurdistan, on the other hand, Soviet Kurdologists, in line with their state's nation-building or empire-building efforts, categorized the Armenians and Kurds within the USSR as people who were "small nations" implying that they lacked a distinctive written culture but possessed forms of folklore (Leezenberg 2015).[1] Such an orientalist[2] theoretical move served to de-link both Kurds and Armenians from their already existing written culture, which flourished in their ancient, Islamicate and

Persianate past (Leezenberg 2015). In addition, in Iraqi Kurdistan, during the uprising of the Kurdistan Democratic Party (KDP) and its Peshmerga against the then-ruling Saddam Hussein regime, the KDP were able to seize government archives, thereby demonstrating the culpability and scale of the Hussein regime's Anfal genocide to the world (Montgomery 2001). Although there have, for the most part, been no official Kurdish archives, akin to the official archives of contemporary and former nation and imperial states, these archives can be studied with a view to answering numerous different historical and theoretical questions.

As the Kurds have historically lived in many different polities and become entangled in various transnational movements, ideas and entities, studying the Kurds also, by definition, involves engaging in global history. Nevertheless, both compiling archives and making use of existing archives involves partaking in various power relations (Stoler 2002). This is because archives can be said to be manifestations and tools of power, since those who create them arrange them in ways that promote the dissemination of certain forms of knowledge at the possible expense of other ways of perceiving reality.[3] The onus is therefore on the researcher to approach archives not just as a historian but also as an ethnographer (Stoler 2002). Through using the tools of ethnography, one can study the archive as a field in which different power relations, differing in form and extent, are present. However, in order to gain a full picture of the ethnographic field, one must be aware of one's own "positionality" within the field in relation to the other actors and entities situated within them, and the power relations that they are a part of. It is the goal of this chapter to provide the researcher with an overview of the considerations involved in engaging in historical archival research on the Kurds (Cousin 2010, 9). In addition, this chapter makes its own stance clear; what is presented here is how a global, as opposed to national or imperial history of the Kurds, can be conducted.[4] Such an approach would also avoid reifying categories,[5] including the meaning of the term "Kurd," to serve imperial or national political goals, since its contention is that such categories are themselves constructed in time through what can be termed transnational entanglements. These instances involve the points in history when new meanings of what it means to be a Kurd or the boundaries of Kurdistan emerge, as different concepts are translated from one language or context to another, new forms of power relations emerge and are removed or replaced and new forms of transnational solidarity emerge and dissipate. Therefore, such a global historical approach, focused on tracing entanglements, does not rule out considering both imperial and national archives, but it does require deploying an "ethnographic sensibility" and being mindful of the representation of the Kurds within these contexts (Pader 2006).

THE RETURN OF HISTORY TO THE SOCIAL SCIENCES: STUDYING HISTORICAL SOURCES FROM AN ETHNOGRAPHIC ANGLE

The recent turn towards combining history and the social sciences, which involves new ways of both conceptualizing and studying archives, provides a promising opportunity to consider how contemporary social reality is shaped by historical patterns (Wagner 2010; Jacobsen Punzalan and Hedstrom 2013; Inglis 2013; Go 2016; Bhambra 2007). As a result, a historical analysis is also indispensable to a critical theoretical study, since it can alert the researcher to how actors can be emancipated from historically present forms of oppression. In addition, historical research can allow one to be mindful of historical patterns, thereby allowing one to avoid the charge of presentism, meaning that one's findings are only relevant for a static time period (Hinnebusch 2010; Inglis 2013). Studying historical patterns can also serve to enable social scientists to make informed guesses about the future, which, although often shunned by historians, may be relevant for social scientific research projects which seek to make generalizations about historical processes and/or mechanisms (Mahoney 2000; Capoccia and Kelemen 2007; Capoccia 2015). The study of archives plays a key role within this historical turn, along with the study of oral history[6] and secondary sources, allowing findings to be cross-examined and triangulated with each other. As with any historical sources, in examining archival documents, the historical researcher must be mindful of the reliability of sources. However, as Foucault (2002, 7–8) argues, archival sources in the form of documents can be considered to be sources sui generis, because of how "history, in its traditional form, undertook to 'memorize' the monuments of the past, transform them into documents, and lend speech to those traces which, in themselves are often not verbal, or which say in silence something other than what they actually say; in our time, history is that which transforms documents into monuments." Relatedly, Arondekar (2005, 10–11) reads Foucault's (1973, 15) and Derrida's (1995, 1–6, 7–23) influential theoretical accounts of archives as demonstrating how the process of constructing and maintaining an archive is inherently related to any attempt to make knowledge meaningful.

Therefore, studying historical sources from an ethnographic angle can also demonstrate how knowledge is produced in time, which requires that one also be reflexive about one's own positionality. Although some have questioned the bold claim of Foucault (2002) and Derrida (1995) that the presence of knowledge is presupposed by an archive, these critiques can also be read as expanding what we take to be an archive to include oral histories, visual histories, and other genres and means of collection not traditionally associated with the concept of the archive (Arondekar 2005, 11–12). Foucault (2002), for instance, advanced this claim to distinguish between what we take to be an archive in the conventional sense, that is, a site with documents, to an archive as referring to the collected documented experiences from a given context. Crucially, the recent turn to focus on race, gender, and sexuality also problematized the focus on the nation as the focus of the archive, which had been upheld by Guha (1983) as a part of his political programme, premised on the idea that India suffered from "collective amnesia" (Spivak 1988, 271–311 as cited in Arondekar 2005, 13; Mathur 2000, 89–106 and Burton 2003, 137–145 as cited in Arondekar 2005, 14; Arondekar 2005, 13–14). The post-structuralist and postcolonial interpretation of the archive therefore resulted in the introduction of a new range of questions, relevant for historical researchers. Most significantly, they led to the question of whether or not the archive refers merely to the sum of all recorded experiences within a given context or to more specific selections of documents. Relatedly, this question also raises the question of how such an archive could be read and what these readings tell us about the power relations that are present in various contexts.

The question of the relationship between state power and the practice of archiving means that the historical researcher must remain mindful of how archives, including postcolonial national archives, may be related to power relations, by adopting an ethnographic stance. This perspective was, indeed, advocated by postcolonial scholars as a means of revealing how the power relations of the dominating and the dominated that were present in the context of colonialism, shaped how the powerful organized information in archives (Stoler 2002; Bastian 2006; Ferguson 2008). Crucially, such information facilitates power by providing blueprints for actors engaged in practices of ruling others and often involves the displacement of existing, local forms of knowledge (Mignolo 2007). Therefore, approaching archival sites, postcolonial theorists have demonstrated how archives ought to be approached ethnographically in order to make sense of the power relations that are manifest within them (Stoler 2002, 2009). This is because the presence of an archive is always both indicative of and enabling towards different forms of political power, as is demonstrated by how both nations and empires seek to ensure their continuity in time by maintaining archives. The layout of archives and the ease or lack thereof in obtaining information also serves to reinforce power relations (Stoler 2002, 2009). The information complied in archives are also often expressive of the anxieties of their architects, with Stoler (2002, 98) identifying how Dutch colonial administrators in Indonesia were focused on compiling information about mixed race individuals in the East Indes, owing presumably to how they threatened existing racial hierarchies which enabled the Dutch colonial project. Such a move entails studying the "archive-as-subject," rather than considering the archive a mere source, since it involves revealing the very logic of storing and presenting information, which is related to power relations (Stoler 2002, 87–199). The subsequent section will accordingly study how these insights may be applied to solving some of the challenges that emerge from studying transnational history by doing Kurdish history.

THE CHALLENGES OF DOING A TRANSNATIONAL HISTORY THROUGH THE KURDS

In the context of Kurdish history, the postcolonial injunction to focus on the power relations embedded in archives becomes all the more pressing for two reasons; the first of which is related to how Kurds have featured prominently in the archives of imperial powers. Several of these archives, such as the archives of the British state, are, in fact, located in physical sites and can be accessed with ease by historical researchers. Yeğen (2012) has, for instance, produced an excellent account of sources relating to Kurdish political and national aspirations by drawing upon the imperial British archive. Deringil (1998, 2003) and others have, in turn, consulted the Ottoman archives, located primarily in the Turkish Prime Ministry archives and the Yıldız Palace archives, to demonstrate how the late Ottoman state aimed to integrate the Kurds into the state apparatus as loyal Muslim subjects. Their consultation of these documents has crucially demonstrated how orientalism was pervasive in the Ottoman state's production of knowledge regarding the Kurds. This is because of how the Ottoman state sought to integrate the Kurds into state structures but did so by first recognising them as savage "others" who needed to be civilized through the formation of the School for Tribes (Aşiret Mektebi) (Deringil 1998, 101–104).

The French diplomatic archives also contain ample sources that can demonstrate how the French engaged in knowledge production and co-optation strategies toward the Kurds in the context of their colonial project in Syria (Tejel 2008, 4–5). The diplomatic archives of the Allied victors of World War I, including France and the United States of America remain to be considered in detail, particularly to understand the international politics of the period following the defeat of the Ottoman Empire in 1918 and the establishment of the Republic of Turkey in 1923. Leezenberg (2015) has, however, demonstrated how the Russian and former Soviet archives have also considered the Kurds in detail as a part of their goal to develop viable domestic and foreign policies. Consequently, the representation of Kurds in works by Western powers would appear to mirror the claims of many scholars of the Middle East and other postcolonial contexts, such as Said (1978, 322) and Scott (1998), who stress how the imagined nature of places and people outside of the West influenced how Westerners understood them.

Researchers must therefore bear in mind that the Kurds appear to have been considered on a lower level in the imperial hierarchies imagined and enacted by these actors.

It is therefore important to note, while consulting such sources, that the producers of the archive intended the knowledge they were accumulating to aid the interests of their own states. Nevertheless, studying these archives can help demonstrate what these states perceived to be their interests, how they sought to pursue them and how they were aided or resisted by local actors, including Kurds. More importantly, they can help reveal how knowledge of Kurdish identity and of the identity of these states were constructed in the course of encounters, involving the construction of the categories of the self and other (Natali 2005). For instance, the construction of the identity of the Kurds as a nation that ought to enjoy the right of self-determination, enshrined briefly in the Treaty of Sevres of 1920, was enabled by the interests of the Allied victors of World War I and the identity construction project of Kurdish elites (Özoğlu 2001; Culcasi 2006). Prior to the establishment of the nation-state as the primary means of ordering the world, however, knowledge pertaining to the Kurds was produced in the course of both Ottoman and Western attempts at empire-building (Houston 2009). From 1910 onward, the Ottoman Young Turk government undertook an extensive attempt at compiling anthropological data about the various peoples of Anatolia, including the Greeks, Armenians, Turkmens, and Arabs (Houston 2009). Such anthropological ventures were motivated by the related goals of constructing a national homeland for the influx of Muslim refugees from the Balkans and the Caucasus, fleeing from war and persecution from expanding Christian states (Dündar 2013). The conclusion of many of these anthropological surveys, such as those undertaken by the Young Turk known only by the pseudonym Habil Amed and the nationalist ideologue, Ziya Gökalp, were that Kurds merely had a folkloric culture and that they ought to be considered a part of the Turkish element (Houston 2009, 28). Consequently, when considering the late Ottoman archives, historical researchers of the Kurds ought to bear in mind how, during the transition of the Ottoman state to new state units, there emerged practices mirroring the practices of the West toward producing orientalist knowledge.

In addition to being present in these colonial archives and their attempt to compile knowledge that would facilitate effective imperial governance and the maintenance of imperial hierarchies, the Kurds have been represented in the knowledge production efforts of various nation-states. This has meant that they are represented in, and at times perhaps removed from, the archives of several nation-states, which emerged out of or were essentially the reconstituted form of former empires, in the course of the early to mid-twentieth century. As Belge (2011) has demonstrated, the destruction of information pertaining to the Kurds was one of the main means by which the Turkish state aimed to deal with the threat they perceived as emanating from the country's Kurdish population. This fear, which emerged after the Sheikh Said Rebellion, continued to be present throughout the twentieth century (Bruinessen 1986).[7] Such an absence is also notable in the archives of Iraq, whose nation-building Baath Party's archives are, however, situated in the Hoover Institution in Stanford, California, following the US led invasion and occupation of the country in 2003 (Ahram 2013, 261). The complexity of the politics of national archives is also revealed by Zeidel's (2014, 124) account of an encounter with the administrator of the Iraqi National Archives in 2007. In the course of this encounter, Sa'd Eskander also noted that he is proud of being both Kurdish and Iraqi, challenging Western researchers who sought to label the Fayli Kurds in Iraq as "Arabized Kurds." Another consideration to bear in mind is that in both Iran and Turkey, state archives tend to empha-size and contain more sorted and readily available documents on the "golden ages" of their past, meaning that one would presumably be able to access far more documents on Kurds during the height of the Ottoman and Safavid Empires. For example, relying largely on Ottoman archival sources, Özoğlu (2004) has demonstrated how the Ottomans were engaged in the construction of an autonomous group of Kurdish emirates in the sixteenth and seventeenth centuries.

The possibility of relying on both of these types of archives is problematic because it means that the researcher is faced with the risk of reproducing many of the power relations that were involved in the production of these archives. A number of postcolonial political projects have accordingly argued that a more inclusive form of political community can only be constructed through the construction of new archives, made possible by efforts toward truth, justice, and reconciliation, which reflect the views of all members of the political community (McEwan 2003). Carrying out a truly global history through studying the Kurds would especially need to avoid reproducing a parochial or instrumentalist perspective on the Kurds, based on the perspec-tive of a particular historical imperial power, such as France or Britain, or a nation-state, such as Iran or Turkey or, indeed, different perspectives held by the Kurds themselves. A crucial means of avoiding such parochialism would be to focus on how the very meaning of "Kurd" or Kurdish space or "Kurdayeti" is constructed relationally in time, rather than referring to a fixed essential identity (Natali 2005, xvii). Such a relational approach would, therefore, involve focusing on the development of Kurdish identity in relation to other projects seeking to develop a specific identity. Following the prec-edent set by transnational histories of entanglement, such an approach would also involve focusing on how the Kurds themselves came to be associated or disassociated with different practices, ideas, and subjects. Such transnational histories of "entanglement," such as Manjapra's (2014a, 2014b) study of the entanglement of Indian intellectuals and activists with their German counterparts in the course of the late nineteenth century, entail focusing on how identities and practices are altered by such encounters. For instance, Manjapra (2014a, 2014b) notes how German strategists sought to foster links with Indian activists in order to detach India from Britain in the course of the First World War but notes how Indian emigrates who came to settle in Berlin subsequently influenced German nationalist attempts at constructing German identity.

In addition, there is also the very real fact of how political restrictions and other concerns may result in the avoidance of these archives as sources of Kurdish global history. Although Kurdish citizens appear to have exploited the lack of knowledge about them to, for instance evade arrest due to illegal activity, the fact remains that there is a notable absence of Kurds in the official state archives of Turkey. Given the greater acceptance of Kurdish identity in Iran, it is probable that archival sources pertaining to Kurds are present in Iran. For instance, Natali's (2005) study of the construction of Kurdish identity in Iran, Syria, Iraq, and Turkey, occurring parallel to the nation-building efforts of these states, drew upon archival research in the Iranian context. However, as is often the case in historical research, one may face restrictions on account of not being fluent in the local language or political restrictions that may be present in different contexts. In this context, it is telling how historical research studying Kurds in Syria has had to rely on sources other than official archives (Natali 2005; Tejel 2008, 2). As with the other states in which Kurds are present, the Syrian state has also been particularly secretive in terms of its archiving and documentation pertaining to Kurds, making research in and about Syria particularly difficult (Bengio 2014). In addition, although the Ottoman Empire contained a rich Kurdish literature within it, works such as the *Şerefname*, written by the Ottoman Kurdish historian Şeref Han in 1597, as a historical sociology of the Kurdish provinces, were also banned and suppressed in Turkey (Bozarslan 1990 as cited in Houston 2009, 28). The case initiated by the public prosecutor to thwart the publication of this book famously involved the suggestion that the book was encouraging strife within the nation by claiming that different peoples dwelled within Turkey (Houston 2009, 29). Finally, the existence of powerful state actors also prevents effective archival research on legal and illegal Kurdish organizations, meaning that scholars researching them, such as White (2000) and Marcus (2007) have focused on other methods, such as interviews, to answer their research questions.

OVERCOMING CHALLENGES THROUGH
PARALLEL PRACTICES OF ARCHIVING,
CRITIQUE, AND TRIANGULATION

Given these considerable challenges, but the continued global interest in the Kurds, a number of means of overcoming these challenges have been devised by different actors. The first means of overcoming these challenges, which has often been pioneered by Kurds themselves, involves the creating of parallel archives and the use of unconventional mediums to convey information. These efforts to compile an archive can be likened to the use of the term archive, as pioneered by Foucault (2002, 144–148) to more broadly refer to all of the memories that are held by individuals in a specific context, rather than an actual collection of documents. An example of such a practice is provided by the use of cinema as an alternative means of constructing an archive by Kurds located in the Kurdish Diaspora in Europe and the remainder of the world (Koçer, 2014).[8] Koçer (2014) notes accordingly how Kurdish Film Festivals, such as the now annual London Kurdish Film Festival, can contribute to the compilation of such an archive. The internet has also emerged as a key site for constructing an alternative archive and can consequently also be studied as a part of the archive of the Kurdish diaspora (Candan and Hunger 2008).[9] The presence of such an archive can be said to allow Kurds to construct an "imagined community," involving the consumption of cultural products that depict and hence archive their experiences (Anderson 2006). Despite a history of extensive restrictions, Kurds and Kurdish political organizations have also been engaged in extensive publishing efforts, motivated also in part by a desire to maintain the different Kurdish languages. Archives held by organizations such as the Washington Kurdish Institute, the Kurdish Human Rights Association, Handicap International, Mines Awareness Group, Amnesty International, Human Rights Watch and L'Institut Kurde de Paris are also able to provide opportunities for archival research to historical researchers (Natali 2005, 161).

As Jackson (2010) suggests, analytical narratives are always heuristic tools, meaning that they can only be challenged by more comprehensive analytical narratives that integrate more sources, which underlines the importance of using different archives to verify information. The triangulation or cross-checking of sources present in different archives can also serve as a means of verifying statements present in archives, in order to maintain an ethnographic distance toward claims being made within archives. When deployed effectively, such an approach can serve as a means of avoiding the reproduction of the power relations embedded within archives. An example of such a study that effectively checks sources available in different archives in order to provide as accurate a picture as possible of Kurdish history is provided by Klein (2007), who uses Ottoman state archives and consular reports from Britain to demonstrate the nature of Kurdish, Ottoman and Armenian relations in eastern Anatolia during the reign of Ottoman Sultan Abdülhamid II. Ateş (2014) studies how the Ottoman-Iranian frontier, inhabited by Kurds, was established by drawing upon Iranian, Russian, Ottoman, and British archival sources to provide a complete picture of the relational process by which the border between the two empires was established. Such an approach has the advantage of seeking to demonstrate how Britain's and Russia's imperial ambitions, combined with the agency of local actors, resulted in the relational formation of the border (Ateş 2014). The downside to this approach can be said to be how the imputation of such intentionality is always potentially problematic, since it involves guessing the interests of actors. However, considering the different declared interests of actors and reading their accounts of each other's practices can help in providing a more complete picture of the process, helping to forge an analytical narrative (Jackson 2011).

Finally, another possible approach to using archives is to subject archival knowledge to critique, in order to demonstrate how archival knowledge is complicit in the production of existing power relations. An example of such an approach is provided by those who claim that archival research follows an inherently "extractive" pattern, meaning that it mirrors practices of seizing wealth from others (Stoler 2002). In fact, these scholars suggest that not only is archival research analogous to such extractive practices, involving the forcible transfer or seizure of capital, but that it is historically tied to such practices, as in the case of orientalist knowledge production playing an important role in empire-building (Stoler 2002). Although Kurds in Turkey, for instance, have spearheaded Kurdish publishing and other activities, with several prominent Kurdish publishing houses being present in prominent cities such as Istanbul and Diyarbakır, such practices can also be subjected to a critique. This is because the production of such extensive knowledge about Kurds within Turkey can be associated with the Ottoman Empire's efforts to secure control over the Kurdish parts of the country through the use of such anthropological data (Houston 2009). As Houston (2009, 21) argues, publishing houses, such as Avesta Publishing in Istanbul, have sought to revive nineteenth century travel literature and its depictions of Kurds from an orientalist angle, such as İsmet Vanlı's 1973 translation of a French text titled *Kurds and Kurdistan through the eyes of Western travellers*. Ultimately, in order to be convincing and successful, a critical theoretical project, which aims its critique at existing archives, would, however, need to provide tools for emancipation to those who are disempowered by the practices it is critiquing. Therefore, scholars who undertake such critical research ought to consider both the intended and the likely audience of such critical theoretical research, in order to ensure that their research achieves its goal of contributing to emancipation (Jackson 2010).

CONCLUSION

This chapter has aimed to provide a number of tools that would be useful to researchers within the broad interdisciplinary field of Kurdish studies who may be aiming to engage in historical and archival research, as part of a global or transnational history approach. The chapter began by demonstrating the merits of adopting a historical sociological approach that can demonstrate the nature of existing historical patterns. The chapter next surveyed how scholars influenced by post-structuralism and postcolonial scholars have reconceptualized what is traditionally taken to be the archive. The understanding of the archive as a collection of documents, and the sum of all documented information from a specific context, introduced by Foucault (2002, 144–148) was articulated, as well as its adoption by postcolonialism. Postcolonial scholars, such as Stoler (2002) have, in turn, read this intervention as implying that researchers ought to approach archives not only as repositories of information but also as spaces that are themselves expressive of and produced by power relations. Approaching Kurdish studies from the angle of a reflexive and transnational or global history in turn requires being mindful of how Kurds have been constructed and represented in various imperial and national archives. Along with the fact that their situation in these archives warrants the considerations of post-structuralist and postcolonial history, the historical study of the Kurds is also challenging because of the presence of state oppression. Although such oppression, in turn, means that sources are restricted or have been destroyed, both this and the other challenges to meaningful historical study can be overcome by various means. The subsequent section of the chapter demonstrated, through various examples, how consulting multiple archives, adopting a more critical perspective toward available sources or archives and operating with a more expansive definition of the "archive" can be employed to remedy these challenges. It is hoped that the challenges involved in each of these possible "fixes" will allow researchers to play to their own strengths and interests in developing their own strategy toward approaching the historical study of the Kurds. Finally, as with all historical studies, limitations in terms of time, money, and the extent of one's linguistic abilities must also be considered in devising a strategy for historical research.

Although various examples of works employing historical studies as a part of Kurdish studies have been included within this chapter as a means of demonstrating certain points, the goal of this chapter has also been to demonstrate how the existing historiography of the Kurds may be improved. In particular, future studies of the global history of the Kurds may want to explore the historical entanglements of Kurdish actors with other actors, ideas, and practices, as a means of also understanding the present. Moreover, many works in Kurdish studies[10] continue to be focused on providing local histories of Kurds in specific, often national contexts. The meaning of what it is to be a Kurd or the borders of Kurdistan or a Kurdayeti have also largely not been considered, meaning that these areas can also benefit from a global historical approach. Finally, it is worth remembering that, as a means of making a broader social scientific contribution to the field, such studies ought to be framed as challenging presentist assumptions that often plague ahistorical works in the social sciences. Doing so can also, ultimately, contribute to demonstrating the contingency of the present and hence open up new political and practical opportunities to scholars and other actors.

NOTES

1. See also Landau (1975).
2. See Said (1978, 73) for a definition of orientalism as the "collection of dreams, images, and vocabularies available to anyone who has tried to talk about what lies east of the dividing line."
3. On this issue see Rouse (2005).
4. For a recent overview and defence of global history see Drayton and Motadel (2018).
5. On the call to challenge existing categories in research see Emirbayer (1998).
6. See Abrams (2016).
7. See also Bruinessen (1992).
8. See also Çiçek (2011).
9. For a more general overview and proposed conceptual framework, see Pybus (2013).
10. See, for instance, Tejel (2008) and Ahmed (2016).

BIBLIOGRAPHY

Abrams, Lynn. 2016. *Oral History Theory.* London: Routledge.
Ahmed, Mohammed M. A. 2016. *Iraqi Kurds and Nation-Building.* Basingstoke: Palgrave Macmillan.
Ahram, Ariel I. 2013. "Iraq in the Social Sciences: Testing the Limits of Research." *The Journal of the Middle East and Africa* 4, no. 3: 251–266.
Anderson, Benedict. 2006. *Imagined Communities: Reflections on the Origin and Spread of Nationalism.* London: Verso.

Arondekar, Anjali. 2005. "Without a Trace: Sexuality and the Colonial Archive." *Journal of the History of Sexuality* 14, no. 1/2: 10–27.

Ateş, Sabri. 2013. *Ottoman-Iranian Borderlands: Making a Boundary, 1843–1914.* Cambridge: Cambridge University Press.

Bastian, Jeannette Allis. 2006. "Reading Colonial Records Through an Archival Lens: The Provenance of Place, Space and Creation." *Archival Science* 6, no. 3–4: 267–284.

Belge, Ceren. 2011. "State Building and the Limits of Legibility: Kinship Networks and Kurdish Resistance in Turkey." *International Journal of Middle East Studies* 43, no. 1: 95–114.

Bengio, Ofra. 2014. "Conclusion: The Kurdish Momentum." In *Kurdish Awakening: Nation Building in a Fragmented Homeland*, edited by Ofra Bengio, 269–282. Austin: University of Texas Press.

Bhambra, Gurminder. 2007. *Rethinking Modernity: Postcolonialism and the Sociological Imagination.* Basingstoke: Palgrave Macmillan.

Bozarslan, Hamit. 1990. "Önsöz." In *Şerefname: Kürt tarihi*, edited by Şeref Han. İstanbul: Hasat Yayınları.

van Bruinessen, Martin. 1986. "The Kurds between Iran and Iraq." *MERIP Middle East Report* 141: 14–27.

van Bruinessen, Martin. 1992. *Agha, Shaikh, and State: The Social and Political Structures of Kurdistan.* London: Zed Books.

Burton, Antoinette. 2003. *Dwelling in the Archive: Women Writing House, Home, and History in Late Colonial India.* New York: Oxford University Press.

Candan, Menderes, and Uwe Hunger. 2008. "Nation Building Online: A Case Study of Kurdish Migrants in Germany." *German Policy Studies* 4, no. 4: 125–153.

Capoccia, Giovanni. 2015. "Critical Junctures and Institutional Change." In *Advances in Comparative-Historical Analysis*, edited by James Mahoney and Kathleen Thelen, 147–179. Cambridge: Cambridge University Press.

Capoccia, Giovanni, and R. Daniel Kelemen. 2007. "The Study of Critical Junctures: Theory, Narrative, and Counterfactuals in Historical Institutionalism." *World Politics* 59, no. 3: 341–369.

Çiçek, Özgür. 2011. "The Fictive Archive: Kurdish Fimmaking in Turkey." *Alphaville: Journal of Film and Screen Media* 1: 1–18.

Cousin, Glynis. 2010. "Positioning Postionality: The Reflexive Turn." In *New Approaches to Qualitative Research: Wisdom and Uncertainty*, edited by Maggi Savin-Baden and Claire Howell Major, 9–18. Abingdon: Routledge.

Culcasi, Karen. 2006. "Cartographically Constructing Kurdistan within Geopolitical and Orientalist Discourses." *Political Geography* 25, no. 6: 680–706.

Deringil, Selim. 1998. *The Well-Protected Domains: Ideology and the Legitimation of Power in the Ottoman Empire, 1876–1909.* London and New York: I.B. Tauris.

———. 2003. ""They Live in a State of Nomadism and Savagery": The Late Ottoman Empire and the Post-Colonial Debate." *Comparative Studies in Society and History* 45, no. 2: 311–342.

Derrida, Jacques. 1995. *Archive Fever: A Freudian Impression.* Chicago: University of Chicago Press.

Drayton, Richard, and David Motadel. 2018. "Discussion: The Futures of Global History." *Journal of Global History* 13, no. 1: 1–21.

Dündar, Fuat. 2013. *İttihat ve Terakki'nin Müslümanları İskan Politikası (1913–1918)*. İstanbul: İletişim Yayınları.

Emirbayer, Mustafa. 1997. "Manifesto for a Relational Sociology." *American Journal of Sociology* 103, no. 2: 281–317.

Ferguson, Kathy E. 2008. "Theorizing Shiny Things: Archival Labors." *Theory & Event:* 11, no. 4. *Project MUSE, muse.jhu.edu/article/257578*.

Foucault, Michel. 2002. *The Archaeology of Knowledge*. London: Routledge.

Go, Julian. 2016. *Postcolonial Thought and Social Theory*. Oxford: Oxford University Press.

Guha, Ranajit. 1983. *Elementary Aspects of Peasant Insurgency in Colonial India*. Delhi: Oxford University Press.

Hinnebusch, Raymond. 2010. "Toward a Historical Sociology of State Formation in the Middle East." *Middle East Critique* 19, no. 3: 201–216.

Houston, Christopher. 2009. "An Anti-History of a Non-People: Kurds, Colonialism, and Nationalism in the History of Anthropology." *Journal of the Royal Anthropological Institute* 15, no. 1: 19–35.

Inglis, David. 2013. "What is Worth Defending in Sociology Today? Presentism, Historical Vision and the Uses of Sociology." *Cultural Sociology* 8, no. 1: 99–118.

Jackson, Patrick Thaddeus. 2010. *The Conduct of Inquiry in International Relations: Philosophy of Science and Its Implications for the Study of World Politics*. Abingdon: Routledge.

Jacobsen, Trond, Ricardo L. Punzalan, and Margaret L. Hedstrom. 2013. "Invoking "Collective Memory": Mapping the Emergence of a Concept in Archival Science." *Archival Science* 13, no. 2–3: 217–251.

Klein, Janet. 2007. "Conflict and Collaboration: Rethinking Kurdish-Armenian Relations in the Hamidian Period, 1876–1909." *International Journal of Turkish Studies* 13, no. 1–2: 153–166.

Koçer, Suncem. 2014. "Kurdish Cinema as a Transnational Discourse Genre: Cinematic Visibility, Cultural Resilience, and Political Agency." *International Journal of Middle East Studies* 46, no. 3: 473–488.

Landau, Jacob M. 1975. "The Kurds in Some Soviet Works." *Middle Eastern Studies* 11, no. 2: 195–198.

Leezenberg, Michiel. 2015. ""A People Forgotten by History": Soviet Studies of the Kurds." *Iranian Studies* 48, no. 5: 747–767.

Mahoney, James. 2000. "Path Dependence in Historical Sociology." *Theory and Society* 29, 4: 507–548.

Manjapra, Kris. 2014a. *Age of Entanglement: German and Indian intellectuals across Empire*. Cambridge, MA: Harvard University Press.

———. 2014b. "Transnational Approaches to Global History: A View from the Study of German-Indian Entanglement." *German History* 32, no. 2: 274–293.

Marcus, Aliza. 2007. *Blood and Belief: The PKK and the Kurdish Fight for Independence*. New York: New York University Press.

Mathur, Saloni. 2000. "History and Anthropology in South Asia: Rethinking the Archive." *Annual Review of Anthropology* 29: 89–106.

McEwan, Cheryl. 2003. "Building a Postcolonial Archive? Gender, Collective Memory and Citizenship in Post-Apartheid South Africa." *Journal of Southern African Studies* 29, no. 3: 739–757.

Mignolo, Walter D. 2007. "Delinking: The Rhetoric of Modernity, the Logic of Coloniality and the Grammar of De-Coloniality." *Cultural Studies* 21, no. 2–3: 449–514.

Montgomery, Bruce. 2001. "The Iraqi Secret Police Files: A Documentary Record of the Anfal Genocide." *Archivaria* 52: 69–99.

Natali, Denise. 2005. *The Kurds and the State: Evolving National Identity in Iraq, Turkey, and Iran.* Syracuse, NY: Syracuse University Press.

Özoğlu, Hakan. 2001. ""Nationalism" and Kurdish Notables in the Late Ottoman Republican Era." *International Journal of Middle Eastern Studies* 33, no. 3: 383–409.

———. 2004. *Kurdish Notables and the Ottoman State: Evolving Identities, Competing Loyalties and Shifting Boundaries.* Albany, NY: State University of New York Press.

Pader, Ellen. 2006. "Seeing with an Ethnographic Sensibility: Explorations Beneath the Surface of Public Policies." In *Interpretation and Method: Empirical Research Methods and the Interpretive Turn*, edited by Dvora Yanow and Peregrine Schwartz-Shea, 161–175. Armonk, NY; London, England: M.E. Sharpe, Inc.

Pybus, Jennifer. 2013. "Social Networks and Cultural Workers." *Journal of Cultural Economy* 6, no. 2: 137–152.

Rouse, Joseph. 2005. "Power/Knowledge." In *The Cambridge Companion to Foucault*, edited by Gary Gutting, 95–122. Cambridge: Cambridge University Press.

Said, Edward. 1978. *Orientalism: Western Conceptions of the Orient.* London: Penguin.

———. 1978. *Orientalism.* New York: Vintage.

Scott, James. 1998. *Seeing like a State: How Certain Schemes to Improve the Human Condition have Failed.* New Haven: Yale University Press.

Spivak, Gayatri Chakravorty. 1988. "Can the Subaltern Speak?" In *Marxism and the Interpretation of Culture*, edited by C. Nelson and L. Grossberg, 271–311. Chicago: University of Chicago Press.

Stoler, Ann Laura. 2002. "Colonial Archives and the Arts of Governance." *Archival Science* 2, no. 1–2: 87–109.

———. 2010. *Along the Archival Grain: Epistemic Anxieties and Colonial Common Sense.* Princeton, NJ: Princeton University Press.

Tejel, Jordi. 2008. *Syria's Kurds: History, Politics and Society.* London: Routledge.

Wagner, Peter. 2010. "Multiple Trajectories of Modernity: Why Social Theory Needs Historical Sociology." *Thesis Eleven* 100, no. 1: 53–60.

White, Paul J. 2000. *Primitive Rebels or Revolutionary Modernizers?* London: Zed Books.

Yeğen, Mesut. 2012. *İngiliz Belgelerinde Kürdistan: 1918–1958.* Ankara: Dipnot Yayınları.

Zeidel, Ronen. 2014. "Forging Iraqi-Kurdish Identity: A Case Study of Kurdish Novelists Writing in Arabic." In *Kurdish Awakening: Nation Building in a Fragmented Homeland*, edited by Ofra Bengio, 119–134. Austin: University of Texas Press.

Part II

FIELDWORK IN TROUBLED TERRAINS

Chapter 5

Troubled Terrain

Lines of Allegiance and Political Belonging in Northern Kurdistan

Marlene Schäfers

"We are very different from each other. We want to reach out to the women one by one. KAHAD works more through projects. Their work focuses more on men, while we have a more holistic approach: we focus on state pressure (*devlet baskısı*) and the feudal structure (*feodal yapı*). After all, these are the source of the male culture (*erkek kültürü*) we have here. Therefore, we also think it's necessary to educate the men. They work more on the legal front, while we want to change the mentality (*zihniyet*). We need social change."

This is how Bêrîvan, a young women's rights activist working at Van's municipal women's organization, explained to me how her own organization's work differed from that of the Women's Rights Association (*Kadın Hakları Derneği*, KAHAD),[1] another women's rights initiative in town. It was August 2011 and, having arrived in the town that was going to be my field site for the coming eighteen months, I had set out to survey the local women's organizations. What I found were activists who seemed deeply invested in defending what separated rather than what united them.

After Amed/Diyarbakır, Wan/Van is often considered Turkey's second Kurdish metropole. Located only about 100 kilometres from the Iranian border, Van is a bustling middle-sized town with a strong Kurdish identity. Its population grew rapidly as a result of forced village evacuations in the 1990s and early 2000s, and currently hovers at around 600,000. The settlement of Kurdish forced migrants has turned the town into a center of Kurdish politics and activism, and it boasts a whole range of civil society organizations. My research eventually came to focus on female singer-poets (*dengbêjs*) as a way of comprehending the gendered ways in which histories of political violence are voiced in Northern Kurdistan. Yet my broad interest in

69

questions of gender and sexuality meant that throughout my time in the field I closely engaged with a variety of women's organizations, not least because their work has had a tremendous influence on how women in the region think about and make use of their voices.

Reconsidering the conversation with Bêrîvan on this hot August day in retrospect, I believe that it illustrates the immense polarization that dominates politics and society in Northern Kurdistan as well as the discursive and social labor that is continuously invested in its reproduction. Bêrîvan's comments worked to delineate a sharp boundary between her own organization and KAHAD as a constitutive other. In this way, her comments were both reflective and productive of a fault line that, I argue, fundamentally structures political, social, and personal life in contemporary Northern Kurdistan. This fault line simultaneously constitutes and separates two major political formations that claim hegemony in the region—namely the Kurdish movement, on the one hand, and the Turkish state, on the other—while rendering political and social activity on the margins of these formations highly precarious.

In this chapter, I want to reflect on how this dividing line shapes the texture of social life in Northern Kurdistan and on the kinds of challenges it poses for field researchers in the region as a result. My analysis draws on an anthropological approach to boundaries as socially constructed markers of division that are central for the making of identities and for the constitution of social and political communities (Barth 1969; Das and Poole 2004). Borders understood in this sense are not just negative elements of stoppage and inhibition that enforce a division between two self-contained entities, but quite to the contrary contribute to producing the very entities they purport to separate. As such, boundaries are a site of conflict and contestation: they are never entirely stable but subject to continuous renegotiation. Boundaries therefore need to be continuously performed and instantiated in order to be maintained. We might usefully think of such performance as a form of social labor whose effect is the production of those subjects and collectives that a particular border is taken to separate (Bartlett 2007).

Bêrîvan's comments, I suggest, represent such a form of social labor. They establish a sense of political identity and belonging both for Bêrîvan herself and for her organization through distinction from others. As such, her comments are also expressions of loyalty to a particular political ideology and the institutions sustaining it. According to anthropologist Caroline Humphrey (2017), expressing loyalty entails giving priority to one type of attachment over possible others. In what follows, I explore some of the consequences of a social situation in which individuals are constantly expected to make explicit their loyalties and choose one object of allegiance over another. Researchers are not excluded from these demands and will likely sense the pulls of allegiance when they navigate their field. Paying attention to such patterns is therefore imperative as much for dealing with the practicalities of fieldwork as for grasping how political subjects are shaped in contexts of protracted conflict and enduring violence.

TROUBLED TERRAIN

Northern Kurdistan today constitutes a politically highly polarized place. Decades of armed conflict accompanied by assimilationist government and violent displacement have unsettled, transformed, and deeply divided Kurdish society. With the political field dominated by two hegemonic formations—the PKK-affine Kurdish movement, on the one hand, and the Turkish state with its associated institutions, on the other hand—a friend-foe logic has come to pervade social interactions, which posits a neat dichotomous division in a conflict that, as any other, thrives on the existence of grey zones and ambiguities. It is a logic that seeks to shore up loyalties and asks for unquestioned allegiance, always ready to accuse of treason those who fail to bow to the demands of exclusive attachment.

Turkish state policy has driven this logic deep into the intimate fabric of Kurdish society. One means by which this has occurred is through the so-called village guard system. By systematically recruiting Kurdish civilians into state service in order to fight Kurdish insurgents who often issued from the same social fabric, the village guard system has contributed to the formation of a deeply divided social and physical topography. Villagers who have taken up village guard roles have been decried as "collaborators" by the PKK and become the target of violent retaliation, while in the eyes of the state villagers' refusal to take on guardianship has been perceived as an admission of support for the PKK insurgency and resulted in the targeted destruction of homes or entire villages (Belge 2011; Özar, Uçarlar, and Aytar 2013). As Evren Balta (2004, 3) has observed, one consequence of the village guard system that goes far beyond individual guards and their families has been "the complete destruction of 'neutral space'" in the region. The war has turned politics into a divisive weapon, which—like the blade of a sharp knife—is capable of tearing right through the intimate fabric of kinship and village relations, of friendship and collegiality.

What does this polarization mean for the ways in which political subjects and communities are shaped in the region and how does this, in turn, impact field research? I want to turn to my own research experience to shed light onto these questions. My research, carried out in 2011–2012, fell into a period that was characterized by a notable relaxation of the grip exerted by violent conflict on everyday life, leading to a certain disintegration of the dichotomous structure shaping the region. As much as this disintegration opened new spaces of social and political engagement, it also provoked a forceful defense of well-established boundaries that had come to be challenged. Turning to the resulting "boundary work" in what follows, my aim is to shed light onto a hegemonic order from the spaces of its margins. It is at these margins, I contend, that hegemony continuously (re)makes itself by vigorously policing loyalty and allegiance (cf. Thiranagama and Kelly 2010).

Considering my fieldwork experience from the vantage point of today it becomes clear that this was a period in which, even if confrontational politics occupied a firm place on the agenda, hope for a resolution of the conflict made a precarious appearance on the horizon. Two years prior to my arrival in the field, in 2009, the Turkish government had declared its "Kurdish initiative" (*Kürt açılımı*), a series of legal reforms that were to ameliorate some of the long-standing grievances regarding Kurdish political and cultural rights. Although the initiative was immensely controversial, it nevertheless encouraged a certain, timid optimism that a more democratic future was awaiting Turkey's Kurdish population. Such optimism was repeatedly curbed by clamp-downs on Kurdish political parties and activists, as well as continuing clashes between the PKK and Turkish military forces.

Still, a sense of hope that long-standing efforts of Kurdish campaigning would eventually bear fruit pervaded my field research (as premature as it might appear in retrospect). It formed the affective atmosphere in which my research took place, profoundly shaping the ways in which people interacted with their environment, with each other and, ultimately, with me. I use atmosphere here in the sense proposed by Kathleen Stewart (2011, 8), who writes of atmospheres "as a proliferative condition [that] not only allows, but spawns the production of different life worlds, experiences, conditions, dreams, imaginaries and moments of hyperactivity, down time, interruption, flow, friction, eruption, and still lifes." As an atmosphere in this sense, hope—timid and full of suspicion but, nonetheless, hopeful—spawned an immense effervescence of activity at the time of my field work. Sustained by (equally timid) legal reforms and a shift in political discourse, it made people dream about a less violent future and nurture ambitions of tranquil growth and upward mobility; it engendered construction booms and provided a taste of middle-class habits and comportments; it triggered a desire to reflect upon and testify to a violent past that, finally, seemed to have passed; it gave rise to a flourishing cultural scene and a host of civil society initiatives.

The political and military relaxation also impacted Kurdish party politics, which saw a loosening of the PKK's hegemony and a budding of new initiatives. While the pro-Kurdish and PKK-affine BDP's popularity reached new heights, several rival pro-Kurdish parties sought to make their inroads into the field engendering, as journalist Fehim Taştekin (2013) put it, a "diversification of politics in Kurdistan" that "raise[d] the prospect of breaking the PKK monopoly" on Kurdish politics. Such developments were paralleled by an expansion of civil society beyond the realm of organizations ideologically associated with and often financed by the Kurdish movement. International donor money aimed at development and human rights projects, which began to flow into the region via EU agencies and other European institutions, made financial means available to organizations associated neither with Turkish administrative structures nor the PKK-BDP bloc.

My fieldwork fell into this setting of atmospheric hopefulness, diluting boundaries and associational proliferation. More than supplying the "context" for my work, this conjuncture shaped its very outline, determining the interests I was able to develop, the questions I would be able to ask and the relations I was able to establish. That I ended up working closely with two women's associations that had emerged in this newly opened up space and that both sought to benefit—in one case successfully, in the other less so—from international funding opportunities hence reflected both a more general "context" and decisively shaped my interest in local struggles over political hegemony, in the status of women's rights activism and Kurdish women's ambition to public voice and representation. In deciding to work with these two organizations, my concern was less to take these as a base for producing generalizable research findings, than to produce detailed and "thick" knowledge of particular individuals, places, and relationships that would shine light onto my research interests (Cerwonka and Malkki 2007; Geertz 1973; Keesing and Strathern 1998).

BOUNDARY WORK

When I first arrived in Van, KAHAD—the association that Bêrîvan had been so careful to distinguish her own organization from—was one of the first organizations I was pointed to by an acquaintance with whom I had established contact thanks to common friends in Istanbul. KAHAD's range of activities included providing counseling services to female victims of gender-based violence, lobbying local government offices on women's rights issues, and carrying out women's rights education programs. Highly critical of the government's conservative politics on gender and sexuality, the organization followed a largely liberal-secular women's rights agenda. It catered to women of all political convictions and ethnicities, including Iranian and Afghani female refugees based in the city and supported Van's small LGBTQ community. KAHAD was well connected to influential Turkish feminist organizations in Ankara and Istanbul, and maintained a number of international connections with European women's organizations.

Such connections and the access they provided to knowledge and other resources were instrumental in making the organization particularly successful in securing European donor money. They certainly also played a role for KAHAD members' readiness to take me into their midst. The women working at KAHAD had assisted foreign researchers before me and would do so after (though I was probably the one who stayed longest). This meant that "being a researcher" was less of a foreign social category than it might have been in other contexts and certainly eased my integration. Moreover, several of the women active at the association were themselves former or current university students with interests in feminist thought and social theory, who would routinely reflect on their activist work and social surroundings through a theoretical repertoire that I was familiar with. In hindsight, I believe that such shared intellectual socialization played an important role for my relatively quick entry into KAHAD's social world.

Although left-leaning, pro-women's-rights and, perhaps most importantly, pro-Kurdish—all ideological markers which one might think would qualify KAHAD to be considered a partner or collaborator in the eyes of the BDP-led municipality—the organization was regarded with much suspicion by the latter, as the remarks I cited at the beginning of this chapter make clear. These remarks show that there existed important ideological differences between the two organizations regarding, among others, the significance attributed to legal reform and women's rights regimes for ameliorating the lives of women in the region.

In other regards, however, the two organizations were less distinct from each other than Bêrîvan's remarks might suggest. Despite their critique of the project-based women's rights and gender mainstreaming work undertaken by their more liberal feminist colleagues, BDP-aligned women's organizations were equally keen to enter international funding circuits. Van's municipal women's organization was no exception in this regard. Over the course of my fieldwork, the organization submitted several applications to EU-funded project schemes supporting women's rights activism and gender mainstreaming. Municipal women's organizations had established contacts with municipalities in Western Europe whom they were lobbying to enter collaborative funding bids. Alongside a rhetoric of revolutionary change, BDP-associated women's organizations also embraced more liberal women's rights discourses with remarkably frequency, for example in leaflets, during private conversations, or at public events. The day-to-day activities of Van's municipal women's organization, moreover, were not entirely different from what I observed at KAHAD: both regularly organized workshops and seminars for local women to inform them about their legal rights, provided individual counseling, and supported women in navigating state bureaucracy.

This is not to deny the ideological and practical differences between the organizations. Yet these differences were by no means clear-cut and the pervasive lure of international funding opportunities articulated through liberal rights discourse only threatened to further dilute them. Precisely for this reason, I contend, marking and reinforcing a line of distinction became all the more important. We may consequently interpret Bêrîvan's comments as a performative enactment of an ideological boundary between the municipal organization and KAHAD through which an existing but increasingly ill-defined distinction was reified and rigidified. While, on its own, the interchange I had with Bêrîvan that day may seem inconsequential, it stands as an example for the numerous social interactions through which "boundary work" was performed on a day-to-day level. Apart from explicit speech acts like the one I quoted in the introduction, it occurred via decisions who to socialize with or which cafes to visit. It shaped the networks of friendship and collegiality making up local society. It was at stake in interactions with strangers, when people would seek to elucidate, through carefully circumscribed questions, on which side of the great political divide a person was positioned.

The challenge for field researchers lies, I believe, in learning how to recognize when and through what codes such boundary work occurs. Reflecting on her fieldwork with Sudanese migrants in London, Anne Bartlett (2007, 225–226) recounts how she became suspect to the community she was working with by striking up friendship with men from an opposed political faction. Only once she had violated the "invisible line" that separated these factions did she become aware of their existence, as she was suddenly denied access to a refugee center she had previously been working at. Based on this experience, Bartlett suggests viewing boundaries as a heuristic device, which—as sites where political tension becomes manifest—allow grasping the complexity of the political terrain.

Yet it is not only through violating them that boundaries become evident. The careful observation of muted hints, a familiarity with discursive codes and aesthetic symbols, and the knowledge of norms of interaction all allow ethnographers to detect lines of difference and distinction that generally remain implicit. Taking my conversation with Bêrîvan as an example, only familiarity with the Kurdish movement's discourse allows me now, in retrospect, to recognize terms like "feudal structure," "male culture," or "mentality" as distinct markers of a specific ideological position. Similarly, only familiarity with Van's social topography allows me to recognize that the decision of Bêrîvan's organization to work within certain neighborhoods in Van and not others may be read as a statement of allegiance to a particular social and political constituency. Or, to mobilize another example, only a keen eye for the minute details of interior design—for that particular logo imprinted on a clock, that particular calendar sponsored by a specific party or NGO—will be able to detect the subtle performances of loyalty in everyday life that so often occur beyond the realm of explicit discourse. At stake is thus to develop what Cerwonka and Malkki (2007, 162–163) term the "anthropological sensibility": a disposition that draws creatively upon a wide repertory of methods in order to critically approach social facts that would otherwise remain invisible.

Researchers will need to develop these skills not only if they are to "read" their field site properly but also in order to negotiate their own position within it. In a context as polarized as Northern Kurdistan, a researcher's position with regards to hegemonic political formations will inevitably come under scrutiny and may crucially determine access to specific individuals, networks, and organizations. For example, my close association with KAHAD meant that the suspicion many harbored toward the organization on the side of the municipality soon began to rub off onto myself. Members of the latter, for example, would sometimes ask me if I was really hanging out with "those women" from KAHAD—indicating they had heard from others this was the case—and when I replied in the affirmative, they would only nod as if I had just confirmed their suspicion. On the other hand, being a foreigner allowed me to partially distance myself from such suspicions and maintain access to people working with municipal and other BDP-associated organizations (cf. Baser and Toivanen 2018). This is not to advocate distance or detachment—for example by emphasizing foreigner status—as a means of ensuring neutrality and hence broad access during field research (Cerwonka and Malkki 2007, 32–33). Ethnographic knowledge production deliberately seeks proximity with interlocutors as a way of producing in-depth insight, recognizing that there can be no such thing as absolute neutrality. This condition is only heightened in a context as polarized as Northern Kurdistan, where researchers will inevitably sense how charged political and social fault lines are as they navigate their fields.

Access, moreover, is not an unqualified condition that one either does or does not have. It is the quality of access that matters, the proximity or depth of relation one is able to build up with one's interlocutors. Thus, even though I was always able to contact people close to the municipality and make inquiries whenever I needed to, these relations were never marked by the same degree of trust and intimacy as those I had developed with other interlocutors, the women at KAHAD among them. Consequently, the type of knowledge I was able to gather from these different relations was of an entirely different kind. My point here is less to judge which type of knowledge is more desirable—that will vary for each research project—than to underline how one's positionality in the field impacts what kind of "data" one is able to collect and the knowledge one is ultimately able to produce.

Understanding my positionality in the field, including different forms of access and varied relations of trust and intimacy, as directly mediated by the ways in which the locally hegemonic Kurdish movement sustained and regulated its dominance allowed me to view what may appear primarily like methodological problems as a heuristic tool for understanding the shape and course of social and political fault lines in my field site. For such heuristics, embodied and affective knowledge should not be underestimated. The sense of rejection when excluded from a specific conversation, the embarrassment when realizing one has asked the wrong question, the feeling of being kept at a distance by an interlocutor one would like to develop a close relation to: all these are visceral and emotional clues pointing to the tensions that become evident at political fault lines. They were also experiences I repeatedly made as I navigated relations with interlocutors embedded in the range of institutions pertaining to the PKK-BDP bloc. They point to the fact that, as Allaine Cerwonka (2007, 153) notes, "It is often at the level of the body that we register the contradictions of fieldwork and the awkwardness of being a person out of category." The body is in that sense both a heuristic tool and a site of ethical negotiation, particularly in contexts marred by violence and conflict (cf. Nordstrom and Robben 1995). From this perspective, what is often referred to quite abstractly as "positionality," needs to be understood as a question of quite literally taking up a position: an embodied and affective stance from which knowledge is produced. In Northern Kurdistan, doing so occurs under enormous pressure. At the same time, this renders positionality an ever more valuable form of visceral insight through which to better understand how political belonging is shaped in this particular context.

HEGEMONY FROM THE MARGINS

Political belonging can be precarious for those positioned at the margins of hegemonic political formations. Negotiating my relation with the municipality and other associated actors as someone who was seen to be associated with KAHAD gave me precious (though comparatively inconsequential) insight into such precarity through bodily and affective registers like feelings of rejection, exclusion, and embarrassment. Despite its fraught relation to the locally hegemonic municipality, KAHAD nevertheless had the advantage of being able to draw on important local kinship networks and was both nationally and internationally well connected. This was not the case for the Women Artists Association, another organization I worked closely with. The Association offered a platform for Kurdish female singers and musicians facing difficulties in a society where women's involvement in public musical performance is often considered morally questionable or shameful (*şerm*).

It was founded only several months prior to my arrival in Van by a group of female singer-poets who had previously been active at the local Mesopotamia Cultural Centre (*Navenda Çanda Mezopotamyayê*, NÇM), which was ideologically linked to and financed by the BDP-municipality. The women were greatly disappointed with how they had been treated at the NÇM, where, so they reported, male artists and staff did not take them seriously as singers and did not accord them space at public performances. Disappointed by these experiences, the women decided to set up their own, all female association.

They found encouragement for doing so in widely circulating ideas about nongovernmental organizations as key access points for vast sums of money and other resources. The women who embarked on funding the association were mostly middle-aged to elderly, of modest backgrounds, and many had never attended school. In this context, the idea of funding an association that would not only allow them to engage in the musical and poetic work they felt passionate about but might also give them access to resources that were otherwise scarce was certainly appealing.

When it was first founded, the association had enjoyed some financial support by the BDP-run municipality, but this never turned into the kind of regular funding with which the municipality supported its own associations. The women singers also soon found that acquiring the funding that seemed so plenty in the realm of civil society was not as easy as it had appeared, particularly in a situation where, lacking literacy skills and bureaucratic know-how, they entirely relied on the goodwill of others to help with identifying bids, writing applications, and submitting them. As a result, the association found itself scrambling each month to pay the rent and charges for its office space in the city center, relying on donations from more well-to-do acquaintances, friends and relatives to make ends meet. Matters were not made easier by the fact that relations with the BDP and municipality quickly worsened. This meant that renting venues for performances the women were planning became a real challenge, and that the endeavor to sell tickets for concerts ran into a wall of indifference from audiences that normally pride themselves for supporting Kurdish culture.

Municipal officers also exerted continuous pressure on members of the association to give up their endeavor and return into the fold of the NÇM and several women took up the offer. Perihan, head of the Artists Association and one of my closest interlocutors, was heartbroken over these developments. She had been a committed supporter of the Kurdish movement from its very inceptions—enduring immense suffering, including torture, for her support— and now suddenly found herself at odds with it. She could not comprehend why her commitment to work with Kurdish women singers, something that she regarded as an important contribution to preserve and revitalize Kurdish culture, could not be embraced by the pro-Kurdish municipality. And indeed, rather than disagreement over the type of work the Artists Association was engaged in, it seemed that the main issue motivating the municipality's attempts to curb the association was its institutional independence.

Hegemony, this makes clear, asserts itself most fiercely at the margins, where the negotiation of allegiance and belonging becomes particularly urgent. Above, I argued that researchers in Northern Kurdistan are well advised to develop an acute sensitivity for the major fault lines and divisions that structure their field in order to negotiate positionality and manage access. What the example of Perihan and her association adds to this insight is the importance for researchers to not only take into account the immense polarization that marks their research context, but also the ways in which their interlocutors themselves navigate this fraught terrain. While such navigation has certainly become the focus of analysis in its own right as indicative of the social relations ethnographers seek to understand (e.g., Thiranagama and Kelly 2010), what it implies methodologically has been somewhat less explored.

Perihan and the women organized through her association were among the most important interlocutors for the research project I undertook at the time. The way in which they negotiated the expectations of loyalty on behalf of the municipality and sought to gain access to its various resources therefore had important consequences for my own research. The socially and financially precarious situation of the association meant that a great deal of its members' activities centered around how to improve relations with the municipality and how to access the financial flows they had heard were so abundantly available at civil society organizations. Engaging in "participatory observation" in this context consequently made me witness more heated debate about local politics and musings about the workings of international funding schemes than performance of customary knowledge or recitation of oral history. The association's precarious position in the field of local politics also had great impact on my own positionality vis-à-vis its members. The women at the association very quickly recruited me—an internationally connected, multilingual young woman with at least minimal technological knowhow—into their various attempts at improving their situation. In my they invested their hopes of accessing the money they had heard was so amply circulating through civil society organizations. In me they also saw opportunities for tapping into the (inter)national fame as singers and musicians they felt they deserved.

As a result, it did not take long before I was busy immersing myself into the intricacies of international funding schemes, drafting applications and working out budget plans. I set up contacts with documentary filmmakers and photographers, and organized a week of concerts in Istanbul. I also initiated an EU-funded project that took some of the association members on a musical exchange to Armenia and culminated in a performance at a large Istanbul concert hall. I was hence far from only an ethnographer while in the field: I found myself hovering between the roles of project coordinator, musical manager, fixer, and researcher. In many ways, I was delighted to be able to give something back to people from whom I learned so much and to do so in tangible and concrete ways. On the other hand, these engagements also created expectations, not all of which I was able to live up to. I did not manage to orchestrate the great international artistic breakthrough, neither did I tap into those mystical flows of money.

Rather than thinking of these experiences as a lamentable divergence from an ideal type of disinterested and impartial research, I would argue for an approach that valorizes them as important insights into how a situation of intense polarization structures our interlocutors' possibilities of action as much as their dreams, aspirations, and horizons of imagination. Impartiality, for one, is not only unattainable, but upholding it as an ideal reproduces problematic binarisms such as objective versus subjective, rational versus emotional, mind versus body (Cerwonka and Malkki 2007, 171–174; Willis 1980). Ethnographic research means participating in the social contexts in which we are working and therefore becoming implicated in the lives of our interlocutors. Instead of disavowing such involvement, we need to ponder the ethical implications that such implication entails. Ethnographic fieldwork inevitably blurs the lines between informantship and friendship, between instrumentality and emotional investment.

Many of my "informants" became close friends over the course of my fieldwork, and these ties of friendship formed the backbone of my research, because they allowed for trust, intimacy and, ultimately, "thick description" (Geertz 1973). I was happy to help with scrambling together resources for the Women Singers Association not only because this was my research project but also, quite simply, because these were my friends. And still, I would have my notebook continuously within reach, ready to treat as "data" what I observed. This intermeshing of personal investment with the instrumentalities of field research poses ethical quandaries. It requires from researchers an ethical "common sense," alongside more formal mechanisms like informed consent or, at a later stage, the rigid anonymization of interlocutors' identities. There are no clear-cut answers to where ethnographic research ought to stop or what sort of "data" should remain outside its reach. Ultimately, as Liisa Malkki (2007, 95) notes, "the question is what one does with research material, and why one wants to know."

This also entails recognizing that our interlocutors are people like any other, who engage with us based on their own motivations and interests, rather than treating them as disinterested, "authentic" informants. In this particular case, recognizing that I was equally instrumental to the people I worked with as they were to me, as well as pondering what exactly constituted my instrumentality proved insightful for understanding the specific impasses and dilemmas my interlocutors faced. My centrality for accessing a particular set of resources sheds light on the ways in which a context of protracted conflict, scarce resources and tightly policed political divisions impacted on the trajectories of action and imagination of the women I worked with. It also highlights how such a context raises or at the very least accentuates the ethical stakes of implicating oneself as a researcher into the lives of the people one works with. Ultimately, I was the one who had the liberty to leave and extricate myself from local networks and relationships at the end. As much as I got to momentarily experience the sense of precarity that reigned at the margins of hegemonic political formations, this precarity was to remain my interlocutors' life world. We are therefore well advised to tread our steps carefully.

CONCLUSION

Let me be clear that my aim in this chapter has not been to pass judgment on either side of the dispute between municipal organizations on the one hand and KAHAD or the Women Artists Association on the other hand. Just as with any dispute, there are many stories that could be told about this one, and the one I have told here is not the only nor necessarily the correct one. Yet, I maintain that the story I have decided to tell holds significance for what it says about the making of political subjectivity in a situation of protracted conflict and intense polarization and, consequently, for how ethnographic research may be conducted in such a context.

My focus has been on the social work of distinction that occurs at the margins of hegemonic formations. It is at these margins—the borderlands, as it were, of poles of allegiance—that political hegemony is established and maintained. In Northern Kurdistan, a decade-long history of warfare and state violence has deeply polarized society, such that norms and expectations of allegiance permeate private lives as much as public discourse. As a result, the demands of loyalty make themselves constantly felt. Researchers, I have argued, are not excluded from these dynamics. The polarized nature of Northern Kurdish society is not only an issue they need to learn how to navigate for themselves, but the way in which their interlocutors, too, navigate existing divisions fundamentally influences their positionality in the field, the kind of material they will be able to gather and the knowledge they will be able to produce.

Focusing on the contested borderlands of political hegemony brings into view the boundary work that is crucial to the delineating of political communities and the shaping of political subjects. From this perspective, we may approach fieldwork as the artful task of tracing boundaries and lines of allegiance, following their meandering course, sensing their energetic pulse or subdued implicitness, and navigating the spaces they delineate, open up or foreclose.

NOTE

1. All names of individuals and organizations in this chapter are pseudonyms.

BIBLIOGRAPHY

Balta, Evren. 2004. "Causes and Consequences of Village Guard System in Turkey." *Mellon Fellowship for Humanitarian and Security Affairs Conference*, CUNY, New York, December 2, 2004.

Barth, Fredrik. 1969. *Ethnic Groups and Boundaries*. Boston: Little, Brown and Co.

Bartlett, Anne. 2007. "The City and the Self: The Emergence of New Political Subjects in London." In *Deciphering the Global: Its Spaces, Scales and Subjects*, edited by Saskia Sassen, 221–242. New York: Routledge.

Baser, Bahar and Mari Toivanen. 2018. "Politicized and depoliticized ethnicities, power relations and temporality: Insights to outsider research from comparative and transnational fieldwork." *Ethnic and Racial Studies* 41, no. 11: 2067–2084.

Belge, Ceren. 2011. "State Building and the Limits of Legibility: Kinship Networks and Kurdish Resistance in Turkey." *International Journal of Middle East Studies* 43, no. 1: 95–114.

Cerwonka, Allaine, and Lisa H. Malkki. 2007. *Improvising Theory: Process and Temporality in Ethnographic Fieldwork*. Chicago: University of Chicago Press.

Das, Veena, and Deborah Poole. 2004. *Anthropology in the Margins of the State*. Santa Fe: School of American Research Press.

Geertz, Clifford. 1973. *The Interpretation of Cultures: Selected Essays*. New York: Basic Books.

Humphrey, Caroline. 2017. "Loyalty and Disloyalty as Relational Forms in Russia's Border War with China in the 1960s." *History and Anthropology* 28, no. 4: 497–514.

Keesing, Roger M., and Andrew Strathern. 1998. *Cultural Anthropology: A Contemporary Perspective*. Belmont, California: Wadsworth.

Nordstrom, Carolyn, and Antonius C. G. M. Robben. 1995. *Fieldwork under Fire: Contemporary Studies of Violence and Survival*. Berkeley: University of California Press.

Özar, Şemsa, Nesrin Uçarlar, and Osman Aytar. 2013. *From Past to Present a Paramilitary Organization in Turkey: Village Guard System*. Diyarbakır: Diyarbakır Institute for Political and Social Research (DISA).

Stewart, Kathleen. 2011. "Atmospheric Attunements." *Environment and Planning D: Society and Space* 29, no. 3: 445–453.

Taştekin, Fehim. 2013. "New Party Linked to Barzani Makes Play for Turkey's Kurds." *Al-Monitor*, November 24, 2013.

Thiranagama, Sharika, and Tobias Kelly. 2010. *Traitors: Suspicion, Intimacy, and the Ethics of State-Building*. Philadelphia: University of Pennsylvania Press.

Willis, Paul. 1980. "Notes on Method." In *Culture, Media, Language*, edited by Stuart Hall, Dorothy Hobson, Andrew Lowe and Paul Willis, 76–83. London: Routledge.

Chapter 6

Working on Communities under Political Domination

Subaltern Kurds in Turkey

Polat S. Alpman

Working in dangerous fields, especially with those with excluded and dominated groups within society, is not preferred by many researchers. The same political domination that plagues minority groups penetrates academia and makes these fields risky, uncertain, and dangerous. Academia in Turkey has been mostly stripped of its independence due to the tremendous pressure of the state apparatus (Beşikçi 2013). Works that challenge the official state narratives on the issues like Kurdish, Cyprus, Armenian problems are seen as dangerous fields where one is discouraged from working. For this reason, it is difficult for researchers to produce critical and objective knowledge on anything, let alone on the issues that are considered "dangerous." Scholars who study these issues often prefer to reiterate them from the perspective of the state. Hence, many of these academic endeavors are done to legitimize or hide political, economic, legal, and social domination.

This chapter has two purposes. The main aim is to understand and explain the position of a researcher who works with subaltern groups under political domination and the pressure toward these subalterns. To accomplish this, I will draw from my research experiences in 2013–2014, involving ethnographic fieldwork with the Kurdish community in Istanbul. The other purpose of this paper is related to a discussion on "dangerous" fields. The chapter also demonstrates that it is necessary to consider the concept of "danger" as a methodological concept for fieldwork (Sluka 1995, 276–294; Peritore 1990, 359–372).

For this reason, I will first discuss the Kurdish question in Turkey, before moving forward to present observations from my fieldwork. While there are certain tendencies to adhere to and reiterate the state's perspectives in such fields, and it is also necessary to mention that critical voices do exist. Such an overview will also demonstrate how a subaltern Kurdish identity is reproduced in different spaces, by focusing on the particular case of the Kurdish community in Istanbul. It will thereby examine the multifaceted nature of subalternity, as experienced by Kurds, which has economic, social, and other dimensions.

SUBALTERNITY AND THE KURDS IN TURKEY

Kurdish society in Turkey is a class-stratified society, and the politics within it is based on the violence associated with class and social privileges. Kurdish society also takes the form of a stateless nation, as Kurds failed to establish a Kurdish state with new boundaries after World War I. They were therefore forced to live under the authority of the political regime in Iraq, Turkey, Iran, and Syria (King 2013, 41–65). The Kurds become minorities within different nation-states, yet they were prevented by the sovereign states from obtaining political rights in their lands (Chaliand 1993). The Kurdish question in Turkey concerns political, economic, judicial, social, and civil rights of Kurds that have not been recognized. Historically, a political regime dominated by Turkish nationalism was created after the establishment of the Republic of Turkey in 1923. This new regime, which is identified as Kemalist Turkey in the literature, aimed to gather all Muslim non-Turkish ethnic groups under the umbrella of Turkishness. Many ethnic groups succumbed voluntarily to the offer of assimilation and were consequently Turkified (Kineşçi 2017; Oran 2015; Yıldız 2015; Atasoy and Ertürk 2010). However, the Kurds mounted resistance to these attempts to assimilate them by rejecting the state's ethnic policy. This led to the unfolding of armed conflict between the Kurdistan Workers' Party (PKK), established in 1979, and the Turkish Republic. In turn, this conflict resulted in the eastern region of the country, where most Kurds live, to remain under a permanent condition of war. Kurds who live in this region have experienced various tribulations because they have been torn between the oppression of both the state on one side, and the PKK on the other.

People who have been stuck in the middle of war and conflict conditions have continued to migrate to Western metropolises, such as Istanbul, fleeing conditions of poverty, unemployment, education, and health problems. These groups experienced oppression both by the state and the PKK. Kurds who migrated to western Turkey confronted hardships such as racism, discrimination, inequality, abasement, exclusion, and othering in their political, economic, cultural relationships and daily interactions. While the Kurdish community experienced the oppression of the state through people who carried the titles of "teacher," "soldier," "police officer," and "doctor" in the Kurdish region, after they migrated to Istanbul, they began to experience oppression within all areas of their daily life.

Nowadays, Istanbul is the city with the largest Kurdish population in the world, and Kurds continue to migrate there. The population of Istanbul is approximately 16 million, and it is estimated that 4 million of this population is composed of Kurds (Sönmez 2013). As a result of the forced migration wave that started in the 1990s,[1] Kurdish neighborhoods emerged in Istanbul (Kurban and Yükseker et.al. 2008). These people, who had become expropriated because of migration, transformed into a cheap labor force to be able to survive in the city. Some of them succeeded in adapting to the conditions after migration. A few have become qualified workers, and even less have become employers or small tradesmen (Kurban and Yeğen 2012).

Tarlabaşı, which is one of the poorest neighborhoods in Istanbul, became one of the neighborhoods where subaltern Kurds settled (Yılmaz 2003a). Tarlabaşı is in the center of Beyoğlu, which is one of the most established districts of Istanbul, and is adjacent to Taksim. Taksim is composed of a central square and surrounding area that is a place of consumption enjoyed by tourists and the middle class. While Taksim is ostentatious, Tarlabaşı is fusty. People who settle in Tarlabaşı are generally socioeconomically from the lowest segments of the society. When it comes to the Kurds, their subjection to political domination and oppression adds to the local population's marginalization. Because Tarlabaşı is a place with higher rates of crime and violence compared to other neighborhoods, the inhabitants of Tarlabaşı are stigmatized with crime and marginalization, and Tarlabaşı is confined within a border made of glass. This border is also the border absorbing the people from the bottom of the society into Tarlabaşı by criminalizing them and preventing their exit from there (Yılmaz 2003b). Subaltern Kurds crossed this border soon after they came to Istanbul. Here Kurds had to take shelter in houses without baths and kitchens as crowded groups of men, or as two, three families together. Subsequently, many of them started to work on the streets or in the unlicensed workshops in Beyoğlu and Taksim, on the opposite side of the street. The Kurds, trapped between illness, crime, poverty, and poor conditions, on the one side, and the carnivalesque space of middle-class consumption and entertainment, on the other, had to deal with not only this but also with being Kurdish as a political existence (Şahin 2010).

WORKING WITH THE SUBALTERN

The concept of "subalternity" refers to a condition of subordination brought about by colonization and other forms of economic, social, racial, religious, linguistic, and/or cultural dominance. Subaltern studies are, therefore, studies of power. Power is intimately related to questions of representation which have cognitive authority and can secure hegemony (Beverley 1999). Therefore, the concept of subaltern is used to define oppressed people with no opportunity to express the desperation they experience in their daily life. They generally suffer from discrimination because of their ethnic, religious, gender or group identity. Furthermore, this concept describes those who are ideologically convinced that they deserve a basement and devaluation through a wide range of catalogue of gestures, mimics, uses of language, and from physical-bodily properties to cognitive-emotional properties. In other words, subalternity is a result of the normalization processes of class exploitation and domination mechanisms.

Subalterns possess both experimental and intuitive knowledge against exploitation, domination, and oppression. For this reason, they construct a deep and silent effort to organize their daily life to be tangent to inequality and discrimination practices as far as it is possible. From Gramsci to Spivak, the common emphasis in subalternity studies is on the typology composed of commonalities formed in the objective conditions framing the subaltern in mutual connections. This typology describes the subaltern as speechless. Hence, when the subaltern can express that s/he is a subaltern, s/he is not a subaltern anymore (Spivak 1990, 158). For that reason, subalternity is an expression of unsubjectivation or, more precisely, of being mutilated by becoming speechless against the sovereign (Spivak 1988).

Hearing the voice of the subaltern and investigating political, social, economic, and cultural representations means paying attention to this voice, which is "a voice for the most part stifled and reduced to silence, marginalized, its utterances scattered to the winds" (Jameson 1983, 71). However, the communication between a researcher, who wants to listen to subalterns under political pressure, and a subaltern should not be understood as the communication between two equals. One of the sides is not a subaltern and has organic relations with the sovereign. Even though the subaltern speaks for themselves, interviews are done between unequal sides with a power dynamic (Beverley 1999). This kind of consideration of the power relations, class position and status of the researcher, separates them, and the symbolic and cultural power they carry materializes during the interview. In the course of the interview, the researcher transforms their respondent into a subject, meaning an empirical material of the study. This transformation inevitably includes a power relation because of the differences between the researcher and the interviewee (Altorki 1994). Working with a community under political pressure can be evaluated as a choice to bypass this power relation. Nevertheless, applying such a bypass, going to the field without thinking about this, carries the risk of speaking on behalf of the subaltern instead of speaking with them.

POSITIONING MYSELF: WHO AM I?

How do we describe ourselves (Adler and Adler 1987) when working in such fields and with communities under political pressure? Who are we, and with which identity do we present ourselves? In my case, I am a member of the dominant identity group in Turkey: I am male, Turkish, Sunni, middle-class, employed, and educated with a certain set of cultural and social capital. The Kurds I met during my fieldwork, regardless of being young or old, uneducated or low-educated, unemployed or employed, married or single, or of having lived in the neighborhood for less or more than five years, had experienced state violence in the course of their encounters with authorities. Therefore, after coming to Istanbul, all of these people encountered the various forms of Turkishness here, in addition to the oppressive state's practices (Tatum 2000, 9–14).

"Who was I, as the person who would interview them?" was the question that I had to answer before starting my fieldwork (Tregaskis 2004; Ellingson 1998). Was I a part of Turkishness? Or was I a part of the state, as an academic working at a state university? Otherwise, should I identify myself with universal values, scientific knowledge, or as a part of the university? Ethically speaking, which values did I represent, and to whom or what were my responsibilities? Whose knowledge was the knowledge I tried to understand and explain, to whom did it belong to and for whom was it necessary? On behalf of whom did I conduct interviews? Did I conduct them as an academic or as an activist, as a state officer, or as a scientist who maintained his/her critical perspective? As a curious Turk, or Kurd? As a partisan who imposed her/his political views on research participants? As a person from Istanbul, or as a person whose ancestors were immigrants?

These questions can be extended, and it is not possible to give a standard answer to how researchers position themselves in the field. I think that the researcher is obligated to find an answer both methodologically and ethically (Coffey 1999). In anthropology, a researcher's attempt to reidentify oneself before the fieldwork is not related "to catch the point of view of the indigenous." In other words, I do not mean that the researcher should rid oneself of their own culture to understand the point of view of the indigenous. Instead of taking Malinowski's (1988) anthropological approach of the researcher as one who is purified from their own culture, I argue that researchers should learn to establish connections with an awareness of class, symbolic, and cultural power relationships.

The methodological and ethical answer for the question of "Who am I?" necessitates being objective while considering the common good and the presence of power (Burawoy 2005). A researcher who works on marginalized identities and groups under political pressure, but does not share the same identity with the group, should be aware of the domination and the inequality that their study causes. This awareness of possible inequalities should be a part of their analysis (Muhammad, Wallerstein, etc., 2015). This is significant because the researcher can be taken to represent the sovereign and its culture when s/he encounters the subaltern (Postholm and Madsen 2006; Kutlu 2015).

A person working with communities under political pressure cannot be expected to operate in the field independently from their own political opinion. Distortions embedded within every research relation can resurface, especially with excluded groups. These distortions are not communication failures. In order to eliminate the symbolic violence caused by being researched, one needs to construct the methodology of listening, which understands and interprets, rather than interrogates and judges (Bourdieu 2000, 608–609). This kind of listening is neither the listening of an unbiased academic apparatus nor the listening of an activist who identifies her/himself with the dominated group. Whenever the researcher listens, it is important to remember that it is not partly an academic and partly an activist listening. Rather, they are apart from all of these. The researcher, who is the owner of the point of view in the field by knowing the trace of sovereign on themselves, is the person who is aware of their class and social privileges. Only with this kind of awareness, can they fulfill their public responsibility when working with subalterns and/ or those under political domination (Burawoy 2004, 1607).

It is necessary to remember that attributing such a mission to anyone working in the field is an ethical discussion. Accordingly, considering the person one presents oneself as in the field is not only a methodological issue but also an ethical one. When I decided who I was in the field, I had to keep the state in my mind because the source of power upon the Kurdish community is the state. At the same time, I am an academic working at a state university, and I think that the state guarantees not only the social, political, and civil rights gained by historical and social struggles of the democratic state, but also scientific autonomy and liberty. In fact, we are obliged to rethink the vulnerable relationship between the state and academia, which is threatened by neoliberal capitalism and corrupt state practices. Especially in countries that have a fragile democracy imposed on them and who have undergone a process of modernization from above, like Turkey, academic autonomy cannot be institutionalized and academia is a mere apparatus used by the state (Beşikçi 2013). Thus, for instance, a researcher who works with subaltern Kurds in Turkey could encounter the pressure of the state even if it is not direct.

The other side of this fact is the armed organizations, and in my case, it is the PKK. I did not meet anyone who claimed that s/he was a member of the PKK, but nearly all research participants had a relative who was a member of the organization. In Istanbul, there was no power or influence of the PKK, but there were sympathizers of the organization who saw some benefit in its success. The PKK should also be seen as a power apparatus. However, in a metropolis like Istanbul, the PKK's political pressure happens indirectly. For that reason, I should have not considered this organization. Rather, I should have taken into consideration the legal and political compounds of the Kurdish movement, especially the *People's Democratic Party* (HDP).

A different dilemma has arisen from working with groups under political pressure in this new junction: the researcher carries the trace of sovereign ideology and power, and the easiest way to escape from it is over-identification with the opposite side. Nevertheless, this situation causes new problems. First of all, this kind of identification is distorted. It eliminates listening to interlocutors. This supposed new level of reality the researcher reaches by the way of over-identification in fact is a distortion. This kind of identification makes it easy for the researcher to manipulate the knowledge of the field personally. In order to avoid over-identification, the researcher should go back to the question about who s/he is against, which raises the question of political pressure (Briggs 2002, 911–922).

How should the researcher situate themselves against the political domination of the state, the media, law, and other oppressive forces? How should they describe themselves against large and threatening organizations such as the state and political/armed groups, even if they are a person who aims to actualize their public responsibility? What is the nature of this responsibility and how are its borders determined by the researcher? In addition, what is their intellectual mission, which presumably includes bearing witness to the era?

A researcher who works with subalterns must therefore primarily answer the question of who s/he is. The issue I personally worried the most about was the fact that I am not a Kurd and more precisely that I cannot speak Kurdish. I knew that research participants could speak Turkish but also, I thought that I had to speak Kurdish because I supposed that this would make a good impression. Of course, if I was a Kurd and possessed the local networks that Kurds had, many things would have been easier for me. However, this situation also could have hindered many things I could have seen in the field because I would have also been exposed to political domination. This is because encountering subalterns under political domination is not related only to the state and identity. It is also a matter that concerns class. Some Kurds are not subaltern because they have higher rank in class and social structure, and they may experience less political domination. Hence, subalternity can determine the intensity of political domination.

Therefore, a Kurdish researcher may carry this kind of class and social privileges. S/he also bears the trace of power. The language the researcher uses, their discourse stereotypes, their types of seeing and hearing, their understanding and interpretation patterns, even their body and mind can be surrounded by a sovereign ideology and the power. Hence, a researcher within this stratum, who is described as a "white Kurd" by some Kurdish writers and who enjoys the privileges provided by the state, has to decide who s/he is. A researcher who wants to work with communities under political domination must regulate her/himself with a methodological and ethical perspective, although s/he has ethnic identity, political belonging, status, and similar demographic properties. Such a kind of regulation is limited by the necessities of the field and should be performed reflexively.

WORKING IN A DANGEROUS
FIELD, OR "WHO ARE YOU?"

The concept of "danger" is usually used for the benefit of or concern for researchers who conduct the fieldwork (Sharp and Kremer 2006; Sluka 1995; Peritore 1990). Nonetheless, when it comes to communities under political domination, not only the researcher but also the research participants may experience danger during fieldwork (Glasius et al. 2018, 17–35). The fact that some of the threats on the scene, such as violence and terror, are more visible than others, does not remove the danger that is more difficult to see. Interviewees in particular can be vulnerable in the face of invisible dangers (Lee 1995; Lee-Treweek and Linkogle 2000). For example, in the context of Turkey, a male researcher who insists on meeting a woman does not know whether or not he will be hurt by a man who is a relative of the woman after the interview. However, this lack of awareness does not mean that he is unaware of the characteristics of the field.

This danger is much greater when political domination is concerned. For example, marginalized identities or immigrants are not under domination only because of class discrimination or racism, ethnic discrimination, and nationalism (Glick-Schiller and Fouron 1990). These identities are subject to all political, social, legal, economic, sexual, religious, and similar social fields, resulting in the obligation stay inside the bounds of this externally defined identity. These dominations can enter the field through inequality and discrimination systems internalized by the researcher who is the member of society. Because the stigma of inequality and discrimination faced by marginalized identities (Jahan 2016) there is a kind of "social contract." The objection and criticism of this stigma are usually defined as treason in countries which do not have a democratic culture, and therefore any attempt to rectify this problem usually adds up to not much more than political correctness. Especially countries claiming a democratic system, when racist political rhetoric arises, it serves as a reminder of the usually hidden "social contract."

To cite a recent example of such a case in the United States, President Trump, referring to African and Haitian immigrants, asked, "Why are we having all these people from shithole countries come here?" This situation indicates the often-invisible face of the dangers in the field for the interlocutors and the researcher. The dangers arising from the sociopolitical structure are not always calculated or predictable, and cannot be regulated. For this reason, for example in Turkey, a man who bullies a female relative just because she had an interview with a male researcher, or a police officer who interrogates or even detains a researcher just because the researcher interviewed people from an ethnic group under political oppression or anyone who sees himself as the representative of the sovereign identity can also be counted as threats in the field.

Therefore, the concept of danger in the field can be used bilaterally and superficially. The first of these ideas is about the dangers originating from the field. The second, on the other hand, refers to the dangers that lie outside of the field but which also have an effect on the field. The dangers originating from the field may change depending on the basis of the attributions of the group worked upon. In the Kurdish community I worked on, dangers were limited. Dangers from interviewees, relatives of the interviewees, people settling there, people wanting to save the group from the dangers outside, and the Kurdish movement are within the bounds of possibility. I was not harmed physically by any of them, despite encountering some dangers. However, I am not sure that my experience could be generalized for all researchers.

One of the dangerous scenarios I encountered involved some Kurdish youth called "qirix" who expressed their weakness in social relations with the Kurdish community, who had no belief in the success of their cultures, who experienced anomie intensely, and continued their daily life by committing crime and violence. Some of them were parts of small gang groups with eight to ten people. Some of the gangs were composed of two or three people. Generally, they used drugs and had no jobs and did not search for a job. *Qirix*s are not a danger encountered by everyone who works upon the Kurdish community. Most often, widespread danger is directly related to political, judicial, economic, social dominations surrounding the Kurdish community. To put it more broadly, a person who works on the Kurdish community may be conceived by the police as a threat.

Moreover, the researcher might not appear in the category of a confidential person. There are many possible ways to eliminate the mistrust. However, in dangerous fields, it needs to be remembered that danger is not only physical and emotional but also occupational and ethical. Thus, people who work in dangerous fields have to determine their occupational and ethical limits, and take care of these limits when they gain the confidence of the interviewees.

Whether being conventional or dangerous, in every field, the researcher must clarify to the interviewees who s/he is, as who and for whom s/he carries the study there. As for myself, a person, who decided to work on the subaltern Kurdish community in Istanbul and did not know the Kurdish language, was not born and grown up in a Kurdish city, described her/himself only by her/his occupational attributes: Could it be enough to work in the field? I was sure that it was not enough, and so I decided to move into the field where I would work in Beyoğlu. By doing this, I decided to approach everyone within the surrounding area, not only the interviewees. I would acquaint myself with the people in my surroundings, my neighbors, shopkeepers, and I would express simply, comprehensibly, and clearly who I was and why I settled there. Thus, I believed, I would not experience problems in the field interviews. However, I must confess that it did not turn out as I had expected.

Describing myself clearly increased the suspicion upon me and was not enough to be accepted as a trustworthy person. When working with communities under political domination, being an academic could not eliminate the security concern even if it provided me with a relative status. Such questions were based on the deep doubt displayed toward me: Why did I do such research; why did I ask such questions; why did I record the voices of the interviewees; by whom were they listened; and did the state make me do this research. The insecurity toward the state was reflected on me, and the explanations I provided were useless. However, in spite of it, most of the interviewees who consented to interviews did not refrain from explaining their opinions explicitly, especially women.

During the interviews, the question asked to me was "who are you?" This question was not always asked with words but with gestures, mimics, or implications. There were some replies I prepared: "I am from Istanbul, from Kocamustafapaşa. I am studying for a doctorate at Ankara University. My subject is about Kurds who came to Istanbul. I work on understanding how they live, how they work, and the problems they encounter because of being a Kurd." This is a simple, conceivable answer but usually it did not work because there was almost no person from Istanbul in Istanbul. Everybody migrated to Istanbul from all around the country. When I said that I was from Istanbul, this did not include any information about my ethnic-religious identity. So, I developed the answer. In fact, the answer is within the answer of the question of "why should I trust you?"

Thankfully I had friends in the neighborhood I lived in, and knowing them and spending time together generated mutual confidence. First of all, I conducted interviews with them, and later with others through their help. Most of the time, they accompanied me, and so many people who did not initially want to speak with me accepted to be interviewed. Of course, accepting the interview did not mean that they replied to my questions.

These problems emerged not only during the interviews. It is about not belonging to the place, and not belonging to the place which is so risky in Tarlabaşı. For instance, for a presentation, while photographing the teahouses in which Kurdish men spend time in Tarlabaşı, a fourteen- or fifteen-year-old Kurdish boy approached me with a knife in his hand, and then he started to swear in Turkish. I did not know what to do or how to react. I did not want to draw back, but the fact was that he could harm me. In that moment, I caught an old man's eyes. He was yelling in Kurdish to the boy while he was coming, and he pulled him away from me. He apologized in an ashamed manner, and he told that the boy was ignorant and he did not have a job so he vagabonded as such. I asked him "would you like to drink tea?" We sat down in the teahouse near and started to talk. I did not record the talk. While I asked him some of the questions from the questionnaire, my main aim was not to conduct an interview with him. Hasan told me his own life story and his living experiences in Istanbul. Soon after leaving him, a man in his mid-twenties approached me and told me in a threatening way not to come here again. I asked why but he swore and walked up to me with a threatening gesture. All these events happened 200 meters from my house. In other words, we were neighbors.

I learned that it necessitates going out of scientific practices to produce an acceptable answer to the question of "who are you?" Even being accepted as a trustworthy person for me was not enough to conduct interviews as part of a reciprocal, trustful relationship. After some interviews, either confirming to the interviewees as "all our talk will stay between us, won't it?" or sending messages about the interviews can be given as the examples to this fact. This is because whoever I am, I am not one of them. I do not mean to be Kurdish, because even if I am a Kurd, I am not one of them.

I was able to conduct some interviews with the help of the networks of some of my Kurdish friends. These friendships may have generally allowed me to skip many of the questions my interviewees usually asked me. While getting further away from this network, the question of "who are you?" took part in the interviews even if it was not verbalized explicitly. This was about what I was rather than who I was, why I did such research, what I would do with the information gathered from the field, and in the name of whom I made it. There was no importance given to my occupational interest, my academic concerns, my political opinions, or even my personal ideas toward Kurdish society. The crucial point was who I was. Especially when the questions became deeper about Turks and the state, interviewees also felt uneasy. Some of them, who thought that these questions were dangerous in themselves, demanded to stop recording by using gestures.

Some interviewees tried to find out who I was by using divergent tactics. For instance, the most widespread one was their idea that I was an intelligence officer. Most of my interviewees did not say it evidently but implied it, and many people recommended that I confess to being a MIT agent. This one is a good example: "Some MIT (National Intelligence Organization) officers come here occasionally, and we discern them. We have no secret. Let them come. Sometimes they come as the secret police. Let them come. It is not a problem for us." In some interviews, it was underlined that the trust was mutual, and I was told: "if you are from MIT or the police, do not hesitate, speak frankly. We are not afraid of anything but let us be honest mutually."

It is normal to develop such kind of behaviors and opinions for eliminating threats, pressure, risks, and dangers upon themselves. In fact, it is also a widespread problem to interpret the researcher working in the field as an intelligence officer. For instance, a similar fact was experienced by researchers working on the Muslim community in the United States after 9/11 (Gaskew 2009). Particularly, it is no wonder that the communities that feel under political domination have such worries. The duty of the researcher is to the quest for the trust of the community s/he works with and to make a convincing explanation as to who s/he is within the interview. Mostly, it is known that these explanations are useless because there are class and social differences between the researcher and the interviewee. These disparities constitute a gap, and this gap cannot be filled in a short time by introducing her/himself of the researcher. It is enough to begin a fieldwork by accepting it in advance, and admitting that the knowledge gained from the field is obtained in spite of this gap, instead of endeavoring for filling the gap.

CONCLUSION

In this chapter, I set out to bring up some of the questions that researchers who study political dominance and oppressed communities must ask themselves before and after entering the field. These questions must be continuously asked during the scope of the research. These questions, whose answers we do not know but still ask, are formulated on the basis of the knowledge gained from our experiences, and remain relevant in this way. The first question among these which I ask myself is "who am I?" When I declare that there are two answers to this question, one methodological and one ethical, I do not suggest that one is more important than the other. Nevertheless, I insist that the methodological answer should be also a public answer. Indeed, the ethical answer is an answer that is between the person and the people situated in this scientific area as well as one that takes care to guard and protect the area. The answer for the question of who I am is also an answer, which should be constructed by the field, attributes of the field, and the intuitions and abilities of the researcher who takes a role in the field. It is not an abstract explanation but it is a concrete and bordered answer. Consequently, feeling sympathy to subalterns, especially people under political domination, endeavoring to help them, wishing wellbeing for them, and establishing a solidarity relationship with them should not be turned into representing them (Beverley 1999).

A researcher, who starts to see themselves in such a position, reproduces the power relationship between her/himself and the subalterns, of whom s/he can never become a part. They also cannot put forward that interviews were made between equals by ignoring the fact that s/he is one of sides due to hegemonic relations and symbolic violence. It should not be forgotten that the researcher, who introduces her/himself as a "prognosticator" announcing and showing the reality of the subalterns under political domination, usually attributes accuracy to her/his own subjective interpretation.

Does this mean that researchers are imposing their own views on these subaltern individuals? Equality cannot be provided no matter how strong the negotiation is, and it cannot produce a satisfactory answer to the question of "who are you?" Nevertheless, this situation does not mean that the consideration of the aforementioned questions should be abandoned from the fieldwork. A person who works with communities under political domination and pressure has to express constantly and explicitly that they are a person, who can be confided in and that the knowledge s/he gathers will not be used against them. It is important to remember at all times that the presence of political domination makes people suspicious and insecure against the society they live in and its institutions.

Our questions and answers will continue to inform the fieldwork that we engage in as long as we continue to work with subalterns, communities under political domination and pressure in dangerous fields. Therefore, situating the self in the field should be incorporated into the research process as the concept of danger arises not only from real people located in the field, but also the political, social, economic, judicial, or security conditions surrounding them.

NOTE

1. Forced migration can often be defined as the movement of refugees and internally displaced people (those displaced by conflicts) as well as people displaced by natural or environmental disasters, political conflict, violence, or development projects. Forced migration policies were implemented in some Kurdish provinces in Turkey during the nineties. "Between 1986 and 2005, it is estimated that between 953,680 and 1,201,200 people were forced to migrate from their villages and towns of 14 provinces in the Eastern and Southeastern Anatolia region (80% from the villages) for security reasons" (Özar 2010, 93; Kurban et al. 2007).

BIBLIOGRAPHY

Adler, Patricia A., and Peter Adler. 1987. *Membership Roles in Field Research.* Newbury Park: Sage.

Altorki, Soraya. 1994. "At Home in the Field." *Endo-etnography* 7, no. 1: 53–71.

Atasoy, Emin, and Mustafa Ertürk. 2010. "Bulgarian Novels from Ethno-Geographical Perspectives." *Eastern Geographical Review* 24: 87–116.

Baker, Carolyn D. 2002. "Ethnomethodological Analyses of Interviews." In *Handbook of Interview Research: Context and Method,* edited by Jaber F. Gubrium and James A. Holstein, 777–795. London: Sage Publications.

Beşikçi, İsmail. 2013. *Bilim - Resmi İdeoloji, Devlet – Demokrasi ve Kürt Sorunu.* İstanbul: İsmail Beşikçi Vakfı.

Beverley, John. 1999. *Subalternity and Representation: Arguments in Cultural Theory.* Durham: Duke University Press.

Bourdieu, Pierre et al. 1999. *The Weight of the World: Social Suffering in Contemporary Society.* California: Stanford University Press.

Briggs, Charles L. 2002. "Interviewing, Power/Knowledge, and Social Inequality." In *Handbook of Interview Research: Context and Method,* edited by Jaber F. Gubrium and James A. Holstein, 911–922. London: Sage Publications.

Burawoy, Michael. 2004. "Public Sociologies: Contradictions, Dilemmas, and Possibilities." *Social Forces* 82, no. 4: 1603–1618.

Chaliand, Gerard. 1993. *A People without a Country: The Kurds and Kurdistan.* Translated by Michael Pallis. London: Zed.

Coffey, Amanda. 1999. *The Ethnographic Self: Fieldwork and the Representation of Identity.* London: SAGE.

Ellingson, Laura L. 1998. "Then You Know How I Feel: Empathy, Identification and Reflexivity in Fieldwork." *Qualitative Inquiry* 4, no. 4: 492–514.

Gaskew, Tony. 2009. "Are You with the FBI? Fieldwork Challenges in a Post 9/11 Muslim-American Community." *Practicing Anthropology* 31, no. 2: 12–17.

Glasius, Marlies, Meta de Lange, Jos Bartman, Emanuela Dalmasso, Adele Del Sordi, Aofei Lv, Marcus Michaelsen, and Kris Ruijgrok. 2018. *Research, Ethics and Risk in the Authoritarian Field.* Basingstoke: Palgrave Macmillan.

Glick-Schiller, Nina, and Georges Fouron. 1990. "Everywhere We Go, We Are in Danger: Ti Manno and the Emergence of a Haitian Transnational Identity." *American Ethnologist* 17, no. 2: 329–347.

Jahan, Yasmeen. 2016. "Intersectionality of Marginalization and Inequality: A Case Study of Muslims in India." *Journal of Political Sciences & Public Affairs* 4, no. 1: 1–6.

Jameson, Fredric. 1983. *The Political Unconscious: Narrative as a Socially Symbolic Act.* London: Routledge.

Kineşçi, Erdinç. 2017. *Nusayri Kimliğinin Oluşumunda Siyasal Katilimin ve Siyasi Partilerin Rolü: Hatay Örneği.* Ankara: Gece Kitaplığı.

King, Diane E. 2013. *Kurdistan on the Global Stage: Kinship, Land, and Community in Iraq.* London: Rutgers University.

Kurban, Dilek, Deniz Yükseker, Turgay Ünalan, Ayşe Betül Çelik, and A. Tamer Aker. 2007. *Coming to Terms with Forced Migration: Post-Displacement Restitution of Citizenship Rights in Turkey.* İstanbul: TESEV.

Kurban, Dilek, Deniz Yükseker, Turgay Ünalan, Ayşe Betül Çelik, and A. Tamer Aker. 2008. *"Zorunlu Göç" ile Yüzleşmek: Türkiye'de Yerinden Edilme Sonrası Vatandaşlığın İnşası.* İstanbul: TESEV.

Kurban, Dilek and Mesut Yeğen. 2012. *Adaletin Kıyısında: 'Zorunlu' Göç Sonrasında Devlet ve Kürtler.* İstanbul: TESEV.

Lee-Treweek, Geraldine, and Stephanie Linkogle. 2000. *Danger in the Field: Risk and Ethics in Social Research.* London: Routledge.

Lee-Treweek, Geraldine, and Stephanie Linkogle. 2000. "Putting Danger in the Frame." In *Danger in the Field: Risk and Ethics in Social Research,* edited by Geraldine Lee-Treweek and Stephanie Linkogle, 8–12. London: Routledge.

Malinowski, Bronisław. 1988. *A Diary in the Strict Sense of the Term.* Cambridge: Cambridge University Press.

McDowall, David. 2004. *A Modern History of the Kurds.* New York: I. B. Tauris.

Modan, Gabriella Amy Shuman. 2011. "Positioning the Interviewer: Strategic Uses of Embedded Orientation in Interview Narratives." *Language in Society* 40: 13–25.

Muhammad, Michael, Nina Wallerstein, and Andrew L. Sussman. 2015. "Reflections on Researcher Identity and Power: The Impact of Positionality on Community Based Participatory Research (CBPR) Processes and Outcomes." *Critical Sociology* 41, no. 7–8: 1045–1063.

Oran, Baskın. 2015. *Türkiye'de Azınlıklar.* İstanbul: İletişim.

Özar, Şemsa. 2010. "Zorunlu Göçten 15 Yıl Sonra." In *Türkiye'de Zorunlu Göç: Hükümet Politikaları,* edited by Serkan Yolaçan and Ebru İlhan, 91–96. İstanbul: TESEV.

Peritore, N. Patrick. 1990. "Reflections on Dangerous Fieldwork." *The American Sociologist* 21, no. 4: 359–372.

Polsky, Ned. 1967. *Hustlers, Beats, and Others.* Chicago: Aldine.

Şahin, Bahar. 2010. "Tarlabaşı: Medeniyetin 150 Metre Aşağısı." In *Hayalden Gerçeğe: Tarlabaşı Toplum Merkezi Deneyimi,* edited by Pınar Uyan Semerci. İstanbul: İstanbul Bilgi University.

Sharp, Gwen, and Emily Kremer. 2006. "The Safety Dance: Confronting Harassment, Intimidation, and Violence in the Field." *Sociological Methodology* 36: 317–327.

Sluka, Jeffrey A. 1990. "Participant Observation in Violent Social Contexts." *Human Organization* 49, no. 2: 114–126.

Sluka, Jeffrey A. 1995. "Reflections on Managing Danger in Fieldwork: Dangerous Anthropology in Belfast." In *Fieldwork under Fire: Contemporary Studies of Violence and Survival,* edited by Carolyn Nordstrom and Antonius C. G. M. Robben. Berkeley, 276–279. University of California Press.

Somay, Bülent. 2008. *Çokbilmiş Özne.* İstanbul: Metis.

Sönmez, Mustafa. 2013. "Artan Kürt Göçü ve Mesajları II." April 10, 2013 at http://mustafasonmez.net/?p=2912.

Spivak, Gayatri C. 1988. "Can the Subaltern Speak." In *Marxism and the Interpretation of Culture,* edited by Cary Nelson and Lawrence Grossberg, 271–313. Chicago: University of Illinois.

Spivak, Gayatri C. 1990. *The Post-Colonial Critic: Interviews, Strategies, Dialogues.* Edited by Sarah Harasym. New York: Routledge.

Tatum, Daniel B. 2000. "The Complexity of Identity: Who Am I." In *Readings for Diversity and Social Justice: An Anthology on Racism, Sexism, Anti-semitism, Heterosexism, Classism and Ableism,* edited by Maurianne Adams, Warren J. Blumenfeld, Heather W. Hackman. New York: Routledge.

Tregaskis, Claire. 2004. "Identity, Positionality and Power: Issues for Disabled Researchers. A Response Paper to Broun and Heshusuis." (See http://dsq-ds.org/article/view/492/669). *Disability Studies Quarterly* 24, no. 2.

Yıldız, Süheyla. 2015. "Being Assimilated, Introversion, Acquiring Identity, Identity Strategies of Turkish Jews since the Republican Era." *Alternatif Politika* 7, no. 2: 257–290.

Yılmaz, Bediz. 2003a. "Coping with the Metropolis. Kurdish Migrants Living in an Inner-City Slum of Istanbul" (Draft Version), *Researching Internal Displacement: State of the Art* Conference, Norwegian University of Science and Technology, Trondheim, February 7–8, 2003. Retrieved May 13, 2013, from: goo.gl/XmtMfh.

Yılmaz, Bediz. 2003b. "Göç ve Kentsel Yoksulluğun İstanbul Tarlabaşı Mahallesi Örneğinde İncelenmesinde İlk adımlar, İlk Sorular." *Toplumbilim* 17: 95–105.

Chapter 7

Feeling Solidarity in an Estranged City

Ethnography in Postwar Diyarbakır under Surveillance

Demet Arpacık

This chapter engages with the implications of insider-outsider researcher debate by drawing upon my experiences during the ethnographic research I carried out in 2017 as part of my doctoral education. I studied the transformation of Kurdish language activism in response to the Turkish government's changing Kurdish language policy and discourse from 2009 to present (from the period of peace negotiations 2009–2015 continuing with the city wars erupted in late 2015, the interim coup attempt in 2016 until today).[1] My analysis identifies the inherent multiplicity of both insider and outsider positions and the effects of the sociopolitical conditions on these positions by reflecting intersectionally on gender, language, and ethnicity. I selected two cities as my research sites: Istanbul and Diyarbakır (Amed, as called in Kurdish). These cities are the most important hubs of Kurdish cultural and linguistic movements; the former being a highly diverse cosmopolitan city in western Turkey with the largest number of Kurdish population of all cities in Turkey with about 3 million comprising 14.8 percent of Istanbul's population (KONDA 2011) and the latter being a predominantly Kurdish populated city, the center of political, social and cultural Kurdish activism, and the so-called capital of northern Kurdistan (southeastern Turkey). In this chapter, I will restrict my analysis of field experiences to Diyarbakır alone, which served as a particularly and overwhelmingly intense site since it was going through a violent transformation after about a year-long war in the city center. As a Kurdish woman growing up in Batman (an hour to Diyarbakır by car) where my family lives, I have had prior insight and relevant personal experiences. However, due to the specific time and space of my research, I have experienced particularly heightened feelings of estrangement and solidarity at the same time. I intend to clarify these contradictory sounding positionalities as I reflect on my observations. Before I do so, I want to clarify my take on the insider-outsider dilemma that serves as a messy, yet conducive ground for critical engagement with the field site, interlocutors, and data.

INSIDER'S BURDEN

Similar to many researchers, who study communities, with whom they share a significant level of affinity, I had also developed anxieties and doubts around my ability to produce objective, scientific work, others' perception of my objectivity, and the reliability of my study. My struggle with my insider identity started before my field research, which is likely the case for other ethnographers. These anxieties and doubts had developed largely due to the positivist expectations of science that still dominate social sciences despite the constructivist turn, a topic that I will explore in what will unfold, and also to the reactions and expectations of colleagues in academia with whom I have shared scholarly conversations and exchanges. I have always viewed, and still do, my study as having transnational and interdisciplinary relevance, yet after being identified a few times by my colleagues as a researcher doing "Kurdish related stuff" or "some ethnic study," I developed an unbeatable urge to develop a discourse which would sound as objective as it could to gain respect and credibility as a scholar and to situate the research with the Kurdish population as academic. An attitude which proved to be self-limiting. As a result, I purposefully remained oblivious to my insider capital both as a Kurd with own experiences regarding Kurdish language in Turkey and as a scholar who has certain background information about the Kurdish language activism. The reasons for my anxiety were twofold: I had the impression that I was either perceived as an "authoritative insider" or a "questionable academic" (Voloder 2014, 4). Both positions stamp out alternative envisioning, dynamic beings, and critical voices. Firstly, I was seen as a person who could and should speak about anything Kurdish related. This perception was particularly strong due to the scarcity of Kurds, especially Kurdish women in the US academic institutions. I was invited to give talks on Kurdish women's liberation movement, anarchist movement, Rojava revolution and the Syrian conflict, and the referendum in the Kurdish Regional Government of Iraq among a few. Not to mention that I started to increasingly receive an astonishing look when people discovered that I am Kurdish due to the mere militant, "sexualized," "fetishized" exotic, and decontextualized depiction and media coverage of Kurdish women from YPJ (Yekîneyên Parastina Jin, Women Protection Units) in the war against IS (Islamic State) in Syria (Toivanen and Baser 2016, 300; Düzgün 2016, 284). Secondly, I developed anxiety because

I rejected my research to be understood as a merely ethnic study not likely to provide academic insight.

The discomforting condition of psychic disequilibrium based on the denial of my insider knowledge has lasted until one of my professors who read my research proposal curiously asked me what my stance was regarding my research topic. She told me that I employ such an impartial voice that I almost equate the repressive practices of Turkish government with the practices of Kurdish language activists and suggested that I read feminist and postmodernist literature that offer constructive discussion with regards to the objectivity of science, the reductionist insider-outsider dichotomy and the researcher positionalities. Urging for constant reflection on one's own role and influence as a researcher and on the power relations at play in the field site (Abu-Lughod 2008; England 2014; Hammersley 1992; Bilecen 2014; Wolf 2018; Brubaker 2004; Narayan 1993), this literature did not only enable me to develop a much healthier mindset as an ethnographer, but also allowed me to develop a nuanced understanding of my overall data from the field. I hope my paper will be an embodied demonstration of this lens.

Cárdenas (2017, 72) cogently stresses the "epistemological value of our embodied experience of ethnographic fieldwork" by posing a strong critique to the expectations of a disembodied, detached and impartial researcher advocated by the conservative social science tradition. I found comfort in Voloder's suggestion for researchers who study worlds that resonate strongly with them and that they are highly engaged in. Rather than being a detached researcher aspiring to arrive at an objective account of their study—such an absolute objectivity is unattainable—one can instead address the ethical concerns of insiderness by developing an "ethnographer-activist" stance (Voloder 2014, 10). Similarly, Cárdenas strongly argues that the research insiders develop is "beyond the quest for knowledge . . . and is not simply a matter of representation, but rather a labour of care, caring about, but also of caring for" (Cárdenas 2017, 72). Cárdenas's words are especially suggestive for scholars working with oppressed, silenced and marginalized groups.

Acknowledging one's insider insight and making peace with this reality is the first step, yet not a sufficient one for a critically situated research. Insiderness is a vague term that can mean many things but also nothing. Voloder (2014, 4) critiques the depoliticized, ahistorical, and uncritical declarations of identity and belonging by researchers and calls for a more critical form of positioning that does not presume certain shared identities or sensibilities with interlocutors. She suggests that while researchers should acknowledge the material consequences of their insider and outsider positions, they should also be concerned about the "historicity" of both otherness and insiderness (4). In other words, the question of under what conditions and structures these identities are evoked or suppressed deserves careful attention. As Bilecen

(2014, 53) suggests, reflecting on ethnographic experiences through the strict dichotomy of insider-outsiderness will undermine the complexities of changing personalities of both the researcher and the research participants and lead to essentialization of ethnic identity. Positions are malleable based on the time and space of research and numerous other factors (Van Mol et al. 2014, 71). The researcher needs to be reflexive of the politics of insider research and develop ethical principles that will both be conducive to developing a non-biased research and a research that will be embraced by participants and contribute to their cause. In response, I opt to cautiously embrace and benefit from my contextually insightful insider capital without making any claims for "authenticity" or "homogeneity" of my insiderness (Voloder 2014, 4). Nevertheless, as I avoid reifying static, bounded notions of identity, I also acknowledge the potential for the pursuit of authenticity and homogenization both by me and by my respondents at a time when there exists a palpable force aiming to uproot. Fortier (1996, 306) argues that as cultural critics celebrate hybridity, fluidity, flexibility of identity, they risk promoting a crude dichotomy between absolutism and transgression privileging the latter; the former referring to "rooting, fixation and exclusivity," the latter to "resistance, subversion, and translocality." She rejects the hierarchizing of experiences and instead calls for "not an either or-duality between conformity and resistance, between inclusion and exclusion, but a complex articulation of all such processes." Faria and Mollett (2016, 81) make a similar observation with regards to the concept of race. They embrace "post-racial" analysis that views race as a powerful construct with material consequences in human relations, but that it is both "antiessentialist" and "antifoundational." This analysis transcends the poststructuralist understanding of race only as it relates to power. My experiences in the field which will be unpacked in this chapter have shaped my positionalities and made salient certain parts of my identity and preempted certain others.

CHANGING POSITIONALITIES AT THE TIMES OF UNCERTAINTIES

I had initially developed my research project idea during the peace negotiation talks in Turkey (2009–2015) when many Kurdish cultural and language institutions were enjoying an unprecedented level of freedom in their practices even when in reality they were quite delimited if we consider international standards for the rights of linguistically minoritized groups. My initial plan was to visit Kurdish language institutions and investigate how their practices around Kurdish language education and education in Kurdish language differ ideologically compared to the Turkish state's general language policy making and educational practice. The limited freedom enjoyed by the Kurdish lan-guage institutions came to an end soon after the negotiation process ended. The very problematic and ingenuine nature of the peace negotiation process paved the way to the intense city wars in many Kurdish cities, one of the bloodiest being Diyarbakır. A report delivered by OHCHR (the Office of the United Nations High Commissioner for Human Rights) notes 2,000 deaths in the Kurdish populated areas between July 2015 and December 2016, 1,200 of which are civilians, and destruction of thousands of houses and cultural heritage (OHCHR 2017, 7). The operations were ongoing in districts and vil-lages of the city at the time of my research. The condition deteriorated after the coup attempt in July 2016 as the ruling government used the coup as an excuse to silence every opposition group. The destruction caused in the city and in the social life of people was furthered by the closure of many Kurdish cultural, civic and political institutions. The government appointed trustees to many municipalities run by the pro-Kurdish HDP (Halkların Demokratik Partisi- People's Democratic Party) party while it detained its officials. Social and cultural services carried out under the previous HDP municipalities were stopped by the appointed trustees. Kurdish private primary schools, Kurdish kindergartens, Kurdish cultural and linguistic centers, and Kurdish theatre are among a few (Letsch 2017; Sims 2016; Kingsley 2017).

The war that was waged to silence the political, social and cultural activi-ties of Kurdish movement was also reflected in the symbolic realm: linguistic landscape of the city (Ahval News 2018; Stockholm Center for Freedom 2017). One of the first works of the trustee was to order pulling down of the Kurdish-Turkish bilingual signboard (in which Turkish and Kurdish were written with equal fonts) of the main municipality and replace it with one that omitted the Kurdish name of the city "Amed," placed Turkish name at the top and added Turkish flag and the abbreviation "T.C." (Republic of Turkey) in the board (Bianet 2016). The trustee of Kayapinar district of Diyarbakır also ordered removal of the signboard of the Cegerxwîn Youth, Culture, and Art Center (Cegerxwîn Gençlik, Kültür ve Sanat Merkezi) because it had the name of the well-known Kurdish writer Cegerxwîn and wanted to replace it with "July 15 Nation Cultural Center" referring to the attempted coup date on July 15, 2016 (T24 2017). After public and media reaction, the name was put in place again. The trustee also ordered the addition of an Arabic word "waw" that means "to serve" in the signboard. The addition of Arabic language needs further attention and can be understood as part of the ruling party's project of Islamization as a strategy to counter the Kurdish liberation movement and the salience of Kurdish language, but this chapter is too limited to elaborate on this topic.

Many of my colleagues and friends believed, rightfully, that after the cata-strophic war in the city and the purges of Kurdish organizations, everything came to an end and that it would take a long time for the movement to revive. People were curiously shocked when I told them that I was going to study Kurdish language activism in Diyarbakır and Istanbul. They typically responded, "But everything is closed, and everyone is inside (imprisoned)." I believe my insider knowledge, or rather familiarity with the Kurdish political history, benefited me the most at this very desperate point because knowing the resistance and historical transformation of Kurdish movement in general, I knew that the Kurdish language activism would continue its activities by transforming them albeit in a more disguised way due to the oppressive conditions. Of course, a lot remained imponderable.

It was not of course easy to explain my instinct to the Institutional Review Board (IRB).[2] The committee asked for eight revisions of my application over a period of six months. In one revision, they asked me to obtain written permissions from each sealed institution whose activities I wanted to observe and also to obtain research permission from an IRB-like institution in Turkey to conduct my research. I have come to understand that the research institution, like many other institutions, was operating with the terms and categorizations that legitimize "nation-state" and its institutions as interlocutors and does not intend to develop alternative forms of management of the research projects that are interested in minoritized groups and their works especially under oppressive regimes. This approach renders minoritized groups even more vulnerable because the nation-state becomes the controlling body for the knowledge production concerning them contributing to a dreadful epistemological injustice. It is counterproductive to one of the most important missions of ethnographic research, that is to work on the lived experiences of discriminated and marginalized groups. Wimmer and Schilller (2003, 308) describe this condition as "methodological nationalism" that privileges and naturalizes nation states as units of analysis. This type of methodology, they claim, not only reinforces the uncritical engagement of researchers with the territorial boundaries of nation states in designing their study, but it also leads to the emergence of a certain type of epistemic logic that further justifies nation states and its boundaries in producing scientific knowledge. Moreover, board members expected stability, officiality, and formality of my ethnographic site, entirely unaware of "the mobility turn" in the social sciences that welcomes "itinerant and siteless ethnographies" engaging with, in my case, people trying different maneuvers to navigate state surveillance radar, and for this reason, need camouflage (Sawaf 2017, 14). I have explained to the board members that it was impossible to get any permission from the state which imprisoned many journalists and activists who reported on the war in the region or who were critical of the government's antidemocratic practices. This declaration further complicated already misguided communication with the members and made them more suspicious of my project. They responded stating that they were worried about my safety. In a further revision, I was asked to explain if then upcoming independence referendum in the Kurdistan Regional Government of Iraq would have any impact on my study and the safety of my participants. I should admit that I was truly charmed by the amount of knowledge that the review board members had regarding the Kurdish politics. However, at that point, I sensed that I could never explain the complex political situation and the board was not in a position to understand. In brief, as a researcher belonging to a minoritized group and conducting study with that group, I had to battle not only with the literature that adopts a commonsensical understanding of nation-state as the natural form of categorization, but also with institutional structures that perpetuate this naturalization. After solving the issue of IRB with the interference of my adviser, I started my journey to Diyarbakır.

WHEN SITE BECOMES DEFINITIVE

Amelina and Faist (2012, 1715) contend that the site of ethnography should be conceived as a political, historical, social and cultural entity. Following the same logic, Elwood and Martin (2000, 649) alert ethnographers to the role of the research site in constructing power and positionalities as it "embodies and constitutes multiple scales of social relations and meaning." In this sense, it is particularly important to describe the condition of the city of Diyarbakır at the time of my research to show how the very way it was being controlled and militarized by the state forces and navigated by the locals was telling about the relations of power and domination in a modern form of colonization. This description will also speak to the situatedness of my narrative influenced by the context in which this research is carried (Dwyer and Buckle 2009, 56).

The surveillance gaze that I have tangibly felt on me the entire time I was in Diyarbakır became apparent during my initial bus trip from Batman (my hometown) to Diyarbakır. There was a presence of armed vehicles and barricades and checkpoints in Batman and soldiers would make sporadic tours on the main streets with huge tanks and armored vehicles, yet I soon realized on the way that this condition could not be compared to what was happening in Diyarbakır, which was practically under siege. There were four separate checkpoints along the road with five to ten special forces on each point together with a few tanks, armored vehicles and barricades with sandbags. Our driver slowed down the van with eighteen passengers as we approached the first checkpoint. One of the soldiers hit our van with his rifle and yelled at our driver accusing him of driving too fast in disdain. Driver avoided any problems by acting apologetic even though he was slow. They took all our identity cards and run a security check on them that lasted about half an hour.

There was fear and anger in the air, yet everyone was silent. An old Kurdish woman murmured a curse "Xwedê bela wan bide" (May God curse them) and a few others responded "Amîn" (Amen). This occasion instilled in me an increased sense of collective solidarity and attachment with everyone in the van compared to the time when the van first took off and when everyone was merely a passenger. From what Baser and Toivanen (2018, 2) discuss in their work, one can describe this moment as a time of increased "politicization of ethnicity and belonging." This moment of increased proximity as a response to the overwhelming hegemonic presence of the other, adversary, clothed in the most violent form and behaving hostile, can be understood meaningfully only if it is contextualized in the "broader societal issues of dominance and discrimination" (Voloder 2014, 7).

Sur district of Diyarbakır, which is bordered by the historical citadel and is the place where the most violent clashes took place, had a stronger alienating effect. At every door of the citadel were located police checkpoints and barricades. In the center of the citadel, Sur, many buildings were turned into police stations. At the center is the main police station that has at least five armored vehicles in its front at a time that spread fear at their mere sight. There are signs of three crescents (the sign of the ultra-right Turkish group), Turkish flag and the abbreviations such as JÖH (Gendarmerie Special Operations), PÖH (Police Special Operations)[3] on the walls and bullet traces on many buildings. Half of the Sur district was entirely demolished, emptied, mainly flattened and was completely caged by the police barricades. One night, one of my respondents, who also became a friend, and I sat at an outdoor café in Sur, where we were soon surrounded by a group of about twenty heavily armed security forces together with a cameraman who was recording the moment. They asked everyone sitting on the chairs to take out their identity cards. This search was more like a performance, compared to regular searchers, perhaps for some pro-government T.V. channel. As male forces asked for male customers, the only two policewomen approached our table and commanded to have our identity cards. One of them had a black t-shirt with drawings of three big grey wolf heads with blue eyes that felt almost alive, an iron wolf head as a necklace, and a bracelet with Turkish flag. Grey wolves are being used as symbols by the ultra-right Turkish groups in Turkey. Hunted by the specter of the wolves, which always terrifies me, my friend and I left the place with feelings of violation, estrangement and desperation.

Diyarbakır was strikingly different compared to when I first visited it during the negotiation talks in 2010. One of my interlocutors, Rûken (all names are pseudonyms) who was previously teaching in one of the three Kurdish schools collectively named Dibistanên Azad (Free Schools) until its closure by the government, resembled the city to a deeply saddened person. Almost all my interlocutors mentioned the drastic change of the city from a vibrant one that attracted many local and international tourists, political activities, researchers and NGOs and hosted many social and cultural events in the last few years during the negotiation talks to one that was left destroyed both physically and psychologically due to the intense city wars and ongoing curfews under the state of emergency. The dizzying rapid shift from a period of relative state of tranquility[4] during negotiation talks to a state of havoc as a result of an intense city war accompanied by extensive surveillance and control system left the city and its residents disoriented. This unrecognizable new state of the city that is socially, culturally and politically deracinated transpired feelings of alienation for me, but more so for my interlocutors who witnessed the radical change firsthand. A few respondents explained that they became very reserved, and to an extent asocial and confined themselves to their homes because the war was too intense to witness, and it changed the city. Their social lives were transformed, their movements in the city were largely fettered.

Contradictorily, this suffocating, tenebrous environment also diffused a strong sense of solidarity and togetherness in the violent presence of the other. This situated feeling of sameness is rather being imposed upon as we become subjected to hostile treatment, humiliating inspections, constant scrutiny and as our freedom of movement and social, political engagement is being largely restricted. Feelings of estrangement, dislocation, lack of agency, violation and relevant humiliation were almost always accompanied by the quest for solidarity, sameness, and comradeship. I was highly overwhelmed by the occupation of the city, surveillance, militarization, and the constant fear of possible bomb explosions,[5] so I have repeatedly asked my respondents about how they were coping with this situation and if they were envisioning any hope for the future. In almost an effort to sooth me, one of my respondents, Roj, replied; "Do not lose hope, our turn is closer than you can imagine. This dark time is a harbinger for a free future." Similar sensibilities were voiced by my interlocutors who used the term "we," including me, to describe their activities and ideas, and "they" to refer to the state forces during research encounters. Here I do not mean to propose insider-outsider dichotomy as one connoting two purely distinct cultural and historical entities, but one that reflects the power imbalance between two groups that enables the breach of social life of one group by the other which represents the state and the dominant group. "They" were materialized in the huge tanks and armored vehicles that toured the streets every five minutes honking the sirens for attention, in the barricades that surrounded every public building for protection, in the huge flags that were hanged over the public buildings, checkpoints featured at each door of the citadel and in other parts of the city, in rifles and guns, and in the dark black sunglasses that were only worn by the special police forces, soldiers, and policeman in plan-clothes, and in the sexist and fascist signs and slogans written by the security forces on the walls of the city center. "We" were sensed each time when new activists were detained or imprisoned, when police entered into cafes or parks for identity checks, when a few protesters were violently silenced, detained by the security forces and taken away in armored vehicles, and when armored vehicles surrounded the location of a Kurdish language related event. Both these positions were result of highly politicized space and time period (Baser and Toivanen 2018).

MULTIPLICITY OF INSIDERNESS

I now want to elaborate on the interactions I had specifically with my interlocutors during which a myriad of other dynamics played a role in shaping our positionalities. These changing dynamics allude to the argument that there are no singular versions of insiderness and outsiderness, rather these positionalities emerge during interaction between individuals who either create or deconstruct boundaries dialogically (Van Mol et al. 2014). Moreover, unlike essentialized understandings, ethnicity is not the only or the most important determinator in these interactions. Rather, other factors such as gender, class, religion, and race come to conflate with ethnicity and together they culminate in "multi-positionalities" (Baser and Toivanen 2017, 4). In this sense, we can define insiderness as moments of proximity and outsiderness as moments of distance that transpire in dialogue. Bilecen (2014, 53) suggests that we can consider the positioning of the researcher and their interlocutors' as "a continuum rather than a dichotomy." In the initial phase of my research, I had a relatively hard time establishing long-lasting contacts or contacts that would help me reach out to people and places. I had assumed that the mere fact of being one of very few Kurdish woman researchers and being from Batman, a nearby city, would open up the doors. Knowing the Kurdish political movement's emphasis on women's liberation, I almost developed a sense of entitlement for respect and help. However, this was soon proved to be inefficient due to a few space and time specific reasons mentioned above.

I arrived at the field at a time when almost all cultural and linguistic institutions were closed and the surveillance and forms of camouflage by the state forces were practiced immensely. Almost everyone I talked had a court case opened against them, had been detained, or imprisoned at least once before. Moreover, they were pursuing the activities of the previously sealed institutions in a disguised fashion all the while trying to prevent any potential breaches to the privacy of Kurdish parents and children who continued to benefit from their work. Therefore, they had difficulty understanding why I was trying to learn what, how and where of these activities almost like an agent. Everyone I met had a justifiably very protectionist attitude and responded to me "I have to ask my comrades" and I later learned that there was a consensus to not talk to anyone outside of the activists' circle about the activities.

I asked every of my informants to see if there was a Kurdish language class for adults which was generally offered by Kurdî-Der (Kurdish Language Association) before it was closed by the government and I was told that there was not any, and it was not planned. After a month of spending hours of work time in the cafe of one of my respondents, Yasin, on a daily basis and therefore developing friendship with him, he approached me one day and told me that there was a Kurdish class and that I could attend if I promised to not share this info with anyone else. He accompanied me on my first day to the course and introduced me to the teacher and explained the situation. It was during these moments where I felt I do not have full control and power over the evolvement of my field, but my respondents also shaped my data collection (Lobo 2014). This condition reveals the agency of my interviewees in determining the boundaries of inclusion, their ability to draw the terms of insiderness by inviting or rejecting me into their activities, and their power in questioning my authority as a researcher (Voloder 2014, 8; Fozdar 2014). Fozdar (2014) further posits that while the researcher has a certain type of power over the researched due to the hierarchy that naturally occurs in the research encounter, power is not always at the hands of the researcher, in other words, it is not unidirectional. Instead, the researcher and the respondents "negotiate from several axes of power" (Fozdar 2014, 42; Van Mol et al. 2014). In this case, I was dependent on my subjects to provide me with access to their platforms (England 2014).

The relation between the researchers and their interlocutors is also shaped by the social and political context in which the research takes place (Van Mol et al. 2014). At the time I was carrying out my research, there were not any other researchers, who were abundant during peace negotiation process, and my interlocutors were surprised of my presence at such an unpleasant time. They also had developed a sense of obliviousness and resentment toward research and researchers because they interacted with many during negotiation talks and none seemed to have altered their ultimate reality. I was a complete outsider in this distinction because I was the person who had not risked her freedom to do the job they voluntarily have performed nor had I sacrificed to contribute to the language movement in the same way they had. Moreover, I would leave the city after my research and they would be left behind in the open-air prison like city, Diyarbakır. This situation also corresponds to the partiality of my insiderness (Halilovich 2014). One of my female interlocutors, Jiyan, told me that they decided to talk to me only because I was a woman from Batman because she was tired of being a research subject, a condition that she believed benefited only the researcher. Another respondent told me that he would respond to my email if I had mentioned that I was from Batman (meaning if I was a Kurd) because he gets too many requests and he is tired of responding. In her response, Jiyan both established a point of sincerity signifying our shared gender and place of origin and made visible our difference in social status, me as a privileged researcher interested in her own work, and she as the person who gives her time and energy for no return (I do not mean a tangible one).

This asymmetry in power relations became most apparent when I interviewed the female cochair of a formerly sealed language institution. Havîn, was imprisoned at the age of nineteen for her political views, as she explained, and remained in prison for seventeen years. After getting out, she married and had two kids, who are under the age of five, and started to work in the linguistic movement. Due to her previous record and her two kids whom she described as her only "treasures," she was reserved and distressed that her statements would get her into trouble. She remarked: "I actually did not want to talk because I am super careful. It is very easy to get in again and I cannot afford that at this stage in my life." Compared to Havîn, I was in a much secure position, funded by my school to carry out my research with no record of imprisonment. However, she added, "I was told that you were a Kurdish woman working on language, which is less dangerous than the politics, so I accepted to talk to you."

Their protectionism and suspicion were solidified due to some of the features that characterized me. I could not speak Kurdish well enough and my knowledge of Kurdish was restricted to basic everyday matters and was not sufficient to hold a political or abstract conversation, which was uncommon for someone grown up in Batman and I surely came about very suspicious. Why would they trust to open up to me at a time when almost all my interlocutors faced the threat of being detained or imprisoned for merely being a teacher or an organizer? Kurdish informants funded by the Turkish Military Intelligence (MIT) are not uncommon. I developed a destabilizing mode of trying to prove that I was not an agent. I used my historical knowledge of the movement in conversations and openly shared my political views or stance to establish closeness. I also specified when useful the tribe my family belongs to, which revolted against the government in late 1930s and were sent to exile in western Turkey where they lived for over a decade before returning to Batman after the declaration of amnesty. My family is well known in the political circles and I was shown instant sympathy when a few of my interlocutors learned this. The tribal names and affiliations, which have largely lost their enactment power, continue to play a facilitating role in establishing and maintaining contacts in the Kurdish community. I intuitively benefited from this context-specific information. During my encounter with my first interlocutor, I specified that the tribe I mentioned was my mother's side rather than father's. His initial excitement and interest seemed to fade away after hearing this. Since blood and identity are believed to transfer from the father's side rather than mother's, the mention of my mother's side would not have much effect, so I decided to not mention this despite my disbelief in this patriarchal family structure. The story of the tribe I belonged to also explained my limited Kurdish. My maternal grandparents grew up in exile not learning a word of Kurdish. They did learn Kurdish after they came back to Batman but have chosen to speak to their children, including my mom, in Turkish out of fear to not experience similar situations. This tradition was sustained. My mother also chose to speak only in Turkish with us. As is manifest with this story, in addition to my aspirations for expanding on the literature on linguistically minoritized groups and finding meanings from interdisciplinary analysis, my study is also driven by my own personal history and my interest in finding answers to some "ontological questions" (Halilovich 2014, 89). Halilovich (2014) states that researchers who are deeply connected to their study at a personal level cannot claim "historical, personal, and human distance" from the subject and ultimately all research is influenced by the autobiography of the researcher. However, this personal connection can produce meaningful knowledge if the researchers reflect on their "politics, principles, and beliefs" and to be "immersed while maintaining a critical distance" (Bott 2010, 170; Halstead 2001, 307).

Language had a determining role in the power dynamics between me and my interlocutors. I told my respondents that they could speak in the language of their choice during the interview, Turkish or Kurdish, since I understand both well, but I would speak Turkish because I am more comfortable in. Fourteen interlocutors chose to speak in Kurdish to me as I was using a mixture of Kurdish and Turkish. I could not help but feel less competent when I spoke Kurdish or when my participants chose to speak Kurdish and I could not answer fluently. In these moments, I have also sensed that I would be given more respect and attention if I could speak Kurdish more fluently especially as someone studying a subject related to Kurdish language. Many scholars remain silent with respect to the role of language during research encounters because, again, the traditional social science research assumes either full linguistic fluency or no knowledge of the language, and therefore, use of translators during interviews (Tanu and Dales 2016). This assumption is also related to the distinction made between native and non-native ethnographers, the former is expected to speak the language and the latter is not. My non-fluent language knowledge also poses a contradiction to my claimed insider status if viewed in monolingual terms. If the researcher claims to know more than one language, they are assumed to be balanced bilinguals proficient in both languages spoken. However, in reality such a balance rarely exists, people use whatever "linguistic features" they have in their linguistic repertoire to express themselves (Garcia 2014; Garcia 2011). This does not reflect the reality of bilingual people's daily communication patterns and certainly was not the case during my interviews. In the Kurdish cities, almost everyone is bilingual, knowing Turkish and Kurdish to differing degrees, and using both in their conversations, sometimes in the same sentences.

Another factor that impacts consciousness, behaviors, and relationships of researchers and their respondents is gender, which plays out both in the conscious and unconscious level. I have had better and more intimate relationships with my female respondents and I still continue my friendship with two. With one of my female respondents, Hülya, later friend, I shared some of the discomfort I felt in the city as a woman and she concurred. As we shared our experiences, it was revealed that we both employed similar strategies to simultaneously navigate and combat the male gaze in the city. There were many women on the streets, especially in the city center where I lived, with different clothing styles and I was able to be outside until midnight with no trouble because the center was very social with many cafes. Before residing in Diyarbakır, I selected certain type of clothes from my wardrobe to feel more comfortable in the city and not attract too much attention. I did not bring, for instance, shorts or miniskirts, while I have seen a few women who were wearing them, but also seeing the increased attention of both male and female crowd toward them. On the other hand, just like my friend, Hülya, I also did not want to give up completely and conform to a more conservative clothing style as many women ethnographers need to or are expected to do out of necessity (Wolf 2018), but rather challenge the male gaze to a certain extent. I did wear sleeveless shirts or mid-length dresses and I felt in solidarity with other women who also, despite the discomforting male gaze, continued to fight for a free space for themselves. Of course, I was in a different position from my friend Hülya or other female locals, because I was still not a local of Diyarbakır and had no relative. While mainly intuitive, I want to give one last example to provide how complex these sorts of decisions are for women in fields that have certain societal expectations about how women should wear or behave. I was having monthly visits to Batman, the nearby city, to visit my family. I had to narrow my wardrobe even further by excluding sleeveless shorts and mid-length dresses. Batman, compared to Diyarbakır, is a more conservative place due to its history of religious extremist groups' organization, such as Hizbullah and other extremists, fueled by the state's Islamization policies in the city (Kurt 2017). Diyarbakır also served as one of the centers of Hizbullah, which was used effectively by the state especially in 1990s in its fight against PKK, but compared to Batman, Diyarbakir's cosmopolitan atmosphere alleviated these groups' influence over the city. Moreover, in Batman, I am a local person with an extended family and due to my mother's constant fear of her daughters' being "besmirched," I decided unwillingly, to act more careful and more in line with the norms. A decision that I am still not very happy with and continue to struggle. I want to open a bracket here and add another analysis of our friendship with Hülya. I see her and almost all my respondents as comrades in future endeavor and I believe they have similar perceptions of me. This kind of relationship also poses a challenge to the expectations of positivity and objectivity of the science as it seeks to destroy hierarchy and exploitation in research encounter and beyond (Wolf 2018).

So far, I have written on the dynamics of interaction between me, as the researcher, and my respondents, I should also add that not all my respondents shared the same political, ideological stance. In fact, I have observed that the political divergence in the Kurdish movement is also reflected in the linguistic realm. The most apparent sign of this was the type of newspaper that each organization or platform that I visited had available daily that differed from one another. This incoherence is neither uncommon nor unanticipated in social movements. As Homi Bhabha (2012, 2) states, the same people who have "shared histories of deprivation and discrimination," can develop different approaches in their struggle for equality and freedom and "the exchange of values, meanings, and priorities may not always be collaborative and dialogical, but may be profoundly antagonistic, conflictual, and even incommensurable." As this can be the case, it is neither abnormal nor abominable to have diverse perspectives and stances in a movement. Indeed, it is inherent in almost every social movement (Urla 2012). Both sides welcomed me, and they referred me to one another for interviews and contact while they critiqued each other's stance, sometimes harshly. I kept seeing both sides in similar events and venues and I asked one of my respondents if they always had such a close relationship. Mehmet responded; "indistinctive attack of the government on all Kurdish institutions made us realize that we are on the same boat and should work together." As is the case in the conversations around insiderness, differences become more or less salient depending on the sociopolitical context.

CONCLUSION

I attempted to provide a nuanced contribution to the already sharply contested crude insider-outsider dichotomy. It was of utmost significance to be exposed to the scholarly debates on insider-outsider debates especially with a critical, and feminist, poststructuralist lens. The literature enabled me to reflect on my senses of entitlement, my assumed feelings of belonging and difference in a constantly changing and unpredictable space and time. As my account of field observations reveal, insiderness or outsiderness are not purely historical, cultural constructs, but they are also political, situational, and imposed. It is this multiplicity that makes it impossible to entirely claim or reject insider or outsider positions by the researchers. The particularity of my account lies in the specific space and time of my research which had a profound impact on the positionalities, subjectivities, consciousness, relationships of all subjects, myself, and my interlocutors alike. All the knowledge and analysis that I have provided remains largely situated and subjective, yet also political, dialogical, reflective and, critical. Diyarbakır's occupation, militarization and its violating surveillance system simultaneously transpired heightened feelings of estrangement and solidary. The very violent and polarizing atmosphere of the city created strict boundaries between locals and security forces, who are the representatives of the state. The alterity was stark and exposed in violent and hostile encounters. The alterity of the locals does not negate the many differences that shape the divergent positionalities in their encounters. Language, gender, ethnicity, political ideologies, and locality in the form of family ties and time spent in the city have all contributed to the diversity of interactions and communications as well as shifting identities and positionalities. As noted above, studying marginalized communities, especially the ones who are silenced and who are omitted in international political dialogues, is not an easy task, perhaps harder for those who have strong forms of affinity with their research population due to their already scrutinized and possibly suspected position. The researcher not only deals with the already systemic challenges that are imposed on a certain people or region, but they also have to handle systems of knowledge production that legitimize nation states, its boundaries, and its ontology.

NOTES

1. I use the term postwar here to refer to the aftermath of the violent confrontation that started in December 2015 in Sur district of Diyarbakır (later leaped to other Kurdish cities) and lasted until March 2016 between the Turkish state forces and members of YGD-H (Patriotic Revolutionary Youth Movement) affiliated with PKK (Kurdistan Workers Party) during which many civilian lives were lost, more than half of Sur was destroyed and thousands left or were forced to leave the city. I use the term war to define this period instead of "conflict" which has been used to define the Kurdish question in the last forty years in Turkey. This period (2015–2016) is different from before and after due to actual violent confrontation in the city center that resulted in huge loss of human lives, and the siege by the military forces, use of airstrikes, bombs, and other heavy weaponry, all within a short period of time.

2. Institutional Review Board is a committee overseen by the Office of Human Research Protection in the United States. The committee was formed after the enactment of the National Research Act of 1974. This act came into being after numerous human rights abuses were reported in various research projects in twentieth century. The board reviews proposed research projects that engages with human subjects to

determine if they are ethical and if the research protects the rights and welfare of human subjects/participants. Similar committees exist in some countries around the world, but not all.

3. The two operations units are special forces that receive intensive training in the Turkish military and are used in high-risk situations.

4. My readers should not imagine an absolute routinized, problem-free life in Diyarbakır even during the negotiation talks because this period only refers to the de facto ceasefire between the state and the PKK. In 2013, police opened fire over protesters who were opposed to the construction of new gendarme stations and Medeni Yildirim (19) died in Lice district of Diyarbakır and the soldier who killed him was released. In 2014, during protests against gendarme stations again, Haci Baki Akdemir (50) and Ramazan Baran (26) were killed as a result of indiscriminatory fire from the soldiers. In 2015, a bomb was exploded in the campaign meeting of HDP party and five people lost their lives. In 2015, the Kurdish lawyer Tahir Elci was assassinated in daylight in front of cameras and his assassins are still not identified by the state.

5. Two bombings are among many; On May 10, 2016, a police bus carrying some PKK members was bombed and three detainees died: http://www.diken.com.tr/pkkdan-polis-servisine-bombali-saldiri-aractaki-uc-pkkli-oldu-onlarca-sivil-yaralandi/. In April 2017, one of the buildings of police headquarters exploded and three police officers died. PKK claimed responsibility for the bombing: http://www.hurriyet.com.tr/diyarbakirda-emniyet-binasina-bomba-saldiri-ka-40715114.

BIBLIOGRAPHY

Abu-Lughod, Lila. 2008. *Writing women's worlds: Bedouin stories.* California: University of California Press.

Ahval News. 2018. "Kurdish language signs removed from Diyarbakır streets." published in April 11, 2018. https://ahvalnews.com/turkey-kurds/kurdish-language-signs-removed-diyarbakir-streets.

Amelina, Anna, and Thomas Faist. 2012. "De-naturalizing the national in research methodologies: Key concepts of transnational studies in migration." *Ethnic and Racial Studies* 35, no. 10: 1707–1724.

Baser, Baser, and Mari Toivanen. 2018. "Politicized and depoliticized ethnicities, power relations and temporality: Insights to outsider research from comparative and transnational fieldwork." *Ethnic and Racial Studies* 41, no.1: 2067–2084.

Bhabha, Homi K. 2012. *The location of culture.* New York: Routledge.

Bilecen, Başak. 2014. On the tide between being an insider and outsider: Experiences from research on international student mobility in Germany." In *Insider research on migration and mobility: International perspectives on researcher positioning*, edited by Lejla Voloder and Liudmila Kirpitchenko, 53–68. London: Routledge.

Bianet. 2016. "Diyarbakır municipality's Kurdish-Turkish plate renewed." published in December 21, 2016. https://m.bianet.org/english/society/181921-diyarbakir-municipality-s-kurdish-turkish-plate-renewed.

Bott, Esther. 2010. "Favourites and others: Reflexivity and the shaping of subjectivities and data in qualitative research." *Qualitative Research* 10, no. 2: 159–173.

Brubaker, Rogers. 2004. *Ethnicity without groups*. Cambridge & London: Harvard University Press.

Cárdenas, Roosbelinda. 2017. "Commentary on 'ethnography as knowledge in the Arab region' by Roosbelinda Cárdenas." *Contemporary Levant* 2, no. 1: 71–74. doi: 10.1080/20581831.2017.1322231.

Düzgün, Meral. 2016. "Jineology: The Kurdish women's movement." *Journal of Middle East Women's Studies* 12, no. 2: 284–287.

Dwyer, Sonya Corbin, and Jennifer L. Buckle. 2009. "The space between: On being an insider-outsider in qualitative research." *International Journal of Qualitative Methods* 8, no. 1: 54–63.

Elwood, Sarah A., and Deborah G. Martin. 2000. ""Placing" interviews: Location and scales of power in qualitative research." *The Professional Geographer* 52, no. 4: 649–657.

England, Kim V. L. 1994. "Getting personal: Reflexivity, positionality, and feminist research." *The Professional Geographer* 46, no. 1: 80–89.

Faria, Caroline, and Sharlene Mollett. 2016. "Critical feminist reflexivity and the politics of whiteness in the 'field'." *Gender, Place & Culture* 23, no. 1: 79–93.

Fortier, Anne-Marie. 1996. "Troubles in the field: The use of personal experiences as sources of knowledge." *Critique of Anthropology* 16, no. 3: 303–323.

García, Ofelia. 2011. *Bilingual education in the 21st century: A global perspective*. Malden: John Wiley & Sons.

García, Ofelia, and Li Wei. 2014. *Translanguaging: Language, bilingualism and education*. London: Palgrave Macmillan.

Halilovich, Hariz. 2014. "Behind the emic lines: Ethics and politics of insiders' ethnography." In *Insider research on migration and mobility: International perspectives on researcher positioning*, edited by Lejla Voloder and Liudmila Kirpitchenko, 1–17. London: Routledge.

Halstead, Narmala. 2001. "Ethnographic encounters. Positionings within and outside the insider frame." *Social Anthropology* 9, no. 3: 307–321.

Hammersley, Martyn. 1992. "On feminist methodology." *Sociology* 26, no. 2: 187–206.

Kingsley, Patrick. 2017. "Amid Turkey's purge, a renewed attack on Kurdish culture." *The New York Times*. June 28, 2017.

KONDA. 2011. *Kürt Meselesinde Algı ve Beklentiler*. Istanbul: İletişim Yayınları.

Kurt, Mehmet. 2017. *Kurdish Hizbullah in Turkey: Islamism, violence and the state*. London: Pluto Press.

Letsch, Constanze. 2017. "In Turkey, repression of the Kurdish language is back, with no end in sight." *The Nation*. December 21, 2017.

Lobo, Michele. 2014. "Negotiating aboriginal participation in research: Dilemmas and opportunities." In *Insider research on migration and mobility: International perspectives on researcher positioning*, edited by Lejla Voloder and Liudmila Kirpitchenko, 1–17. London: Routledge.

Narayan, Kirin. 1993. "How native is a "native" anthropologist?" *American Anthropologist* 95, no. 3: 671–686.

Office of the United Nations High Commissioner for Human Rights. 2017. *Report on the human rights situation in South-East Turkey July 2015 to December 2016*. Geneva: Switzerland.

Sawaf, Zina. 2017. "Ethnography in movement: Bounding the field between the compound and the trailer in Riyadh, Saudi Arabia." *Contemporary Levant* 2, no. 1: 12–23.

Sims, Alexandra. 2016. "Turkish authorities shut down first Kurdish all-female news agency." *The Independent*. November 1, 2016.

Stockholm Center for Freedom. 2018. "Turkish authorities remove Kurdish language signs from Diyarbakır streets." April 11, 2018.

T24. 2017. ""Cegerxwîn Gençlik ve Kültür Merkezi'nin ismi '15 Temmuz Millet Merkezi' olarak değiştirildi" ("Cegerxwîn Youth, Culture and Arts Center's name was replaced as 'July 15 Nation Cultural Center'")." published July 13, 2017. http://t24.com.tr/haber/cegerxwin-genclik-ve-kultur-merkezinin-ismi-15-temm uz-millet-merkezi-olarak-degistirildi,414167.

Tanu, Danau, and Laura Dales. 2016. "Language in fieldwork: Making visible the ethnographic impact of the researcher's linguistic fluency." *Australian Journal of Anthropology* 27, no. 3: 353–369.

Toivanen, Mari, and Bahar Baser. 2016. "Gender in the representations of an armed conflict." *Middle East Journal of Culture and Communication* 9, no. 3: 294–314.

Urla, Jacqueline. 2012. *Reclaiming Basque: Language, nation, and cultural activism.* Reno: University of Nevada Press.

Van Mol, Christof, Rilke Mahieu, Helene Marie-Lou De Clerck, Edith Piqueray, Joris Wauters, François Levrau, Els Vanderwaeren, and Joris Michielsen. 2014. "Conducting qualitative research: Dancing a tango between insider-and outsiderness." In *Insider research on migration and mobility: International perspectives on researcher positioning*, edited by Lejla Voloder and Liudmila Kirpitchenko, 69–84. London: Routledge.

Voloder, Lejla. 2014. "Introduction: Insiderness in migration and mobility research, conceptual considerations." In *Insider research on migration and mobility: International perspectives on researcher positioning*, edited by Lejla Voloder and Liudmila Kirpitchenko, 1–17. England: Routledge.

Wimmer, Andreas, and Nina Glick Schiller. 2003. "Methodological nationalism, the social sciences, and the study of migration: An essay in historical epistemology." *International Migration Review* 37, no. 3: 576–610.

Wolf, Diane L. 2018. "Situating feminist dilemmas in fieldwork." In *Feminist dilemmas in fieldwork* edited by Diane L. Wolf, 1–55. London: Routledge.

Part III

INSIDER, OUTSIDER, OR SOMETHING BEYOND?

Chapter 8

Outsiders Twice Over in Kurdistan

Francis O'Connor and Semih Celik

This chapter discusses a period of fieldwork we conducted in September 2012 in Northern Kurdistan, which was a relatively bloody month in the ongoing conflict resulting in ninety-six reported deaths: fifty-three members of the security forces, thirty-nine PKK guerrillas, and four civilians.[1] Violence had resumed in August 2011, marking the end of the so-called Kurdish Opening initiated by the AKP a few years earlier (Gunter 2013, 442–43). The three Kurdish majority cities where we conducted interviews, Kızıltepe (Qoser), Mardin (Mêrdîn), and Diyarbakır (Amed), did not witness any fighting or significant disturbances in that period, but there was certainly a pervasive atmosphere of tension. Our local contacts expressly warned us and essentially prohibited us from traveling to Hakkari and Yüksekova due to a number of large-scale counter-insurgency operations. Undoubtedly, the conditions there would have been significantly more challenging and more akin to the situation described by other authors with experience of research directly in conflict areas (Sluka 1989, 9–43; E. J. Wood 2003). Yet, many of the people, with whom we socialized and conducted interviews, had been directly or indirectly affected by the state's clampdown on Kurdish civil society which had resulted in the imprisonment of thousands of Kurdish activists, as well as politically non-mobilized Kurds (Casier, Jongerden, and Walker 2011). Accordingly, although our physical safety was never in question, the research environment was profoundly influenced by the broader security situation. It rendered us more cautious in spontaneous interactions and likely ensured that people were more hesitant in agreeing to speak with us and also impacted the material they felt comfortable discussing.

Before our field research, we had preconceived notions of how our "outsiderness" would likely impact our efforts to do research there. We were warned by other academics and activists with experience in the area that it was not the best time to go to Kurdistan due to an escalation in the conflict. This advice strengthened our self-perception as outsiders even before our journey began, outsiders who would be in danger and struggle to comprehend the everyday struggles of the "natives" of a distant land of conflict. Although we have dismissed the advice not to go there, we remained concerned about the success of the fieldwork. We presumed that a dark-haired Turkish speaker with a tanned complexion from Istanbul (Semih) would be less of an outsider than a pale-skinned, physically stereotypical Irish person and a nonspeaker of Kurdish and Turkish (Francis). It came as a shock to both of us, when all public attention was directed toward Semih, who repeatedly found himself the target of mischievous admiration by bands of children and adult men, who relentlessly pursued him because of his physical resemblance to a Fenerbahçe Brazilian football player, Cristian Baroni. The ostensibly more physically obvious outsider—the freckled Irish person—attracted little or no attention on the street. While a relatively simple anecdote, it highlights that one's positionality is a dynamic construction and can confound preconceptions.

The series of interviews we conducted were one of the core sources of primary data for Francis's PhD dissertation (O'Connor 2014), which was concerned with the relationship between the PKK and its support networks from the 1970s to the 1990s. We conducted around twenty interviews with former members of the PKK, PKK sympathizers and supporters, people who had personal encounters with the movement, and a smaller number of Kurds who opposed the PKK.[2] This chapter is based on the transcripts of these interviews, which also included substantial sections on their metadata describing interview locations, and interactions beyond those between us and our interviewees. This was complemented by a twenty-page document that Francis completed reflecting on not simply the interview process but the broader experience of fieldwork in Kurdistan. Issues related to memory in interviews are well known (Portelli 1981), but despite our extensive documentation of our experience there, it is six years since our trip and as much as our interviewees at the time, as authors we too are subject to retrospective interpretation and vagaries of inconsistent memory.

This chapter most certainly does not outline an example of best methodological practice or a research design that ought to be replicated by other researchers lacking in local language capacities. It rather details how less than ideal technical circumstances (time and language constraints) and an authoritarian research environment certainly inhibit certain forms of data gathering, and also generate unforeseen advantages. It also highlights the practical as well as the social and emotional benefits of field research with a trusted partner and the joint production of knowledge inherent in interview situations with at least three persons. In this chapter, we will first analyze our experiences of "dual" outsiderness and explain how it was not a binary cleavage in either of our cases but rather a dynamic and disaggregated process, constructed and influenced by the authors' self-perceptions, interactions between the authors and with their interview partners, all shaped by the physical and socio-spatial environment. We will then proceed to detail some of the technical and logistical elements of conducting translated interviews and how we attempted to mitigate some of the evident associated disadvantages.

OUTSIDERNESS

Simmel argued that the outsider perspective is "freer practically and theoretically" and that the external researcher "surveys conditions with less prejudice; his criteria for them are more general and more objective ideals; he is not tied down in his actions by habit piety and precedence" (in Merton 1973, 124). A contrary approach argues that outsiders can never empathize with the subjects of research because they are alien to their cultural values (Kusow 2003, 592). Our experiences in the field confirmed that such a dichotomous differentiation (often understood in national terms) simply privileges particular cleavages and denies the salience of existing solidarities (e.g., as leftists, as historians, as persons from a rural background) and precludes emergent solidarities which develop through the research process. That is not to deny the relevance of being a national outsider/insider but rather to contextualize in it a broader field of identities.

The salience of our different national backgrounds (as non-Kurds) did play a big role; our national "outsiderness" led our interviewees to presume that we were profoundly ignorant of the realities and history of the Kurdish struggle. This manifested itself in two distinct reactions: some felt that it was necessary to provide us with a potted "history" of the Kurds and the Kurdish struggle, while others felt inadequately equipped to engage with us. The first group usually began by giving an extended explanation of the movement, its origins, and its underlying philosophy. On more than one occasion, these mini-lectures were characterized by somewhat of an accusatory tone. This was almost universally directed to Semih rather than Francis, as if it was understandable for a total foreigner to be ignorant of Kurdish history but not for a Turk. Interestingly, we were never asked about our degree of the familiarity with Kurdish history by these specific interviewees; rather they took it as given that a Turk would either be uninformed or misinformed about the Kurdish struggle. Our strategy for the initiatory stages of interviews had been to encourage our interviewees to get used to talking to us. Our preferred choice was if they recounted their earlier lives, childhood, and family background to help us subsequently contextualize their experiences of the conflict but on the occasions where they preferred to regale us with a historical

summary of the Kurds, we felt it was preferable to not interrupt them immediately. However, this resulted in significant portions of interviews dealing
with idiosyncratic interpretations of the Sheikh Said (Şêx Seîd) rebellion and
the writings of Öcalan rather than any relevant first-hand experiences of the
conflict. Many of these interviewees hoped to redirect us to areas of history
and politics of their own personal interest, such as the "early Turkish Republic," and some were surprised and irritated by our focus on what they held
to be unimportant matters. Interestingly, some of these interviews contained
the most blatant examples of false information. One interviewee in Mardin,
presented to us as a BDP (Barış ve Demokrasi Partisi/Peace and Democracy
Party)[3] party intellectual, openly denied that the PKK guerrillas targeted village guards and their families in the late 1980s. He argued that such attacks
never happened and that in reality things were not as they were presented in
Europe by the "positivists" and the Turkish lobby. This outright denial makes
little sense when at the Fourth PKK Congress in 1990, the PKK's leader Öcalan himself publicly criticized the attacks and distanced the movement from
them (in Imset 1992, 345).

The second tendency we experienced was the incredulity of certain people
that we were actually interested in their experiences. On one occasion, we
spontaneously dropped into the BDP office in Sur, Diyarbakır. We were
warmly welcomed by a large group of middle-aged to elderly gentlemen
drinking çay (tea). Semih explained to them what we were working on and
if they would be interested in sharing their personal experiences with us.
They dismissed the possibility of doing interviews personally, arguing that
we should talk to the party members as their stories could not possibly be of
relevance to people like us. We stayed and drank çay with them for an hour
or so where they provided us with their interpretations of the history and
philosophy of the movement in which they described the PKK as a Kurdish
Nationalist, Islamist, and Marxist organization. This confused summary was
enlightening in itself, as it showed that the numerous ideological changes
of the PKK are not necessarily fully internalized by its potential sympathizers. Even when on occasion, their stories drifted to personal matters,
one gentleman showed us a bullet wound in his leg he received in the late
1970s, they could not be persuaded to systematically share their personal
experiences. This could of course be related less to our outsiderness per
se, than to us being "unvouched" outsiders as we were not accompanied
by any of our local acquaintances. Perhaps the location in the BDP offices
rendered them reluctant to speak to us on a personal basis as they did not
wish their accounts to be conflated with official BDP policy. Nevertheless,
they seemed generally amused that people could be interested in them specifically and our impression was that their reactions were at least in part,

informed by excessive humility, directly in contrast to the aforementioned type of interviewee.

On occasions Semih's Turkishness did generate certain tensions. On one occasion an interviewee criticized Francis for bringing a Turkish rather than a Kurdish translator, thus starting an interview on a negative footing. One notable incident highlighted the small errors that can undermine efforts at trying to create interview networks. Close to the apartment in which we were staying, we noticed a Kurdish language school. As we passed it every day of our stay, we considered calling in and introducing ourselves to see if anybody there would be interested in helping us with our research. One afternoon, in the presence of a local friend, we dropped in unannounced. We were ushered into an office which had a few portraits of guerrillas and one of Öcalan among other explicitly political materials, where we met two men in their thirties who we presumed to be teachers in the school. Our friend, in a well-meaning effort to help us, introduced himself and then bluntly presented us as people studying the PKK. In an effort to redeem the situation, Semih sought to explain in more detail who we were and on what our research actually focused. However, when saying the word PKK, he pronounced it the Turkish rather than the Kurdish way. One of the men brusquely interrupted Semih, declaring that was not how the word was pronounced there. The pair then perfunctorily stated that they had security concerns and would not be able to help us with their research and escorted us to the door in a manner which showed that our presence was clearly unwelcome. If Semih were to have been a Kurdish speaker he would certainly have known better than to pronounce the term PKK in the Turkish fashion. However, while the pronunciation was undoubtedly a mistake, the biggest error was that our friend had directly mentioned the PKK. From thereon we avoided any direct mention of the PKK, using more generic terms such as the Kurdish movement or in more specific cases referring to guerrillas. Naturally, once a degree of reciprocal trust had been established, and if interviewees were comfortable with referencing the PKK or even specific subdivisions within it, we also used them but only ever after they were first introduced to the conversation by others. A final lesson we learned was, when we were being first presented by local friends and contacts, that we had to be aware of their specific local reputation and position. In the case described above, our friend comes from a family which is not locally known as supporter of the Kurdish movement, which when combined with the casual use of the term PKK would likely have resulted in our interviewees being ill disposed in our regards.

A repeated point of immediate affinity was Francis's Irishness: when introductions were made by our Kurdish contacts to interviewees or simply their friends and family, they inevitably focused on his national background. Most people, who were involved in organized Kurdish politics, were well informed about the conflict in Ireland, the peace process, and in particular the hunger strikes of the early 1980s, although this was not necessarily the case when we spoke to less politicized people. The first Irish republican prisoner to die on hunger strike in 1981, Bobby Sands, was the subject of noted admiration. The Steve McQueen film *Hunger* (2008) detailing Sands's final weeks and months appears to have been widely seen in Diyarbakır and was referenced repeatedly in interviews and conversation. The hunger strikes in Ireland occurred at the same time as the Kurdish resistance in Diyarbakır prison after the military coup in 1980. One long-time political prisoner explained how an article in the *Günaydın* newspaper on the Irish hunger strikes was secretly shared among the prisoners.[4] Considering the extremely harsh conditions in the prison at the time, it took substantial efforts to preserve and pass it on; it was hidden in a pipe during the day before being shared at night time.

However, similar to how as authors we tried to avoid the reification of "Kurdishness," Francis's Irishness was not simply accepted by our interlocutors. He was intensively questioned about where he was precisely from (they were often visibly disappointed when he explained he was not from the North) and his specific politic views and family stance on the conflict. This led to a somewhat of an ethical dilemma for Francis: although a socialist and a sympathizer with the republican struggle, he is not an uncritical Irish Republican Army (IRA) or Sinn Fein supporter. On occasion, to avoid lengthy debates he allowed his views to be understood in a less nuanced fashion than would ordinarily be the case. There is absolutely no doubt that the combination of Francis's political views and being Irish led to a form of innate solidarity with our interview partners. It seems unlikely that a person from a country with a colonial background would have benefited from the immediate presumption of solidarity. In practical terms, those awkward first minutes of meeting an interviewee were filled with questions regarding the conflict in Ireland rather than our research or motivations for engaging in it, thereby lessening the power disparity between interviewers and interviewees. It also had the unforeseen benefit of somewhat mitigating any concerns they might have had regarding Semih's Turkishness.

Our self-perception of our outsider position was further called into question by instances of transversal solidarities with interviewees, beyond interviews. Interviews as shared experiences at times created a suitable environment for the sharing of further knowledge, expertise, and comments on totally unrelated curiosities. Semih as a historian was asked by one of the interviewees to help reconstruct the story of his genocide survivor Armenian-Muslim grandmother. As these examples demonstrate, outsider and insider as dichotomous positions were constructed more in our minds in most cases, rather than in the minds of our interviewees.

Outsiderness between Cautiousness and Paranoia

The literature on fieldwork suggests that in conflict environment, societies tend to be self-protective, and suspicion and mistrust against the outsiders prevails (Ergun and Erdemir 2009). Having thought so, we had self-positioned ourselves as potential targets prior to the fieldwork which led us to make non-spontaneous decisions on a number of occasions. On one occasion, our interview with the then head of the BDP in Diyarbakır, Zübeyde Zümrüt, was postponed due to a guerrilla funeral taking place not too far away from the party headquarters. Even though some party members suggested to us to go there, and despite our interest in participating in the funeral, we were too apprehensive to take a cab and tell the driver to take us to the cemetery, where everyone knew a guerrilla funeral was taking place. On another occasion, we were strolling around the streets when our friend pointed out an old Armenian church to us. While we were having a look at it we were approached by the custodian of the church who warmly welcomed us. When he heard Francis was Irish, he immediately expressed his support for the IRA and asked questions about the peace process in Ireland. We subsequently learned that he was in fact a BDP local councilor. In retrospect, in light of his political engagement and age profile he would have likely made an interesting interviewee. This chance encounter occurred shortly after our botched interview experience in the language school; however, we felt it better to stick to interviewees to whom we had been introduced by reliable "gatekeepers."

At times our caution almost lapsed into paranoia. One of our interviewees in Diyarbakır warned us that her phone was under surveillance and for us to be careful about the words we used while talking to people we hoped to interview. Although at no time did we have any encounters with the security forces, we had been repeatedly warned before the trip about the inevitability of attracting their attention. Accordingly, we were certainly in a state of cautious alertness, which particularly in Diyarbakır with its huge visible presence of security forces lapsed into paranoia at times. This was also related to the knowledge that the security forces and police have a heavy undercover presence in the city and operate a comprehensive network of informers. In the Ofis neighborhood of Diyarbakir, while waiting at a traffic light on a very crowded street, we were both suddenly grabbed by our arms by a seemingly blind young man, who wanted us to bring him to a certain point in the street. He had a white walking cane but at least to our ophthalmologically uninformed perspective did not really seem blind as he was looking left and right and walked confidently. He immediately spoke to us in Turkish with a Western accent, and he was intrusively interested in what we were doing in Diyarbakır. We deflected his questions by saying that we were students traveling around Turkey. When he learned Francis was Irish, he explained how much he admired the IRA before proceeding to declare that he used to work for the Turkish army in Northern Iraq. His insistent questioning and incongruous story triggered our paranoia sensors and we were extremely relieved to leave him at his destination. The episode was almost certainly harmless; he probably grabbed our arms by chance, had some partial vision and his questions derived from excitement at a coincidental encounter with tourists. Yet, it was illustrative of our latent paranoia, which knowingly or unknowingly would have affected our fieldwork experiences.

On another occasion, out of the blue, one of our interviewees Nuri called Semih on his phone and asked if he could meet him again, when Semih asked him why, he said that he could not talk about it on the phone, triggering our suspicions that something untold may have been at hand. The following day while walking past the large military base in Yenişehir, Semih was grabbed from behind, naturally leading him to believe that "this time it is definitely the cops." But it was of course, nobody else but Nuri himself. Nuri was on his way to the nearby office where we had previously interviewed him and he spotted the pair of us. In the end, it turned out that the issues he did not wish to discuss with Semih on the telephone were related to his interest in learning more about his Armenian grandmother rather than anything more sinister. He wanted some advice from Semih about the feasibility of conducting research in some Ottoman archives with which Semih was familiar. This funny incident and others show that researchers can exaggerate their own self-importance and relevance to the security forces when in fact we were most likely not on their radar at all. However, this form of paranoia conditioned how we interacted with random people and regrettably denied us the possibility of arranging spontaneous interviews. In retrospect this was a mistake but if we were to conduct further research in the near future, in light of the authoritarian turn in Turkish politics and the persecution of academics and activists, such paranoia although exaggerated in 2012, would be perhaps in 2018 be more than well founded.

THE SAMPLING PROCESS: WHOM WE DID AND DID NOT INTERVIEW?

A significant limitation of field research on topics related to armed conflict is the impossibility of obtaining a representative sample (Malthaner 2014, 182). It is simply unfeasible to expect sampling standards, data transparency, and methodological expectations, that pertain in other sectors such as the use of control groups to be conducted in insecure environments. Additionally, such expectations should be rejected in principle due to the sensitive nature of material gathered in the course of interviews and obligations to protect one's interviewees (Parkinson and Wood 2015, 23). Nevertheless, greater transparency about sampling methods and acknowledgment of their limitations would enhance the credibility of qualitative research based on interviews (Khalil 2017, 5). Our interviews were arranged through a form of opportunity sampling, which Silke describes as conducted "with conveniently available groups or individuals and little effort is made to sample systematically" (2001, 8). Central to the sampling process is the necessity of negotiating access (Balsiger and Lambelet 2014, 154). We had numerous informal points of access through "gatekeepers" to the broader Kurdish movement. It has been suggested that providing a formal letter from one's institution can help negotiate access (Horgan 2012, 204). However, we did not make use of formal institutional introductions. We had in fact been specifically warned against carrying any institutional material on our person by an academic who had previously conducted fieldwork in Kurdistan. We were told that if we were stopped by police this would trigger their suspicions and endanger both ourselves and our interviewees as well as our other friends and contacts.

Francis had previously conducted fieldwork in Istanbul and in Germany and many of his interviewees provided him with details of people to contact in Kurdistan thus providing multiple entry points, which would hopefully mitigate sample bias. The geographical distribution of these interviews did not reflect any analytical focus on Kurdish diaspora mobilization but was rather a result of the reality that millions of Kurds were displaced from the places where the phenomena analyzed in Francis's PhD thesis occurred. This was also the case for our interviews in Kurdistan itself. The overwhelming majority of events discussed occurred in rural Kurdish areas often geographically distant from where the interviewees currently reside but also very socially and culturally different from them. This draws into question the spatial dynamic of the "field" and what impact physical displacement has on interviews. We sought variation in our interviewees by interviewing people who chose not to join the movement but were sympathetic to it and others who were resolutely opposed to it (e.g., Kurdish Islamists). We also found interviewing family members to be highly useful (Speckhard 2009), as they were often close to the movement but sufficiently distant to express dissent and to not have internalized the "party line" like some former militants. Nevertheless, there were some blatant issues with our sample even with the aforementioned caveats of the authoritarian research environment. Notwithstanding, the prominent role of women in the Kurdish movement, we managed to only interview three. This might have been simply a question of chance but most likely it reflects some underlying gender dynamics and the fact that our principle gatekeepers were all male.

Our most important gatekeeper was Welat,[5] the cousin of a Germany-based Kurdish friend of Francis in Diyarbakır. As Francis's friend had strongly vouched for him and his research, our relationship with Welat was rooted in a familial trust, highlighting the advantages of preexisting friendships in such research contexts (Malthaner 2014, 179). We explained the type of people we hoped to interview and through his own personal contacts Welat arranged for us to interview several people. It is also worth mentioning that chance plays a large part in fieldwork; while drinking çay with Welat in a café popular with people affiliated with the broader Kurdish movement, by pure coincidence a number of people who we subsequently interviewed passed by and Welat introduced us and our project and convinced them to give us an interview. Through these initial contacts we got in touch with more interviewees in a classic example of snowball sampling. We asked our interviewees if they could recommend other people who would be useful for our research and open to meeting with us. Accordingly, spirals of trust expanded into a network of interviewees, in our experience it was personal relationships rather than formal letters or institutional endorsements that were central to our acceptance.

Although having a local gate keeper is a prerequisite for gaining access, one's gatekeepers can also undermine other potential connections. Researchers become locally associated with their gate keepers rendering it difficult to meet people who might have a grudge against that family or distrust their politics (Malthaner 2014, 180). Furthermore, while it is necessary for gatekeepers to trust researchers, for motives of personal security it is also critical for researchers to know and trust their gatekeepers and not simply assess them on their capacity to access networks. In a recent case, an Italian PhD student Giulio Regeni conducting research on labor unions in Egypt was betrayed by one of his gatekeepers and brutally tortured and murdered by the Egyptian regime (Walsh 2017). Another issue worth mentioning is that over reliance on gatekeepers as one's intermediary with the movement renders it difficult to maintain relationships with interviewees and acquaintances after fieldwork is completed. It is important to maintain relationships, primarily because it might be necessary to consult with them subsequently about specific points raised in the interviews and potential future research (Oikonomakis 2016).

It is also incumbent on researchers to try and reciprocate the generosity and support of their interviewees and host communities by sharing some of the findings of their research (Wood 2006, 382). Years after the fieldwork in Kurdistan, while doing research for another project in Istanbul, Semih was told by a Kurdish teacher in his mid-forties active in a pro-refugee movement that people like him go to Kurdistan, finish their research, never go back nor bother to concern themselves with the people who helped them with their research often at potential personal risk. Regrettably, there is a strong element of truth in this observation, although we have both remained engaged in different ways with developments in Kurdistan, it is something of which we (Francis in particular given the onus on non-Turkish citizens to support those within Turkey) are striving to be mindful for future research.

There are also more mundane concerns with relations with gatekeepers and their social context. As mentioned in a preceding section, for the duration of fieldwork you are incorporated into the everyday world of the locals who host you and with whom you socialize. In a Kurdish society, hospitality is highly valued and expected social norm. This of course resulted in many rich and very enjoyable experiences, eating fabulous food, visiting cafes and bars, and simply the hours spent chatting about issues unrelated to our research. However, at times this hospitality can be overwhelming and actually impede one's research. For some time, we were hosted by family friends of Semih, some of whom knew we were there to conduct research and others who believed that we were merely there for tourism. It seems that at times, an escalatory competitive hospitality dynamic developed across their wider family and they sought to outdo one another in showing us around and taking us to restaurants. As much as this was appreciated, it left us with very little time to prepare for our interviews and to transcribe our completed interviews. This was problematic because our data protection obligations demanded that we immediately type up our reports and dispose of all hand-written notes, which could potentially have imperiled our interviewees or indeed ourselves. Similarly, in Diyarbakır, we were hosted by friends of Welat in their student apartment. We were sleeping in their living room and the warmth of their welcome had left us little time to process our interview data. Additionally, some of the people living there were involved in an ongoing trial on some trumped-up charges related to the Kurdistan Communities' Union (KCK) trial,[6] and we felt that our presence as outsiders, associating with people directly involved in the Kurdish movement could potentially complicate their legal difficulties. Eventually, we concluded that it would be best if we stayed in a guest house where we could better manage our spare time and not render our hosts' lives any more complicated. Unfortunately, it seems that we might have poorly communicated our reasoning to our hosts and it seems that our departure was viewed as an insult to the hospitality they had offered us.

Another element of local hospitality is that it obliges the researcher as outsiders to adapt to certain social hierarchies that are not always inclusive. On occasion, younger male family members (around our own age at the time) were often excluded from socializing with us, the "honored" guests. The inevitably male social hierarchies resulted in us being brought places while younger family members were left at home. We were rarely ever afforded time with female family members beyond occasional shared meals. It is certain that if we were female researchers the social dynamics around the fieldwork would have evolved in a much different fashion. Our "inclusion" into the social group (i.e., family, flat mates, and so forth) was always a matter of exclusion of certain members of the group. That was not only a matter of practicality—that is, lack of space, time, and so on—but further a matter of reestablishing internal hierarchies. Those who had known we were actually there for field research, not for touristic motivations, were over-mobilized to help us. In Mardin, we were constantly told by our hosts whom to trust, who to take seriously, and who to follow while doing our field research. It was great hospitality, however, at the expense of us acknowledging their hierarchies—therefore in a way compromising our independence—and being part of those hierarchies to a certain extent.

The negotiation of access and trust building though are perpetual processes (Fielding 2006, 238). They are certainly related to preexisting trust and connections but also related to one's own behavior in the field. We certainly made mistakes which shut down potential networks of interviewees, but we also did things which enhanced our reputation in the eyes of our gatekeepers and their social milieus. First, waiting around for interviews can seem interminable, is often fruitless and extremely boring. However, we were very aware that our interviewees were taking hours of their spare time to recount often horrific personal experiences, potentially dredging up upsetting memories. The very least researchers can do is to be patient, even when at times potential interviewees can be rather brusque. Second, we were careful to understand the language and terms that are employed by the movement themselves and were careful to learn from our mistakes (as outlined above). Finally, trust is often sometimes built by supporting people. On one occasion in Diyarbakır, a friend of Welat asked us to accompany him home to his apartment. He explained that he did not like to walk alone on the street at night because he felt that the police were following him and he was afraid that he would be detained and beaten. We of course agreed and in the course of the—as it turned out uneventful—walk, he explained that both his brothers had died as guerrillas in the mountains and that he felt his family was as a result being targeted. Although, it is recommended not to pay for interviews or provide other material benefits, basic empathetic behavior which acknowledges one's interviewees (or their friends) as more than simply sources of data but as people and political subjects should be encouraged. Beyond the moral imperative of respectful behavior in this regard, researchers are also being assessed by their interviewees and by the general social milieu around them, positive and basic empathetic interactions in the course of interviews and outside them can create a local, positive reputation. Word spreads quickly and inappropriate behavior in a specific context could negatively affect the possibility of doing any further interviews.

THE CHALLENGES OF THE INTERVIEW PROCESS

In addition to the general challenges of research in an authoritarian research environment (Malthaner 2014), our interviews were also historically focused which entails a whole array of further methodological challenges. It is well established that "vocabularies of motive are often furnished 'after the act'" (Blee and Taylor 2002, 105). Furthermore, militants often emphasize "justifications for their behaviour which are in line with their political and ideological beliefs, and to link their own individual choices to an historical—class or generational destiny" (Della Porta 1992, 182). Of course this distortion can be marginalized by rigorous triangulation (Bosi 2012, 153) but as one of the principle advantage of qualitative interviews is the meaning interviewees attributed to their decisions and actions, it is harder to rectify the reinterpretation of meaning by the prevailing climate at the time of interview. However, a way of obtaining answers to the "why" questions is to rephrase them as "how" questions (Horgan 2012, 201). Although, we did not have the benefit of reading Horgan's article prior to fieldwork, through trial and error we arrived at a similar conclusion regarding the futility of directly asking about motivations to act from decades previously. Responses to these questions resulted in long-winded historical explanations which adhere to the narrative of Kurdish exploitation without providing any relevant micro-details regarding their individual behavior in the period we were interested in. Accordingly, rather than asking why individuals joined the PKK or supported them, we asked specific questions such as when did you first ever hear about the PKK (or *Apocular* as they were known in the 1970s) or when did they first knowingly encounter a PKK member. Given a concrete context, it was easier to ask specific questions pertinent to that experience: if they mentioned that guerrillas came to their village, we proceeded by asking questions related to where they met (e.g., in their homes or out in the fields), what they talked about, did the guerrillas ask for something in specific, and so on. As a means to counter the difficulties inherent to historical interviews, such as chronological confusion and simply forgetting, we framed our questions around memorable events such as the 1980 coup[7] or locally relevant ones such as destruction of their villages.

A first step in the interview process is obtaining the interviewees informed consent, understood by Wood (2006, 379) as the process of making it clear to interviewees what the purpose of the research is, and potential risks associated with it so that they could make a fully informed decision to participate or not. In line with our determination not to leave any paper trail related to our research, we obtained oral consent (Fujii 2010, 380). We did not even consider asking for written consent because it was evident that it would have been rejected. It was not always easy to explain to some interviewees the nature of our project; trying to explain that we were working on university research rather than journalism was often futile. In fact, many interviewees seemed disappointed when we explained that we were not journalists who in their eyes would have been best suited to raising awareness of the Kurdish struggle. Naturally, others were very clear on the differentiation and were also very interested in the more conceptual and theoretical aspects of the project. We explained that all of the interviewees (with the exception of information related to public representatives in their official capacity) would be anonymized for their security. Some argued in favor of using their real names because they had "nothing to hide" but in line with academic best practice we anonymized them in all written material based on the interviews. Many of our interviewees also good-naturedly ridiculed our security concerns, reasoning that they can always be arbitrarily arrested without pretext and that speaking to us would have no impact on the likelihood of personal repercussions. We also invited our interviewees to disregard questions they felt overly invasive or that they were not comfortable discussing.

Although, many of the interviews that Francis had previously completed in Istanbul and Europe had been recorded, it was not possible to record them (with a few exceptions) in Kurdistan. In our early interviews we enquired if it would be possible to record them but we were firmly told that it was not possible given the security situation. We then stopped asking in subsequent interviews to avoid starting off interviews on the basis of a "refusal." The absence of recording is of course a profound disadvantage for transcription and regrettably precludes the use of direct quotes in subsequent publications. However, the absence of a recording device ensured the interview took on more of a conversational than an interrogational character. It provided a form of enhanced intimacy. As the majority of our interviewees had at some point been interrogated (and many tortured) by the Turkish security forces, this is a notable advantage. As we were keen to keep a low public profile, interviews were usually held in offices of political associations or parties, or in private office spaces. However, toward the end of our stay in Diyarbakır, we understood which cafes and bars were politically welcoming environments, and we conducted some there; again, highlighting that fieldwork is a learning process. After the interviews, Francis typed up his notes and then Semih read and added to them, thus the writing up process was itself a collective endeavor where we reflected upon aspects of the interview. We also did some "self-criticism" of our own interview "performance"; did we lose the interest of the interviewee at any point, should we have pressed further on one issue or insufficiently on another, what impact did interruptions (çay breaks, telephone calls) have on the interview? In so doing, we were able to improve in subsequent interviews. We then disposed of the hand-written notes, tearing them into pieces and distributed them into multiple bins on the street, rather than directly in our guest house as dozens of shredded pages in English might have elicited some suspicions by staff. In retrospect, the fact that we did not encrypt our data was an error that the authors have not repeated in fieldwork in other projects afterward.

COMMUNICATING ACROSS POLITICAL, CULTURAL, AND LINGUISTIC CLEAVAGES

Translating interviews on the spot (not simultaneously) might seem not like the most appropriate methodology to follow. Anthropologists and ethnographers take both linguistic and cultural translation during and after the fieldwork as a crucial aspect of knowledge production (Borneman and Hammoudi 2009; Watson 1999). "The first unwritten stage of ethnographic translation" that normally takes place following the interview (Beatty 1999, 94) was already taking place during our interviews. Such a method left us with—at least—three different versions of a single event; first narrated by the interviewee, received by Semih and translated into English in a more condensed language, and written down by Francis immediately. While it is true that this way many details that could be of crucial importance were lost in interpretation, the necessity to understand the interviewee kept both Semih and Francis alert, more sensitive to the narration, gestures, and the interaction itself, than in an interview with sound recording, or in one's mother tongue. Fujii (2010, 232) argues that this metadata, "the spoken and unspoken expressions about people's interior thoughts and feelings, which they do not always articulate in their stories or responses to interview questions," is in itself data. Through translation the binary nature of the interview—the interviewee answering questions and the interviewer taking notes to be interpreted later (which Allison calls "freeze-framing" 1999, 117)—is broken with immediate interpretation connecting the three of us more intimately. In this fashion, the interview became a shared experience, as meaning was created partially on the spot with the participation of all three of us. Each interview ended with conversations on the significance of the interview as an experience—and at times just silence—rather than the content of it.

The need to transmit their memories and ideas to the wider world makes language a more curious issue in the Kurdish case. This becomes more apparent when some of the interviewees asked Semih to translate particular sentences and expressions to Francis, emphasizing the importance of transmitting certain messages. Using body language, showing scars (Herzfeld 2009; Hastrup 2010; Luhrmann 2010), or even silences at times revealed the will to establish a "politically intimate" connection with us. Positions of outsider and insider blur and boundaries dissipate in an emotional landscape laden with memories of torture, death, and constant political struggle. Drawing maps, showing photographs, making efforts to recall a few words in a foreign language were all attempts at creating a new political landscape based on a rather new language. One interviewee from the 78ers Association[8] in Diyarbakır draw us a map of the Middle East not only to explain the realpolitik of the region, but also to express how the region looks like in his own mind (see Figure 8.1). At the end of the interview, he showed Francis a photo of his own mother praying with tears between the graves of a PKK guerrilla and a soldier; praying for both of them, and for the termination of decades-long war. This and other examples demonstrate how meaning can be transmitted beyond words and speaking in the same language does not necessarily preclude understanding personal experiences and opinions.

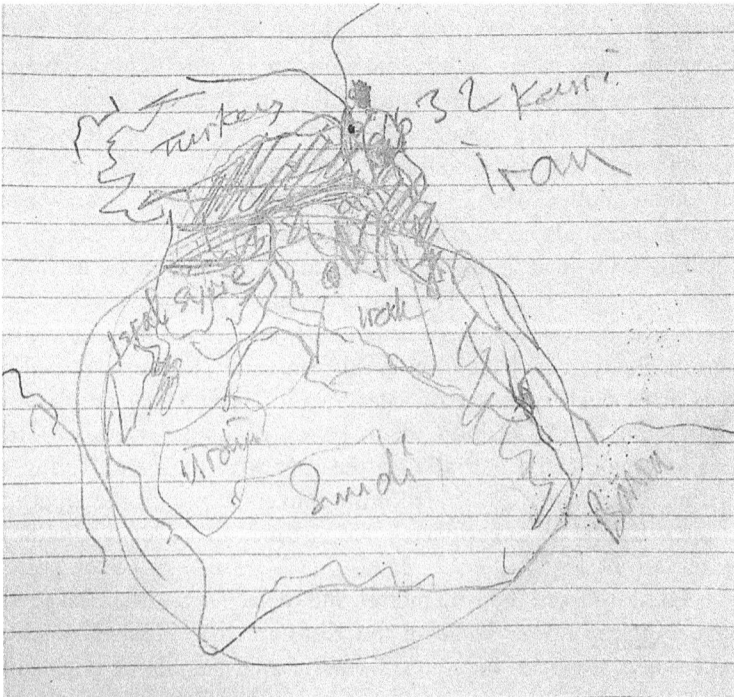

Figure 8.1 Middle East Map Drawn by One of the Interviewees. *Source:* Interviewee.

CONCLUSION

While many researchers have confined their arguments into the conceptual space of outsider and insider defined as belonging to one social group or another, we would echo the position of Baser and Toivanen who argue for the need to "adopt a reflexive approach to different positionalities in the research field, and to look at particular moments of insiderness and outsiderness rather than taking insider and outsider positions as a starting-point for understanding researcher positionality" (2018, 3). The positionality of the researcher vis-à-vis the researched is not a mere technical problem, but it is also inherently political. Our interviewees were all aware that the interaction between us and them was not limited to asking and answering questions. For them, and for us we can now say, interviews were in fact debates where we both repositioned ourselves within a different level of political consciousness, through a new language that is not Kurdish, Turkish, or English (Simmel 1971, 14–45; Herzfeld 2009). Our experience shows that the positionality of researchers regarding their interviewees is rather dynamic and continuously changing. For us reassessment of the interviews has never ended. Years after the fieldwork, we have consulted these field notes and joint memories to try to understand certain instances more deeply in order to reflect on the ongoing conflict. That is also to suggest that researchers' positionality should not be categorized according to whether they are outsiders and insiders, but on their being organic or inorganic. Being outsiders is not an obstacle to establishing an organic relationship with the researched, nor is being an insider a precondition to do so. An organic relationship with the interviewees, especially in conflict areas like Kurdistan allows the necessary space for the shifting of positionalities between outsider and insider, without harming the trust between the researchers and the people they interview.

Our experience as outsiders in Kurdistan was also mediated by the fact that we were two people. The peculiarity of Francis's experience there being largely conducted vicariously through Semih dramatically altered his understanding of it. At the same time, Semih's Turkishness was repositioned by Francis's presence as an "organic comrade" of whom it was anticipated that by being Irish he could understand and empathize with the Kurdish struggle. Our relationship went far beyond that of Semih simply acting as a translator.

None of this would have been possible if we were simply professional acquaintances. In 2012, we were close friends, housemates (even roommates for a while) and profoundly trusted one another. As Romano argues there is indeed power in numbers (2006, 441), everything about our trip was made easier by our mutual support. While our period of field research was very short in comparison to that carried out by many other academics, the possibility of openly discussing some of the more harrowing things we learned in interviews was undoubtedly a moral and psychological support (Wood 2006, 384). It was a joint voyage where we learned about the Kurdish struggle, challenged our own preconceptions and were genuinely emotionally struck by the hardship decades of conflict has brought to Kurdistan. The collaborative fieldwork experience, in a rather "technical" sense, helped us to translate the "ethnographic discomfort and awkwardness" built in our case on the aforementioned feeling of outsiderness and paranoia into sources of insight and revelation (Hume and Mulcock 2004). However, from an "epistemological" perspective, translation during the interviews in fact resulted in the dialogic negotiation of meaning. As Bakhtin emphasizes, "The speaker talks with an expectation of a response, agreement, sympathy, objection, execution, and so forth," (Bakhtin 1986, 69), and our presence as two research comrades provided the necessary grounds, which allowed for the building up of a *space between* (passim. Davies 2010, 11); a shared subjective space through which knowledge was produced collaboratively through a seemingly unsystematic dialogue. The most visible expression of that dialogue was when our interviewees most of whom did not understand English participated in the translation process by interrupting Semih to encourage him to emphasize certain instances of their stories, or when means other than speech were used in order to facilitate a better dialogue between the three of us.

In conclusion, the possibility of joint fieldwork is not feasible for most researchers, particularly early career ones. It is even less conceivable for two friends to conduct research together. Accordingly, this chapter is not an outline of how best to do fieldwork in Kurdistan or elsewhere. Rather it can be considered as an account of fieldwork as a process and a learning experience. Mistakes we made in the first days were not repeated, questions we did ask in later interviews would have been also asked in previous ones and vice versa, questions not asked earlier were asked later. We would have been less cautious and more open to spontaneous interactions and in hindsight it would have of course been worth the risk of attending the guerrilla funerals. This leads us to the conclusion that one's insider-outsider status is not fixed, it changes across interactions with individuals, different settings, and by researchers' own behavior. This is not to argue that being an insider or outsider does not matter but rather that it matters differently at specific times and places. It is crucial to remain reflexive about this, and to continue to reflect on it long after fieldwork has been completed.

NOTES

1. https://www.crisisgroup.org/europe-central-asia/western-europemediterranean/turkey

2. A further forty people were interviewed in Western Turkey and in several European countries. Semih did not participate in these interviews. These interviews were conducted in various languages with many of them through contemporary translation from Kurdish or Turkish.

3. The BDP was a Kurdish parliamentary party that preceded the contemporary HDP (Halkların Demokratik Partisi/Peoples' Democratic Party) and the DBP (Demokratik Bölgeler Partisi/Democratic Regions Party). The HDP participates in national Turkey-wide elections and the DBP runs in municipal and local elections in Kurdish majority regions (see O'Connor 2017).

4. *Günaydın* was a mainstream newspaper founded in 1968 and later became one of the best-selling newspapers in Turkey. The newspaper reflected the official mainstream nationalist-conservative ideology of the state. Various journalists such as Hasan Cemal, Ruhat Mengi, and Bekir Coşkun, who went on to become prominent journalists in the 2000s, worked there at different stages in their careers. For a detailed history of the *Günaydın* newspaper, see Tekin (2006).

5. We have chosen to employ a pseudonym.

6. In the mid-2000s the PKK underwent dramatic restructuring and the PKK was formally incorporated into a broader political structure known as the KCK. The Turkish government has used alleged membership of the KCK as the legal basis to detain thousands of Kurdish civil society activists and politicians.

7. In 1980 elements of the Turkish Army overthrew the government and imposed military law and established a new highly authoritarian constitution (1982). Although the pretext for the coup was the growing violence and insecurity in Turkey between left- and right-wing movement, Kurds and leftists experienced vastly disproportionate state repression.

8. The 78ers organization (78'liler Derneği) is composed of former prisoners of Diyarbakir prison in the postcoup period where systematic torture was inflicted on them and a large number of deaths among prisoners were recorded.

BIBLIOGRAPHY

Bakhtin, Mikhail. 1986. *Speech Genres and Other Late Essays*. Trans. Vern W. McGee, Austin (TX): University of Texas Press.

Balsiger, Philip, and Alexandre Lambelet. 2014. "Participant Observation." In Donatella della Porta, ed. *Methodological Practices in Social Movement Research*, 144–72. Oxford Scholarship Online. Oxford: Oxford University Press.

Baser, Bahar, and Mari Toivanen. 2018. "Politicized and depoliticized ethnicities, power relations and temporality: Insights to outsider research from comparative and transnational fieldwork." *Ethnic and Racial Studies* 41, no. 11: 2067–2084.

Beatty, Andrew. 1999. "On Ethnographic Experience: Formative and Informative (Nias-Indonesia)." in C. W. Watson, ed. *Being There. Fieldwork in Anthropology*, 74–97. London: Pluto Press.

Blee, Kathleen M., and Verta Taylor. 2002. "Semi-Structured Interviewing in Social Movement Research." *Methods of Social Movement Research* 16: 92–117.

Borneman, John, and Abdellah Hammoudi. 2009. "The Fieldwork Encounter, Experience and the Making of Truth: An Introduction." In John Borneman and Abdellah Hammoudi, eds. *Being There: The Fieldwork Encounter and the Making of Truth*, 1–24. Berkeley: University of California Press.

Bosi, Lorenzo. 2012. "Explaining Pathways to Armed Activism in the Provisional Irish Republican Army, 1969–1972." *Social Science History* 36 (3): 347–90.

Casier, Marlies, Joost Jongerden, and Nic Walker. 2011. "Fruitless Attempts? The Kurdish Initiative and Containment of the Kurdish Movement in Turkey." *New Perspectives on Turkey* 44 (April): 103–27.

Davies, James. "Introduction: Emotions in the Field." In James Davies and Dimitrina Spencer eds. *Emotions in the Field: The Psychology and Anthropology of Fieldwork Experience*, 1–35. Stanford (CA): Stanford University Press.

Della Porta, Donatella. 1992. "Life Histories in the Analysis of Social Movement Activists." In Mario Diani and Ron Eyerman, eds. *Studying Collective Action*, 168–93. Beverly Hills (CA): Sage.

Ergun, Ayça, and Aykan Erdemir. 2010. "Negotiating Insider and Outsider Identities in the Field: 'Insider' in a Foreign Land; 'Outsider' in One's Own Land." *Field Methods* 22 (1): 16–38.

Fielding, Nigel. 2006. "Working in Hostile Environments." In Clive Seale, Giampietro Gobo, Jaber F. Gubrium, and David Silverman, eds. *Qualitative Research Practice*, 236–48. London: Sage.

Fujii, Lee Ann. 2010. "Shades of Truth and Lies: Interpreting Testimonies of War and Violence." *Journal of Peace Research* 47 (2): 231–41.

Gunter, Michael M. 2013. "The Kurdish Spring." *Third World Quarterly* 34 (3): 441–57.

Hastrup, Kirsten. (2010). "Emotional Topographies: The Sense of Place in the Far North." In James Davies and Dimitrina Spencer, eds. *Emotions in the Field: The Psychology and Anthropology of Fieldwork Experience,* 191–212. Stanford (CA): Stanford University Press.

Herzfeld, Michael. 2009. "The Cultural Politics of Gesture: Reflections on the Embodiment of an Ethnographic Practice." *Ethnography*, 10 (2–3): 131–52.

Horgan, John. 2012. "Interviewing the Terrorists: Reflections on Fieldwork and Implications for Psychological Research." *Behavioral Sciences of Terrorism and Political Aggression* 4 (3): 195–211.

Hume, Lynne, and Jane Mulcock. 2004. "Introduction: Awkward Spaces, Productive Places." In Lynne Hume and Jane Mulcock, eds. *Anthropologist in the Field: Cases in Participant Observation*, xi–xxvii. New York: Columbia University Press.

Imset, Imset G. 1992. *The PKK: A Report on Separatist Violence in Turkey (1973–1992)*. Ankara: Turkish Daily News.

James, Allison. 1999. "Learning to be Friends: Participant Observation amongst English School-Children (The Midlands England)." In C. W. Watson, ed. *Being There: Fieldwork in Anthropology*, 98–120. London: Pluto Press.

Khalil, James. 2017. "A Guide to Interviewing Terrorists and Violent Extremists." *Studies in Conflict & Terrorism*. DOI: 10.1080/1057610X.2017.1385182.

Kusow, Abdi M. 2003. "Beyond Indigenous Authenticity: Reflections on the Insider/Outsider Debate in Immigration Research." *Symbolic Interaction* 26 (4): 591–99.

Luhrmann, Tanya. (2010). "What Counts as Data?" In James Davies and Dimitrina Spencer, eds. *Emotions in the Field: The Psychology and Anthropology of Fieldwork Experience,* 212–39. Stanford (CA): Stanford University Press.

Malthaner, Stefan. 2014. "'Fieldwork in the Context of Violent Conflict and Authoritarian Regimes.'" In *Methodological Practices in Social Movement Research,* 173–95. Oxford Scholarship Online. Oxford: Oxford University Press.

Merton, Robert K. 1973. *The Sociology of Science: Theoretical and Empirical Investigations.* University of Chicago Press.

O'Connor, Francis. 2014. *Armed Social Movements and Insurgency the PKK and its Communities of Support.* San Domenico di Fiesole: European University Institute.

———. (2017). "The Kurdish Movement in Turkey: Between Political Differentiation and Violent Confrontation." PRIF Report 147.

Oikonomakis, Leonidas. 2016. *Which Way to Social Change Compas?: Exploring How Revolutionary Movements form their Political Strategies through the Experiences of the Zapatistas and the Bolivian Cocaleros.* EUI PhD Theses. European University Institute.

Parkinson, Sarah Elizabeth, and Elisabeth Jean Wood. 2015. "Transparency in Intensive Research on Violence: Ethical Dilemmas and Unforeseen Consequences." *Qualitative & Multi-Method Research* 13 (1): 22–27. https://doi.org/10.5281/zenodo.893081.

Portelli, Alessandro. 1981. "The Peculiarities of Oral History." *History Workshop Journal* 12: 96–107.

Romano, David. 2006. "Conducting Research in the Middle East's Conflict Zones." *PS: Political Science and Politics* 39 (3): 439–41.

Silke, A. 2001. "The Devil You Know: Continuing Problems with Research on Terrorism." *Terrorism and Political Violence* 13 (4): 1–14.

Simmel, Georg. 1971. *On Individuality and Social Forms.* In Donald E. Levine, ed. Chicago: The University of Chicago Press.

Sluka, Jeffrey A. 1989. *Hearts and Minds, Water and Fish: Support for the IRA and INLA in a Northern Ireland Ghetto.* Greenwich (CT): JAI Press.

Speckhard, Anne. 2009. "Research Challenges Involved in Field Research and Interviews Regarding the Militant Jihad, Extremism, and Suicide Terrorism." *Democracy and Security* 5 (3): 199–222. https://doi.org/10.1080/17419160903183409.

Tekin, Akgün. (2006). *Türk Basınında Kayan Yıldız: Haldun Simavi'nin "Günaydın"ı.* Istanbul: Doğan Kitap.

Walsh, Declan. 2017. "Why was an Italian Graduate Student Tortured and Murdered in Egypt?" *The New York Times,* August 15, 2017, https://www.nytimes.com/2017/08/15/magazine/giulio-regeni-italian-graduate-student-tortured-murdered-egypt.html.

Wood, Elisabeth Jean. 2003. *Insurgent Collective Action and Civil War in El Salvador.* Cambridge Studies in Comparative Politics. Cambridge: Cambridge University Press.

———. 2006. "The Ethical Challenges of Field Research in Conflict Zones." *Qualitative Sociology* 29 (3): 373–86.

Chapter 9

The *Omnipresent* Absentee?

Challenges in Researching the Kurdistan Workers' Party in Europe and Turkey

Marlies Casier

In the winter of 2007 I paid my first visit to the building of the Kurdish National Congress (KNK), originally founded as a Kurdish parliament in exile and situated in the heart of Brussels. I was to interview one of its leading members, an exiled Kurdish MP from Turkey. Before the interview could start, some of the activists present insisted on showing me around the whole of the first and second floors of the building. Feeling I could not really refuse, I joined them but, to my surprise, found myself being given a tour around desolate offices, while my "guide" proceeded to open up empty cupboards. I could only assume he was intent on assuring me that they had nothing to hide.

As of 2002, the Kurdistan Workers' Party (*Partiya Karkerên Kurdistan*, the PKK) found itself designated an international terrorist organization by the European Union and the United States. Having waged an insurgency war against the Turkish state since 1984, the PKK had long been branded "terrorist" by the Turkish state, and the civil disruption and criminality associated with the organization and its affiliates in Europe had led Germany and France to order the closure of the organization's branches in their territories during the mid-1990s. Nevertheless, the classification of the PKK as an international terrorist organization in the wake of 9/11 was particularly hard to digest for the party and its followers—so much so that the Europe-based PKK-related organizations devoted much of their time divesting themselves of the "terrorist" stigma, seeking to rebuild the organization's legitimacy as a social-political movement (Casier 2010a).

It was in this era—and against the background of many European countries aligning with the United States' "War on Terror"—that I initiated a

PhD research in Political Sciences at Ghent University. The research sought to answer the question of how Kurds from Turkey living in Europe were able to affect the decision-making process on Turkey's accession to the European Union. The research was timely, starting in 2006, one year into the official opening of the accession negotiations. That time there was still a genuine—though not undisputed—engagement from both Turkey and EU member states to advance Turkey's integration into the European Union.[1] Departing from transnationalism and diaspora studies, the research aimed to uncover the transnational political activities of Kurdish immigrants and refugees in Europe, directed to bring about political change in Turkey. I was interested to find out if and how Kurds from Turkey could take advantage of the accession negotiations with the European Union. How were they organizing themselves? What matters did they prioritize? And how were they framing their grievances vis-à-vis European politicians? I conducted extensive interviews and held formal and informal conversations, with Kurdish political activists and Kurdish politicians in Brussels, Strasbourg, and London as well as in Diyarbakır, Ankara, and Istanbul in Turkey. I also interviewed Members of European Parliament and their staff, and national politicians in Belgium. This, combined with observations, in Europe and Turkey, document analysis, and literature review, allowed to build an understanding of Kurdish transnational political activism toward the European Union.

The fieldwork for this research showed that it is difficult to untangle the actions of European Kurds from the actions of Kurdish activists in (and from) Turkey. Indeed, the transnational political activities involve both "homeland politics," that is, political activities toward the country of origin undertaken by Kurdish activists in Europe, as well as "oppositional politics" for those Kurdish activists (including elected politicians) based in Turkey, but engaged with the internationalization of the Kurdish issue in Europe. Diaspora members were and are thus reinforcing the oppositional politics of the Kurdish movement. Or, put differently, in the Kurdish case I found oppositional political actors (PKK and affiliated associations and parties) to be transnationally active and making use of existing (as well as new) Kurdish (diaspora) associations in order to establish a transnational political space and extend their sphere of influence. The Kurdish transnational political activism vis-à-vis the EU institutions consequently turned out less a matter of initiatives originating from Kurdish refugees and migrants per se, but more the work of a transnationally organized opposition movement, actively fed and supported (as well as at times opposed) by European Kurds. Thus where I started my research (naïvely maybe) as an attempt to understand Kurdish migrants' and refugees' activism vis-à-vis national and EU institutions, I gradually started to grasp the weight of the PKK and PKK-affiliated parties on Kurdish transnational political activism in Europe and realized that my research was very much about "the Kurdish movement," understood here as the whole of associations, organizational bodies, and (successive) Kurdish parties that are (to different degrees) inspired and steered by, and depending on human resources and other types of support from, the PKK. In this research, I thus tried to "make sense" of the Kurdish movement, which required an active engagement (Jongerden 2016).

In this chapter, I reflect upon the challenges of doing ethnographic research about the "diplomacy" activities of the PKK, being an outsider to the Kurdish movement. The chapter engages with the "elusiveness" of the PKK: being labeled a "foreign terrorist organization" compels members of PKK-affiliated political bodies and associations to conceal the nature of their relationship to the political movement. This leads to situations where the PKK seems to be "nowhere" while practically being "everywhere." What is more, the criminalization of the PKK brings about particular methodological and ethical challenges for the researcher. I will discuss these, drawing on my experiences with ethnographic field research in the transnational community of Kurds in Europe on the one hand, and in Turkey, on the other.

THE OMNIPRESENCE OF THE PKK

In a post-9/11 era, no single individual or association, let alone political party, could openly present him/her or itself as being (part of the) or inspired by the PKK, rendering the PKK rather elusive. Yet, my own field research in Europe and Turkey, as well as previous field research-based studies on the PKK in Europe (particularly Grojean 2008), testified of both the dominance and omnipresence of PKK's influence in the transnational political space (in) between Turkey and Europe.

Pro-PKK associations have been active in Europe since the mid-1980s and have proven successful in obtaining public and political support among European Kurds, within a section of European public opinion and from a number of European politicians at the local, national, and international levels (Casier 2011a; Casier 2011b). This provided the PKK and its sympathizers with concrete means to advocate their cause and to publicize the plight of Kurds living in Turkey.

The PKK established its presence particularly in Germany and France, where it sought to organize the growing diaspora of Kurds from Turkey (Østergaard-Nielsen 2001; Grojean 2008; Grojean 2011; Baser 2015). PKK militants would collect financial contributions from European Kurds, call for hunger strikes and mass rallies, set up a satellite television station, radio stations, and newspapers (Grojean 2008; Watts 2004; Eccarius-Kelly 2002) and develop their own small network of "diplomats," all of which gave leverage to an increased visibility of the Kurdish cause.

The tolerance for PKK activities on European soil, as well as European politicians' adoption of criticisms vis-à-vis Turkey, enraged the Turkish authorities, whose embassies and diplomats were continually engaged in attempts to discredit the Kurdish organization (e.g., as funded by the narcotics trade and extortion from the European Kurdish populations). Turkey pressured the Western European governments to crack down on PKK activities on their soil, threatening them in turn with withdrawal from economically important contracts and lucrative arms deals (Grojean 2008). This pressure gradually began to take effect, with increased governmental surveillance of PKK activities in a number of European countries. And although this being largely ineffective—as PKK-affiliated bodies would continue to find ways to meet, organize, broadcast, and publish—it did pave the way for Europe's acceding to Turkey's request to list the PKK as an international terrorist organization (Casier 2010a).

Turkey's push for the PKK's international categorization was not just meant to curb PKK activities. It was in essence meant to deny the PKK, and by extension its affiliated associations and affiliated legal sister party, its recognition as being legitimate political actors representing a particular constituency (both in Turkey, and abroad), a policy which marks the continuation of a history of denialism of Kurds' existence (Yegen 2011). My research showed the labeling of the PKK as terrorist organization had profound effects on the political and societal space for the Kurdish movement both in Turkey and in Europe (Casier 2010a)—even though the movement continued to remain omnipresent and active, both nationally and transnationally. And while it is true that the PKK had always needed to organize and operate rather secretly since the days of its inception, the designation of PKK as "terrorists" further complicated this.

THE ELEPHANT IN THE ROOM

Researching the transnational political activism of an elusive, yet omnipresent illegal political actor brought with it a range of challenges. Indeed, at many times, and particularly in the fieldwork in Europe, it seemed as if PKK was the elephant in the room. Not only could PKK sympathizers and militants in Europe not openly admit their affiliations, as a researcher I was also inclined not to ask for this, fearful as I was to increase my research subjects' suspicions. I wanted to overcome possible distrust from the research subjects toward my "being there" and my questioning. I had many questions on my mind that I did not dare to raise in a direct manner, fearing that these moments of intense contact with my research subjects would be experienced as "interrogations" and consequently result in rejection of the researcher. The fact that the PKK had been listed as a terrorist organization implied that its leaders and militants were under the surveillance of state security agencies, as instances as the one in the aforementioned desolate offices described. Clearly some of the research subjects wanted to put my presence to the test, and wondered if they would find a secret agent across the table.

Concerns over endangering my research subjects, and the felt need to build up some level of confidence, both in me as a researcher and in the sincerity of the project, affected the way I conducted interviews throughout the course of the research. I refrained from recording interviews with Kurdish activists, both in Europe and Turkey, out of the double concern that I would unnecessarily frighten research subjects, and thus find them censuring themselves, and also that the collected data might—if seized—be misused against my informants. During and following each interview, I would take extensive notes by hand, and type out and complete them later. The exception to this were interviews I conducted with Flemish politicians who had been politically invested in the Kurdish issue, who often spoke in retrospect and for whom anonymity and personal security was not an issue. Many of the research subjects were also kept anonymous, except when I would be quoting persons' public speeches, stated during conference panels or press conferences, given the already public nature of these events.

In his account of his own experiences in the field, Grojean described this as *se développer un système d'autocontraintes* or to develop a system of self-control (Grojean 2008, 5), which prevented him from, for example, daring to ask about the clandestine activities of the PKK or the real party positions of informants (in case they were militants or cadres). I never inquired into this kind of information either, nor did I inquire into the line of command; for example, what possible instructions or directives would have come from where within PKK's hierarchy. Instead I opted for a patient and cautious approach to my research subjects and did not try to engage into detective-style inquiries into people's backgrounds or the very specific ways of operating. Looking back, I might have contained myself too much at times and I equally encountered activists who were open and did not meet me with distrust. Thinking about it, I do believe I found it easier to establish report and gain trust with other, non-Kurdish Europeans who were actively engaged with the Kurdish cause at that time. Maybe they were more able to assess my position as an academic researcher, and what that would entail, but maybe also the recognition of some level of "sameness," for example, having an outspoken interest for the "Kurdish issue," yet being an "outsider," positioning oneself as politically leftist have played a role, as well as a felt need, on their part, to share experiences in being involved with the movement. Overall though, conveying what has meaning to me (Ahmed 2016), revealing shared values and beliefs, is likely to have been decisive in the report I managed to establish with many of my research subjects (Ahmed 2016).Yet, while persons' relation to the PKK was rarely made explicit, the research subjects' closeness to the PKK revealed itself indirectly: in PKK's ideological "jargon" which often formed an integrated part of individuals' speech; in the ways individuals paid tribute to PKK's founder and ideological leader Abdullah Öcalan; in the display of important PKK imageries, such as portraits of the leadership and iconic martyrs. And, most clearly, in many of the advocacy and awareness raising activities and messages that aimed at the delisting of the PKK, the improvement of the living conditions of its imprisoned leader, or that sought to promote Öcalan's envisioned role as a peacemaker. But also, on a more personal level, I found it telling how activists, in Europe but equally in Turkey, were very much invested in trying to convince the researcher of the wrongness of the terrorist labeling. And thinking through the initial distrust I encountered, these conversations might also have been a kind of "inquiry" from their side into my personal positioning vis-à-vis the terrorist designation. Also, their concern with the criminalization of the movement might have been exactly one of the reasons why—even though I was an outsider—I was allowed to participate as an observer to activities such as delegation visits to European politicians, for example, accompanying mayors or members of parliament of the Demokratik Toplum Partisi (DTP, later changed into the Baris ve Demokrasi Partisi or BDP)[2] or lawyers of Abdullah Öcalan. Other researchers have equally experienced how insurgency movements do their best to present themselves to researchers (as well as journalists and international organizations) as open and competent, governing actors, doing their best to refute references to the use of violence (Gerharz 2017).

During these kinds of delegation visits by pro-PKK activists and elected officials to the EU institutions, the PKK was also seemingly absent. Indeed, even though it has been argued that European politicians do not recognize the PKK, despite the longtime objective of the PKK itself to establish international recognition (Grojean 2008, 171), the realities on the ground were ambiguous. I witnessed how members of the European Parliament did make time to receive political activists who were affiliated to the PKK and showed willingness to take certain actions in support of their cause, even though they would never openly support the PKK as such. The "keeping up appearances" appeared to be mutual, with the PKK discussed in the "third person" as if it was an entity outside of the meeting rooms. Political activists who'd accompany members of the DTP did not present themselves as militants of the PKK, and European politicians, sometimes aware of the fact that they were facing a militant and with some former politicians acknowledging this in retrospect,

would go along with the game. For them it was less costly to pretend ignorance about the true identity of their discussion partners (Casier 2011a). Apart
from that, in some cases politicians' sensitivity to the plight of Turkey's
Kurds could be traced back a couple of decades (Casier 2011b), and thus their
doors would be open, no matter what labeling Kurdish activists would befall.
By engaging with Kurdish political activists, who had strong affiliations
with the PKK, presented its demands and addressed developments in Turkey
from that perspective European politicians showed their recognition of and
support for some of the goals of the Kurdish movement. Nevertheless, while
the demands could be seen as rightful and legitimate, European politicians
did not want to (be seen to) legitimize the PKK's leading role in formulating
and presenting them. There was no public acknowledgement of the PKK as
the main representative of Kurds from Turkey, far less as the major political
force that they undoubtedly were and are. This in contrast to the recognition
that befell DTP (as political peers), which, nevertheless, was urged (both
in Turkey and Europe) time and again to clearly distinguish itself from the
PKK (Casier 2011b). This reaffirmed the international public image of the
PKK as no more than an armed guerrilla at best or a terrorist organization at
worst, and prevented recognition of it as, at the same time, a social-political
movement enjoying considerable popular support (Eccarius-Kelly 2002;
Romano 2006; Akkaya 2016).

AVOIDING COMPLICITY IN THE CRIMINALIZATION
OF THE KURDISH MOVEMENT

Throughout my research it has been a concern that my research might reveal
networks, tactics, and strategies of various political actors that have generally
remained hidden from or ambiguous to the outside world. Would uncovering
what happens behind the scenes of Kurdish political activism weaken activists' efforts to bring about change? Could my research endanger those who
already found themselves in a compromised position, both in Europe and at
home? This concern was particularly present at the start of my research, as
the activists themselves took great pains not to reveal their own affiliations
openly either to me or to other counterparts in conversations. Parallels can
be drawn to the ways in which ethnographic researchers have struggled with
the questions of the potential disempowering effect of their research during
Cold War times, such as the excellent work by Bourgois on his research of
the guerilla movement in El Salvador (Bourgois 2001). Exemplary is Bourgois' concern over the harmfulness of the prevailing vocabulary about the
guerilla war. The political strictures of the Cold War made it important, and
imperative for him to write about the fourteen-year-old who was shot in front

of him as a "little boy," rather than a "teenage fighter," since adolescents carrying automatic weapons would have deserved to be killed (Bourgois 2001, 12). In the Cold War political climate, Bourgois consciously downplayed the possible relationship of victims to the guerilla movement (the FLMN or Farabundo Martí National Liberation Front), when writing about the effects of the counterinsurgency warfare. In my initial writings, I consciously avoided any engagement with the Kurdish activists' and politicians' relations to the PKK. Later on, appreciating more and more the monopoly of the PKK in the transnational political space of the Kurds, and assured by the work of other researchers (such as Grojean 2008 and Marcus 2007), I did start to address this relationship in my writings. Looking back, I believe the change in my position was strongly informed by my field research in Turkey, as opposed to my field research in Europe.

At the outset, my encounters with Europe-based Kurdish activists, often people who had fled Turkey after the 1980 coup or the war years that followed, had installed in me fear about the realities inside Turkey.[3] Diaspora members' narrations contributed to an imagery of the Kurdish Southeast as if in a continuous state of war. This, at the time of my research, was not the case, as there were only incidental clashes between the Turkish security forces and PKK guerilla units in the mountainous border regions and occasional attacks on military personnel in cities. Yet, activists' stance was not surprising as some of the activists I had come to spend time with had lived through imprisonment, torture, the loss of loved ones and forced exile, which shaped their imagination of contemporary Turkey (in the mid-2000s that is). It was their particular (past) experience with the Turkish state that explained their fears and the reproduction of these fears in their dialogues with the ignorant outsider, in this case me, reinforcing my own fears and my concerns as to "do no harm."

It was thus with a sense of great uneasiness that I arrived and spent the very first days of my fieldwork in Diyarbakır (Amed), the metropolis of Kurdish activism. I kept my notebook stuck to my body in case anyone might take it and uncover whom I had spoken to, what they had said, and what the ultimate purpose of my being there really was. Purposefully I drafted my notes in Dutch (my mother tongue—and clearly not a world language) rather than in English, and virtually uploaded the transcriptions in case my laptop would go missing. Indeed, having entered the country on a tourist visa, I knew that there really was reason enough for me to be put straight back on an airplane to where I had come from. It was only after a couple of weeks' intensively interviewing people and visiting local NGOs and politicians—without anything out of the ordinary happening—that I became more confident in this research setting. Yet, what was even more revealing than the relative quiet and peace I encountered were the mass gatherings I would later take part in.

Indeed, my participation in and observations of public events in the Kurdish southeastern provinces of Turkey were the real "game changer" in my understanding of PKK's omnipresence and my consequent revisiting of the censorship I had taken part in. Particularly revealing was my participation in the Newroz celebrations of March 2008 in Diyarbakır (during my second field visit to the city). Delal Aydin's work on the reinvention and use of Newroz by the PKK (and subsequently the Turkish government's own attempts to "claim" Newroz as "Nevruz") has shown how Newroz has become "a discursive site where different parties of the conflict settled scores" (Aydin 2014, 79), and a very powerful means for popular mobilization and national identity building of the Kurdish masses. This is what I was about to experience myself upon entering the premises of the festival, set-up on the outskirts of the expanding city. More than half a million people—some optimistic voices reporting even up to one million—had gathered to celebrate the start of spring and the Kurdish New Year, revealing the popularity and support for the PKK and its affiliated party. DTP politicians were conveying messages from Öcalan to the audience and songs revering resistance and martyrdom were blasting through the speakers. I saw women of all ages wearing colorful head scarfs with handmade PKK embroideries. The crowds were cheering and confidently making the victory sign, and old women respectfully introduced to me as martyrs' mothers. Turkish police officers were present yet observing quietly, stationed at a distance from the colorful singing and dancing masses. What I witnessed was a public display of allegiance to the movement that was mirrored in parallel gatherings in other towns and cities throughout the region and beyond, in the mega cities of Western Turkey where Kurds moved following their forced resettlement.

The ultimate contrasting event to my initial "State of Imagination" (Hansen and Stepputat 2005) of Turkey—imagined as a state with extensive sovereignty over its (claimed) territory and people—was the 2009 Mesopotamia Social Forum in Diyarbakır. Here, under the auspices of the DTP-led Diyarbakır Büyükşehir Belediyesi (the Diyarbakır Metropolitan Municipality), Kurdish activists, anarchists, ecologists, and leftists from different parts of the world gathered to discuss the need to rethink social, political, and economic realities of Turkey and the Middle East, with imageries of Öcalan and other PKK symbols and publications openly displayed (Casier 2011c).

Conducting fieldwork in Turkey alongside that in Europe allowed me to see for myself the developments in the conflict-affected region of the country, to learn about the concerns of local activists and politicians, and to start to assess the relations and contestations between the southeastern-based associations and local and national political representatives on the one hand, and the central government on the other. This in turn allowed me to better understand the kind of lobbying activities that were being developed in Europe.

Most importantly though, it enabled me to understand how the PKK had become engrained and institutionalized, not only in the transnational space, but both in the political and civil society of Diyarbakır city and inside several nationally organized NGOs. This increased my understanding of what was at stake in the so-called Kurdish issue, the shortfalls of the EU politicians' and bureaucrats' approach toward it, and the (international) blindsightedness regarding the PKK. This in turn convinced me to let go of some of my initial fears with addressing PKK's presence and centrality.

Also, during the second half of my four years of research, the DTP at times more openly declared its support for and attested to its organic relationship with the PKK—this is partly to reject the recurring demands to distance itself from the "terrorists" (which both Turkey and the European Union were calling for). The political party began to feel strong enough to do so, at least in a limited way, as it became more confident in and emboldened by its established political position in the Southeast.[4] Represented in the national parliament as of mid-2007, the DTP/BDP was also increasingly in control of the local authorities and taking bolder decisions, especially in respect of symbolic politics—that is, expressions of Kurdish identity in the public domain (see also Watts 2009). In concert with this, I found the lines between the PKK and civil society becoming ever more blurred, since I understood that activists in the movement who would once have joined the guerilla in the mountains could now be just as, or more effective by living and working or campaigning in the cities (in Turkey).

Both my fieldwork in Turkey and my understanding of developments inside Turkey (at that time) made me conclude that the intertwining of the PKK and Kurdish civil society in Turkey were something of an open secret.[5] I reassured myself that I could and maybe also even *should* more openly address this in my academic writings and presentations. In this way, I believed my work might contribute to a better understanding of the social and political embeddedness of the PKK in Turkey, which, at the time was still lacking in a lot of the literature on Turkey's Kurdish issue, let alone the (European) media coverage of the subject. I thought this could maybe help counteract the image of the Kurdish movement as a "terrorist" organization. I thus reconsidered the way I had initially censured myself when it came to addressing PKK's involvement and thus had been—in some way—complicit in downplaying PKK's role (although I sometimes continued to do so, as I will explain in the incident below).

THE RESEARCHER AS AN ALLY?

Baser and Toivanen (2018) have reflected extensively on their own positionality as apparent outsiders from the Kurdish diaspora, and the different power dynamics that play out during the research and even within single interviews, relating to (perceived) differences regarding the ethnicity, class, gender, language, educational background, and ideology of the researcher. Because of my interest in their "struggle" and because of being a member of the Flemish speaking part of Belgium, I was considered pro-Kurdish and Flemish nationalist, funnily enough, regardless of my personal (and often opposing) take on the Flemish nationalists' goals, discourse, and strategies. I did not pretend to be sympathizing with Flemish nationalists, but I equally did not try to actively "undo research subjects" projections on to me. Looking back, these projections in some ways provided something—an assumed similarity?—that might have helped bridge the distance between me and the research subjects. Research subjects' use of references to the Flemish struggle for cultural and political autonomy also bore testimony to research subjects' efforts to—as experienced by Toivanen—reframe their cause in a way that would (so they assumed) resonate with the researcher (Baser and Toivanen 2018). Also, some of them had been using this frame successfully as part of their transnational advocacy toward Belgian and particularly Flemish politicians (see Casier 2011b). Being seen as first and foremost "Flemish," which I would only regard as one out of many constitutive parts of my identity, and definitely not a very determining one, and being pointed at assumed commonalities of Kurdish and Flemish trajectories, as well as to Flemish nationalist allies, challenged me to gain a better understanding of the Flemish nationalist movement and its engagement with the plight of national (linguistic) minorities. In this sense, my own positionality as a researcher also directed the orientation of my research into this specific part of the history and the dynamics of Kurdish transnational political activism. Something I had not foreseen at the onset of my research.

One of the difficulties I faced during my fieldwork in Europe was the rise of expectations research subjects invested in me. The people I regularly met with started to develop expectations with regard to my position as an academic and thus to my ability to speak intelligibly as an "expert on Kurds" that might contribute to the decriminalization of the Kurdish political movement. Adams has extensively reflected upon the "role" researchers might feel forced to play (Adams 1999). Field research is always a process of collaboration in which the researcher is not all-powerful, and over the course of the fieldwork power flows between the researcher and her informants (Adams 1999, 332). The researcher is not the one who "takes," with the research subjects as those who are "taken from," but fieldwork is deeply reciprocal (Cerwonka and Malkki 2007). A delicate balancing is thus required between being answerable to the expected role informants want the researcher to take on, and the need to protect one's own autonomy and personal integrity. Being an academic, as well as a European, Belgian, and a Flemish citizen, I was implicitly linked to the power structures of effective communication; the activists' cause was so manifestly, indisputably a just one; hence, the obvious conclusion that I should somehow advocate or facilitate for my research subjects. And indeed, I did sympathize with their history and present situation from a human rights' perspective.

Suggestions to organize "something" at the university were bound to come. Some contacts suggested they could come and lecture during our classes, while others proposed to organize a conference or wanted me as a panelist to their own public events. I managed not to accede to these suggestions without appearing to reject the people themselves or the cause they embodied. I always felt a need to keep the PKK at arm's length and did not want my research or my specific position as an academic to be instrumentalized. This doesn't mean that I refrained from any kind of pro-Kurdish activism myself, yet always on my own initiative and my own terms; for example, writing more lengthy opinion articles for the Flemish and Dutch press criticizing the Turkish government's so-called Kurdish Opening (in 2009), the prosecution of DTP and later BDP officials and subsequent party closures. Also, following many requests to copublish with the Kurdish Institute of Brussels—one of the main gatekeepers to my research—I wrote a small booklet on the Flemish politicians' engagement with the Kurdish cause in Dutch, popularizing some of the insights of my research for a broader, nonacademic audience. This way, I hoped to do something in "return" for the time the Institute had invested in me and the research project.

How high expectations had risen, however, became clear to me in early March 2010, the final year of my research project. Some twenty-five Kurdish-linked locations in Belgium were raided by the police (including a satellite broadcasting station), and Kurdish activists arrested (including two ex-MPs), suspected of involvement with the PKK and various drugs, and so on related crimes, organized to fund the organization's activities. These raids broadly coincided with similar raids elsewhere in Europe, and with heavily criticized raids on supposed PKK affiliates in Turkey which netted several top Kurdish politicians (as part of the ongoing KCK prosecution[6]).

At the time of the arrests and their coverage in the Flemish media in Belgium, I did not publicly express any opinions, through writing or interview. For various reasons, I was reluctant to commit my thoughts to the public sphere at that time—and thus refused to denounce (or support) the actions undertaken. My inaction was reproached by some of the leading PKK diplomats in Brussels about two weeks after the arrests, when they called me to ask "Where I had been."

This phone call stunned me. It felt as if they were treating me as one of them and thus disloyal to their organization and their cause, whereas I had always considered myself as clearly positioned outside of the movement, not adhering to its ideas, goals, or leadership (although recognizing their popular appeal). The criticisms also came as a surprise as my absence in the series of events had been a conscious one: several Flemish broadcasting stations and radio journalists had actually contacted me in order to talk to me, as an "expert" about the accusations. Was it indeed true that the people arrested were members of the PKK? Was the satellite TV station to be considered the broadcasting arm of this organization? I had provided some off the record clarifications, yet, insisting that they wanted to tape a real interview, and with me being one of few academics doing research on the PKK in Belgium, they confronted me with a crisis of conscience. The journalists' request forced me into action, even if this was the conscious decision to refrain from any act.

The reasoning behind my decision went to the heart of my personal investment in the project and my involvement in its subject. To begin with, I did not want to hold up lies in public. Of course, I knew about the nature of these associations and their strong affiliation with the PKK, even though this was always—and given the terrorist labeling necessarily—officially denied by its members. Yet, to have denied these relationships as a researcher would have meant stepping out of my academic position and into that of an activist, lying for the sake of a greater cause (which was not my cause). On the other hand, to have affirmed the relationships would have, so I assumed at that time, ended up in contributing to the further criminalization of the Kurdish movement in Europe, narrowing it down even more to "a terrorist organization," a definition the usefulness and theoretical justice of which I had become very skeptical about and which I had started to question in my academic publications.

Of course, I could have testified to the relationships, while arguing against the PKK's terrorist designation. However, I doubted that much media time would be left to communicate any semblance of a nuanced picture of the whole conflict and the Kurdish movement, as surely an elaboration as to why the PKK was not necessarily well defined as a terrorist organization would require. Elaborating on the PKK would take at least half an hour instead of the sound bite or two I would eventually be afforded on this. My participation in a serious, lengthy media discussion was one thing, but a snapshot in popular media was something rather different. I was of interest for what I had to offer, my knowledge of the subject, but it was precisely this, and with it my academic integrity, that, I felt, would be lost.

There were also personal considerations. On the one hand, any implicit incrimination of the PKK on my part would have quite likely led my contacts to withdraw and stymie my further investigations, while, on the other, any suggested support of the illegal, deemed terrorist organization could have had repercussions for me in terms of relations with the Belgian and Turkish authorities. Either way, any participation in interviews on my part would have risked compromising the research as well. Also, the commitment that I had come to feel through my engagement was best served, I felt, precisely through my research project, and, in other words, by my seeking to maintain my personal integrity in this matter.

THE "TERRORIST BOX"

Doing research on the PKK or any kind of Kurdish political opposition is highly contentious in Turkey. In her book *Muslim Nationalism and the New Turks*, anthropologist Jenny White shares her memoires of her participation in a 2008 conference on anthropology in Turkey, at the Yeditepe University. White quotes the former mayor of Istanbul and the university's founder Bedrettin Dalan saying: "There are a hundred thousand anthropologists behind the PKK. . . . Someone takes an X-ray of us, finds the small cracks and learns how to break us apart" (Dalan quoted in White 2013, 54).

Anthropologists are seen as a direct threat to the integrity of the Turkish state, and so is any inquiry from within the Humanities and Social and Political Sciences that touches upon the imaginary of Turkey's unity and its indivisibility. What is particularly disturbing for Dalan and people like him is, I believe, how, as social scientists, we are trying to "make sense" of the PKK (Jongerden 2016). We try to make their ideas and actions intelligible—which does not mean that we "agree" as to their content or shape (as my own research experience showed). Yet "making sense" requires, as Jongerden has argued, that we become engaged with the movement, enter into a dialogue, and spend time with the people who are the constitutive parts of it. Yet, exactly this engagement is troubling for many outsiders, deemed to undermine the assumed neutrality of the researcher and the objectivity of the research. Worse, in Turkey, researchers might end up being categorized as "PKK mouthpieces" or can find themselves labeled "terrorists," as many Kurdish and Turkish colleagues have come to endure (following their support for the Academics for Peace petition and/or during the witch hunt that has followed the 2016 failed coup attempt [Baser et al. 2017; Özkirimli 2017]). In such a climate, it has become ever more difficult to engage in an open, unprejudiced research inquiry into the PKK's sympathizers, militants, and pro-PKK elected officials: both the research subjects *and* the researchers risk being *put away*—sometimes *literally*—(and) into the "terrorist box."

Looking back at how the social-political situation in Turkey has evolved since spring 2009, with the first big waves of arrests and investigations into Kurdish political activists and politicians for alleged membership of the KCK, which would be followed by other rounds, notably in spring 2010. But particularly the situation post-2015 elections and the aftermath of the failed 2016 coup attempt, I do not believe I could do the same kind of research in Turkey, and engage in a similar way as I was able to do during the second half of the 2000s. Yet, despite pessimism reigning and a stream of critical voices leaving the country for a life in exile, one might wonder whether the developments in Turkey reinforce European Kurdish activism—or broader oppositional politics for that matter—and consequently could increase the academic inquiries into them.

However, as my own research experiences testify, the terrorist labeling affects how European Kurdish activists can present themselves in Europe and how they can or cannot elaborate PKK's role in the societal and political make-up of Turkey's Southeast (and equally so as to PKK's role in the political project of Rojava, in Northern Syria[7]). Also, given the labeling, academic researchers in Europe are likely to feel a need—as I did—to navigate concerns as to "do no harm" to their research subjects and themselves, sometimes becoming complicit in a "keeping up appearances" and down playing the actual role of the PKK in Kurdish political activism.

CONCLUSION

In this chapter I have reflected upon the outsider's challenges of doing ethnographic research about the activities of an officially deemed illegal actor, in this case the Kurdistan Workers' Party. I was faced with the "elusiveness" of the PKK as its official labeling as a "foreign terrorist organization" by the United States and the European Union, compelled members of PKK-affiliated political bodies and associations to conceal the nature of their relationship to the political movement. This gave rise to situations where the PKK seemed to be "nowhere" while practically being "everywhere." The PKK was "absent" yet at the same time turned out to be "omnipresent." Indeed, even though the PKK is well established in Europe, making its presence felt among the Kurdish diaspora, and is actively engaged in transnational political activism (in) between Turkey and Europe, very often the PKK seemed like the elephant in the room, with the PKK discussed as an independent entity, situated outside of the actual meeting rooms. This ambiguity was felt both in direct conversations with me as a researcher as well as in observed encounters with European politicians whom Kurdish activists rallied for their cause.

It is not straightforward if, when, and how to address this ambiguity. I personally found myself tiptoeing around it at times and this had everything to do with the prevailing political climate. In a climate, wherein the research subjects were (and *are*) subject to criminalization and prosecution, I practiced a kind of self-censorship, both in my actual day-to-day encounters with the research subjects "in the field," and in the process of writing, publishing, and communicating about my research findings.

Concerned to "do no harm" to our research subjects and ourselves, we can, as academics, become complicit in a "keeping up appearances" and might find ourselves down playing the actual role of the PKK in Kurdish political activism (or any other illegal actor, for that matter). I believe this has been contributing to the PKK's elusiveness and the secrecy around the PKK, as opposed to the recognition of its actual weight, and developing a better understanding of its presence, its work, and the appeal it continues to have, in Europe, Turkey, and the Middle East.

It was by combining my fieldwork in Europe with field research trips to Turkey, and particular Diyarbakir/Amed, and my participation into mass events and critical political gatherings in the political heartland of Turkey's Kurds, that I came to understand the social and political embeddedness of the PKK. These lived experiences made me reconsider how I spoke, wrote, and published about the Kurdish movement. I decided to acknowledge their "omnipresence," as opposed to being accessory to their ambiguous "absence." At the same time, I explained why and how I have not *at all times* been able to actually do so. I closed this chapter by returning to the contemporary political climate in Turkey, where this kind of open academic engagement with political dissidence has come at a very high cost.

NOTES

1. This started to change after conservative parties took office in Europe's leading member states, particularly Germany and France, with Merkel and Sarkozy advancing the alternative of a privileged partnership with Turkey rather than EU membership.

2. DTP, the Demokratik Toplum Paritisi or Democratic Society Party, was the successor to previous Kurdish parties (respectively DEHAP/HADEP/DEP/HEP) which were all closed down or dissolved themselves faced with closure. The DTP was succeeded in 2009 by the BDP (Barış ve Demokrasi Partisi or Peace and Democracy Party), the party from which HDP (Halklarin Demokrasi Partisi or Peoples' Democratic Party) and DBP (Demokratik Bölgeler Partisi or Democratic Regions Party) originated, with HDP functioning as a party for the whole of Turkey with MPs in the Turkey's national assembly, and the DBP functioning as a regional one, holding municipalities and elected provincial councilors. Following the failed coup attempt of August 16, 2016, the judiciary has been prosecuting members of HDP on the basis of its antiterrorism law and since June 2017 the then leadership of the party as well as other MPs have been imprisoned and HDP MPs' parliamentary immunity was lifted following a majority vote by MPs from the AKP (Adalet ve Kalkınma Partisi or Justice and Development Party) and the MHP (Milliyetçi Hareket Partisi or Nationalist Action Party). At the time of writing, eleven HDP MPs had been stripped from their parliamentary seats.

3. In September 1980, Turkey's government was overthrown with a military coup and a civilian government was only reinstalled in 1983. The coup was the third in a row of takeovers, with first and second coups being the ones that took place in 1960 and 1971. In 1980 the military sought to end daily clashes between extreme right and extreme left armed groups and reinstate its own position as "guardians" of the republic and protectors of Mustafa Kemal Atatürk's legacy. The coup and the years under military control led to numerous human rights violations and beheaded most

of the Kurdish as well as other (armed) revolutionary movements in Turkey at that time. The PKK was one of the few parties to survive the coup—as its leadership had already fled to Syria by the time of the coup. From Syria and the Turkish-Syrian border region it continued its plans for an armed insurgency against the Turkish state, which it launched in August 1984. The Turkish state met the guerrilla with counterinsurgency measures that disregarded the rights of the population living inside the Kurdish inhabited provinces, and led to gross human rights violations extending to regular extrajudicial killings. First, following the withdrawal between 1983 and 1987 of the nationwide martial law imposed after the 1980 coup, the Kurdish inhabited provinces of Turkey were governed under a state of emergency law (known by its Turkish acronym OHAL), equivalent in some parts of the Southeast to military occupation. Despite this, however, the PKK insurgency proved successful as the guerrilla force took effective control of large tracts of land in the region. Therefore, the government and army responded to PKK success with the implementation of a new strategy. This involved a cleansing of the countryside, with the destruction of hundreds of village and hamlets and wholesale eviction of a million people, perhaps more (Jongerden 2007). During the early days of the war, a great number of internally displaced persons (IDPs) and others seeking safety and ways to sustain their livelihoods escaped to the big Kurdish cities (Diyarbakir, Van, Batman) and migrated to the Western Turkish metropolises (Istanbul, Ankara, Izmir). Many went to Europe, including political asylum seekers, where some continued to be or became politically active.

4. This changed again to a more cautious approach at a later stage, in 2014–2015, when the Halklarin Demokratik Partisi (HDP, or Peoples' Democratic Party, which grew out of DTP and later BDP) presented itself as a party for Turkey, and actively sought to rally the support from voters across the country with a social democratic program (first in the 2014 local elections and presidential elections and followingly in the parliamentary elections of 2015).

5. Obviously the later developments in the Kurdish Southeastern provinces, with the KCK prosecutions and trials, and particularly the set-backs for the Kurdish movement following the electoral success of DTP's successor HDP in 2015, with the increase of prosecutions of politicians and activists, and the return of heavy violent clashes inside Kurdish majority towns and cities in the second half of 2015 and early 2016 called an end to the relative peace and consequent flourishing of Kurdish civil society in Turkey.

6. KCK is short for Koma Civakên Kurdistan , which means the Kurdistan Communities Union and functions as an umbrella movement for the PKK and sympathizing organizations and parties. With the establishment of the KCK a "KCK contract" was adopted, which stipulates the kind of political project and self-government the PKK seeks realize in Turkey, and by extension in Syria, Iran, and Iraq. In Turkey individuals have been prosecuted for KCK membership as it was considered membership of the PKK and thus of a "terrorist organization." The KCK trials can be considered a means to break the influence of the PKK within the Kurdish politics and civil society in Turkey.

7. Rojava is how Kurds refer to West-Kurdistan and short for the Kurdish de facto autonomous region in Northern Syria, established in 2012 by the PYD (Democratic Union Party) and its armed revolutionaries of the YPG (People's Protection Units),

which were founded and supported by members of the PKK. Rojava was renamed to "Democratic Federation of Northern Syria." The political project of Rojava is considered a direct threat to Turkey's integrity and Turkey has actively sought to finish it off by, inter alia, criminalizing it as "terrorism" and bombarding some parts of the area, as well as pressuring states not to (militarily) collaborate with the PYD and YPG.

BIBLIOGRAPHY

Adams, Laura. 1999. "The Mascot Researcher. Identity, Power and Knowledge in Fieldwork." *Journal of Contemporary Ethnography* 28, no. 4: 331–363.

Ahmed, Shamila. 2016. "Reflections on Conducting Research on the 'War on Terror': Religious Identity, Subjectivity and Emotions." *International Journal of Social Research Methodology* 19, no. 2: 177–190.

Akkaya, Ahmet Hamdi. 2016. The Kurdistan Workers' Party (PKK): National Liberation, Insurgency and Radical Democracy Beyond Borders. PhD diss., Ghent University.

Argun, Betigul Ercan. 2003. *Turkey in Germany: The Transnational Sphere of Deutschkei*. New York and London: Routledge.

Aydin, Delal. 2014. "Mobilising the Kurds in Turkey: Newroz as a Myth." In *The Kurdish Question in Turkey: New Perspectives on Violence, Representation, and Reconciliation*, edited by Cengiz Gunes and Welat Zeyndanlıoğlu, 68–88. London and New York: Routledge.

Baser, Bahar. 2015. *Diasporas and Homeland Conflicts: A Comparative Perspective*. Surrey: Ashgate.

Baser, Bahar, Samim Akgönül, and Ahmet Erdi Öztürk. 2017. "'Academics for Peace' in Turkey: A Case of Criminalizing Dissent and Critical Thought via Counterterrorism Policy." *Critical Studies on Terrorism* 10, no. 2: 274–296.

Baser, Bahar, and Mari Toivanen. 2018. "Politicized and depoliticized ethnicities, power relations and temporality: Insights to outsider research from comparative and transnational fieldwork." *Ethnic and Racial Studies* 41, no. 11: 2067–2084.

Bourgois, Philippe. 2001. "The Power of Violence in War and Peace. Post-Cold War Lessons from El Salvador." *Ethnography* 2, no. 1: 5–34.

Cerwonka, Allaine, and Liisa Malkki. 2007. *Improvising Theory: Process and Temporality in Ethnographic Fieldwork*. Chicago/London: University of Chicago Press.

Casier, Marlies. 2010a. "Designated Terrorists. The Kurdistan Workers' Party and its Struggle to (Re)gain Political Legitimacy." *Mediterranean Politics* 15, no. 2: 393–413.

Casier, Marlies. 2010b. "Turkey's Kurds and the Quest for Recognition. Transnational Politics and the EU-Turkey Accession Negotiations." *Ethnicities* 10, no. 1: 3–25.

Casier, Marlies. 2011a. "The Politics of Solidarity. The Kurdish Question in the European Parliament." In *Nationalisms and Politics in Turkey: Political Islam, Kemalism and the Kurdish Issue*, edited by Marlies Casier and Joost Jongerden, 199–121. New York: Routledge.

Casier, Marlies. 2011b. "Neglected Middle Men? Gatekeepers in Homeland Politics. Case: Flemish Nationalists Receptivity to the Plight of Turkey's Kurds." *Social Identities* 17, no. 4: 501–521.

Casier, Marlies. 2011c. "Beyond Kurdistan? The Mesopotamia Social Forum and the Appropriation and Re-Imagination of Mesopotamia by the Kurdish Movement." *Journal of Balkan and Near Eastern Studies* 13, no. 4: 417–432.

Cerwonka, Allaine, and Liisa Malkki. 2007. *Improvising Theory: Process and Temporality in Ethnographic Fieldwork*. Chicago: University of Chicago Press.

Eccarius-Kelly, Vera. 2002. "Political Movements and Leverage Points: Kurdish Activism in the European Diaspora." *Journal of Muslim Minority Affairs* 22, no. 1: 91–118.

Gambetti, Zeynep. 2008. "Decolonizing Diyarbakir: Culture, Identity and the Struggle to Appropriate Urban Space." In *Re-exploring the Urban: Comparative Citiscapes in the Middle East and South Asia*, edited by Kamran Ali and Martina Rieker, 97–129. Karachi: Oxford University Press.

Gerharz, Eva. 2017. "Navigating Unpredictable Sites. Methodological Implications of Positioning During and After Fieldwork in Conflict Societies." *Social Analysis* 61, no. 3: 1–18.

Grojean, Olivier. 2008. *La cause kurde, de la Turquie vers l'Europe*. PhD diss., Paris: Ecole des Hautes Etudes en Sciences Sociales.

Grojean, Olivier. 2011. "Bringing the Organization Back in." In *Nationalisms and Politics in Turkey: Political Islam, Kemalism and the Kurdish Issue*, edited by Marlies Casier and Joost Jongerden, 182–199. New York: Routledge.

Jongerden, Joost. 2016. "Making Sense: Research as Active Engagement." *Kurdish Studies* 4, no. 1: 94–104.

Marcus, Aliza. 2007. *Blood and Belief: The PKK and the Kurdish Fight for Independence*. New York: New York University Press.

Özkirimli, Umut. 2017. "How to Liquidate a People? Academic Freedom in Turkey and Beyond." *Globalizations* 14, no. 6: 851–856.

Østergaard-Nielsen, Eva. 2001. "Transnational Political Practices and the Receiving State: Turks and Kurds in Germany and the Netherlands." *Global Networks* 1: 261–282.

Østergaard-Nielsen, Eva. 2003. *Transnational Politics: The case of Turks and Kurds in Germany*. London/New York: Routledge.

Romano, David. 2006. *The Kurdish Nationalist Movement: Opportunity, Mobilization and Identity*. Cambridge: Cambridge University Press.

Watts, Nicole. 2009. "Re-considering State-Society Dynamics in Turkey's Kurdish Southeast." *European Journal of Turkish Studies* 10, at http://ejts.revues.org/4196.

White, Jenny. 2013. *Muslim Nationalism and the New Turks*. Princeton and Oxford: Princeton University Press.

Yeğen, Mesut. 2011. "The Kurdish Question in Turkey. Denial to Recognition." In *Nationalisms and Politics in Turkey: Political Islam, Kemalism and the Kurdish Issue,* edited by Marlies Casier and Joost Jongerden, 67–84. New York: Routledge.

Chapter 10

"She's Turkish but Good"

Researching on Kurdish Internal Displacement as a "Turkish" Female Researcher

Yeşim Mutlu

I did not have an identity card until the age of fourteen. We went to the registry office with my father. The officer asked [my father] "Where have you been for fourteen years, do you live in the mountains? Why didn't you issue his identity documents until this time." This is always on my mind; from time to time I think about meeting him one day . . . I did not use it [ID card] for two years, I did not want to use it; insomuch that I nourished hatred against the Turkish State. Yet still I have to use it in some cases: at the hospital, while traveling etc. For example, when I came to Diyarbakır I do not carry it with me.

(Diyarbakır, male, 22)

The above words were the answer of a male interviewee in his twenties and living in Diyarbakır, to a question asked by a woman researcher in her twenties and coming from Ankara for a field research. Given our identity cards, we are both citizens of the same country and hence we should have equal citizenship rights, but we did not. I was the one who benefited from all protections that citizenship ensures and my interviewees were those who were discriminated against at all levels due to their Kurdish identities.

The Kurdish question in Turkey has been one of the most complicated political issues ever since the establishment of the Republic of Turkey. Kurds in Turkey, in quest for equal citizenship rights, revolted against the Turkish state several times starting as early as in the 1920s in the republican history. Turkish state responded every such attempt with various means of oppression ranging from assimilation policies to closing off Kurdish political parties, from decades lasting state of emergency in the regions where Kurds are the majority to punishment of any thought and expression advocating the collective rights of Kurds with allegation of "terrorism" (Gunter 2011, 97). Besides other means, policies of (re)settlement and practices of forced migration have always been one of the most frequently used tactics by the authorities. The fact that PKK launched an armed struggle against the Turkish state in 1984 precluded a normal life for the Kurds living especially in Eastern and Southeastern regions of Turkey. The armed conflict between PKK and TSK[1] that has been going on for almost forty years now, not only "caused significant Kurdish migration from Turkey to Europe" (Baser and Toivanen 2018, 6), but it also regenerated the phenomenon of internal displacement whenever the conflict intensified. Accordingly, from the late 1980s onward and continuingly until the end of the 1990s, Turkey passed through a relentless example of conflict-induced displacement practice through which at least 1.2 million citizens,[2] many of whom were Kurds, were forcefully migrated, or were obliged to leave their habitual residences without any state support.

Taking advantage of the transformations that have occurred particularly in the last two decades in the field of critical ethnography[3] (Sherif 2001, 437), this study focuses on the interplay of ascribed and/or internalized identities that are sometimes conflicting and sometimes reconciling during the field research. Yet, needless to say, these identities are not fixed positions in which the researcher and participant are trapped, but rather they vary in time, space, during and even after the field research. In light of these discussions, this study focuses on the role of attributed ethnic identity and gender in field research. Through a self-reflexive perspective, it aims at both understanding and depicting the story of a female researcher who was attributed the "Turkish" identity in the research field. Moreover, this study focuses on how the researcher was isolated in her own environment while conducting a field research on forcefully migrated Kurdish women and youth.

RESEARCH QUESTION AND METHODOLOGY: VALUES AND QUERIES

Regarding my research, I can trace the first signs of my interest in the aforementioned field up to a class I took in the third year of my sociology undergraduate studies. This class not only changed my perception about Turkish history, which had been taught for years and at each level of the Turkish education system, but it also paved the way for me to confront the Kurdish issue in Turkey, which would become my field of inquiry for my master's thesis. First, I thought about working on Kurdish nationalism. When I shared this with one of our department assistants, the answer I got was: "Do you want to get into trouble? Study another topic." As a result of the literature review I made for my master's thesis (Mutlu 2009) and in time when the forced migrants' problems became more and more apparent, I decided to conduct a research on internally displaced[4] Kurdish youth and women living in Diyarbakır and Istanbul, in the context of state and citizenship relations. The reason I focused on the experiences of youth and women is rooted in the fact that there was a gap in sociological literature on this particular subject in Turkey. I also considered that understanding experiences of forcefully migrated Kurdish youth would give insight into the course of Kurdish issue in Turkey. This is because they were dispersed among blighted areas in metropolises without necessary skills to maintain their lives and became pioneers of the Kurdish insurrection at the cities particularly after the 2000s. Moreover, as Graça Machel puts it: "The recovery and reintegration of children will affect the success of the whole society in returning to a more peaceful path" (Machel 1996, 56). Furthermore, the number of internally displaced[5] children and women are high due to the fact that "the regions of the world characterized by conflict and displacement have relatively high fertility rates and young populations. Women and children thus constitute around eighty percent of" internally displaced persons (hereafter IDPs) (Buscher and Makinson 2006, 15). Herewith, with the guidance of my thesis supervisor, I decided to study the issue of Kurdish youngsters and women's experiences on forced migration and social integration with a comparative perspective of Istanbul and Diyarbakır.[6]

As it is well known, deciding on the methods of field research and of writing process are as important as identifying the studied topic in a research process. This point is also worth mentioning in this study. First of all, it is possible to consider the IDPs in Turkey within the scope of "sensitive groups" as understood in sociological literature. Moreover, it is recommended that ethnographic and/or other qualitative research methods should be given priority, especially in studies on forced migration (Castels 2003, 30). Because interviews have gained acceptance for being suitable for the studies of "people's understanding of the meanings in their lived world, describing their experiences and self-understanding, and clarifying and elaborating their own experience on their lived world" (Kvale 2007, 46), I have deemed it suitable to make face to face in-depth interviews in order to be able to get a sound grasp of the IDPs' experiences.

The main aim of this study was to sort out the social consequences of internal displacement experienced during the late 1980s and 1990s in Turkey's Eastern Anatolia and Southeastern Anatolian regions. To specify, the purpose was to give voice to individuals' experiences of forced migration, look into the integration levels of internally displaced women and youngsters settled down in Diyarbakır and Istanbul and to analyze whether spatial disparity had significance in their integration. In addition to the interviews I conducted in Diyarbakir and Istanbul, I have examined the historical background of forced migration dating back to the Ottoman Empire by going through laws on (re)settlement and their implementation for this study. I started to study the subject in 2007 and carried out the field research in 2008.[7] My sample included twenty-nine young men and women, aged between fifteen and thirty and most of whom had witnessed practices of forced migration after the 1980s. Interviews also included eight women above thirty, two lawyers representing the NGOs working on forced migration, and a party manager of Democratic Society Party[8] (hereafter DTP). The semi-structured in-depth interviews consisted of three parts: socioeconomic characteristics; memories and narratives of the life before internal displacement and of experiences during forced migration; and lastly the life after forced migration, level of social integration and relations with the host population. I recorded all the interviews with the permission of my interviewees.

THE FAMILIAR PENDULUM: RESEARCHER
AS AN INSIDER VERSUS OUTSIDER

The aim of this part is to focus on the role that my attributed identities played in the field and on the positions I experienced and the reasons for them while conducting a field research on Kurdish IDPs as a "Turkish" woman. Positioned as a "Turkish" female researcher, when I decided to study this subject, my personal perspective and academic interest had already headed toward the precedence of human rights in lieu of ascribed ethnic identities and the accompanying conflicts. Additionally, I had thought that I had ridden myself of the possible prejudice against my research topic. Nonetheless, as I read more and more and entered the field, I realized that I increasingly began to position myself and my political attitude toward the Kurdish movement. In my own way, I was not in the same ballpark with "Turkish" ethnic identity and did not prefer to identify myself as "Turkish." This was why I got more and more disturbed by being identified as a "Turk."

My field of study and studied topic were kindly and excitedly received in my own academic community. Yet, my supervisor was the first to warn me about the uneasiness that would arise from any study on the Kurdish issue and that would fall outside the framework established by the official ideology in Turkey: "Are you aware that you can get into trouble?" The purpose of this warning was to act out of concern for me rather than to discourage or threaten me. This was not the last warning I received before I started my research. My research subject, which created excitement for me and for the academic community I was in, to say the least, disturbed my family and friends.

As might be expected, my eagerness to study a topic, which is readily taken as untouchable, was intolerable for my family that identified themselves as middle class with the related everyday practices, tastes and interests and political support to the CHP (Republican People's Party).[9] First, they thought that I would change the topic sooner or later. Then, connotatively they tried to persuade me to change my position. Yet, when those around me realized that I was determined, they relinquished worrying over me and placed their final judgment: "Anyway, you will go up in the mountains soon."[10] This was due to the fact that my study did not categorize the Kurdish issue as pertaining to "terror," "threat of division," or "security." So, in their point of view, I was betraying the "national," setting greater good at naught and was therefore "one of them." These negative responses hardened my tone and had negative impacts on my personal relations.

Although I initially thought that I had put all the warnings and my prejudices aside, in time I noticed that this was not realistic at all. Especially, before I started the field research in Diyarbakır, the questions I asked people who had been to the region before were actually apparent signs of my anxiety: How small is Diyarbakir? Is it known that I was there to do research on such a topic?, and so on. My anxiety also manifested itself in other decisions I made throughout the field research. For instance, in the first days I arrived at Diyarbakır, there was an event called Migration Week, which was organized by the NGOs working on forced migration. Within the context of this event, I was invited to an excursion to an evacuated village to which returns were still banned. Despite the fact that I could benefit much from this for my study and had an urge to join the group, I got nervous and with difficulty decided not to go. This was because I did not know the region well and could not make out whether I would encounter a hitch. Furthermore, what actually tied me up in knots was my ethnic identity. As the literature on insider/outsider dichotomy and its constant fluidity implies, ethnicity, a central dynamic in the research process, plays an important role in the acceptance of the researcher (De Andrade 2000, 26–70). That is to say, before I started the field research, regarding my ethnic identity, I did not know for certain whether I would be considered as an insider and whether my interviewees would share their experiences openly with me. However, after I started the field research, I realized that my ethnic identity did not actually put me to a very disadvantageous position. As a matter of course, there were some supporting factors and they helped me out with establishing rapport with my interviewees. First of all, as I have heard many times before, I have not been perceived as a "Turk" in the first stage because in my interviewees' own words "I resemble Kurds." I was directly asked whether I was Kurdish on many occasions and my answer to this question was "I am not Kurdish as far as I know." In my opinion, this was pointing out to a prejudice that a Turk would not carry out or even not want to carry out such a research and would not make an effort to understand the Kurds' experiences of forced migration. The next question concerned my hometown. When I said that my father is from Erzincan[11] and my mother from Çanakkale,[12] the reaction I received was "It's already obvious." As it is known that Erzincan is habited by a Kurdish population and situated within the borders of Kurdistan, I was not an outsider, but was very much an insider.

POWER RELATIONS IN THE FIELD:
BUT WHOSE POWER?

At this point, it is crucial to mention the importance of space since it is one of the main problematics of this study. Although the fact that my phenotype resembles that of Kurds and that it made a positive impact during my research in Istanbul, it was not sufficient. My reliability at this point was measured by questions that I hardly encountered during the field research in Diyarbakır. The questions directed to me in Diyarbakir were mainly on well-accepted perceptions of the city, on whether I was afraid of going there, what I thought about the city, whether I found it beautiful, and so forth. However, in Istanbul, establishing trust with the participants did not build up as it did in Diyarbakır, but rather it was a "continuous effort" (Kalır 2006, 242) that I was to repeat again and again. For example, many interviewees, especially youth, asked at the beginning questions such as "Why are you researching on this issue?" "Does your family allow you to study this issue?" During the interviews that started with such questions, my credibility changed and my political identity rather than my ethnic identity aroused curiosity: Do I have a relationship with patriotic youth?[13] Do I know X from patriotic youth in Ankara? Do I follow the Özgür Halk magazine?[14] Did I read Abdullah Öcalan's defences?,[15] and so on. Beyond doubt, the answers I would give to these questions would and did affect the direction of the interview. Moreover, my answers could put the interview and subsequent ones in jeopardy. Nevertheless, I preferred to answer the questions honestly and said that I did not have any relation with patriotic youth and did not read Özgür Halk magazine or Öcalan's defences because I did not think that they were relevant for my research. The choice I made could have led me to lose some relationships I had established for my research, but this did not happen. Even so, my interviewees kindly warned me that if I wanted to understand the Kurdish issue I should read them, comments made with a sarcastic tone.

This experience has been very instructive for me on how the power relationship is established between the researcher and the interviewee, a widely discussed topic also in the social sciences (Tedlock 1987; Lee and Ackerman

1994; Bravo-Moreno 2003). First of all, for my interviewees in Diyarbakır to interview with someone they did not know required a well-grounded relationship of trust despite my perceived role as a "researcher" coming from university, a "teacher," and/or "the possessor of knowledge." This was especially so due to the topic, which hardly ever is touched upon in Turkey and when it does, with consequences. At this point, despite the fact that the trusty relationship I had established with my key persons was undeniable, I believe the real issue was that of space. That is to say, I was conducting this research in a place that belonged to them, and this gave them a self-confidence and therefore the power originating from being in their own places. Yet, in Istanbul, what a Kurdish mother in mid-fifties said was the summary of the aforementioned spatial disparity: "We are just guests here" (Mutlu 2009, 102). Accordingly, the Kurds, who accepted meeting me in Istanbul, indeed, were not as comfortable as those who were displaced in Diyarbakır, and probably they felt their identity being under threat.

Another point that attracted my attention was the fact that I had no problem in using the voice recorder in Diyarbakır. Some interviewees even said: "I have nothing to be leery of, you can also record it with the camera." Yet, although none of the interviewees in Istanbul opposed recording, some interviewers were nervous about it. I think what was even more important was the fact that the interviewees wanted me to turn off the voice recorder when they were about to tell stories about the evacuation of villages, firing of houses, and/or their experience with PKK or TSK. For example, a male interviewee from Istanbul, though later he said he was joking, could not go on without saying: "I just said, I do not know who you are, I do not know you. I gave everything out. If I get in trouble, I will have your fingers burnt." Considering the topic I studied, this point was very important since it pointed out to the significance of spatial disparity. In other words, the IDPs in Istanbul did not feel as safe as did those in Diyarbakır, and actually felt the need to hide their identity. This feeling required them to protect not only themselves but also the woman who came to listen to them by taking their "dangerous positions" into consideration. Just as a female interviewee living in a neighborhood where Kurdish population is not intense in Istanbul, put it very clearly: "Neither you nor me will get hurt." Even if they were not living under conditions of conflict anymore, the oppression and discrimination of the Turkish state continued with various means, changing from detention to forced disappearances, from forbidding education in the mother tongue to political activism. Accordingly, it can be considered that the uncertainty of becoming a target of the state at any moment is fueled by this apprehension, which paved the way for the protective approach that they adopted.

"I DO HAVE KURDISH FRIENDS" VERSUS
"SHE'S TURKISH BUT GOOD"

When conducting the field research, it is important with whom and with which institutions the researcher gets in contact in the first stage since it directly affects the subsequent stages of the research. This point not only may lead to the dismissal or consolidation of existing prejudices toward the studied topic by the researcher, but it also has the potential to affect the progress of the research in a positive or negative way. In my experience, I have noticed that not only the relations established for the field research, but also personal relations other than the institutional ones can affect to a great extent the researcher and the research as well. To begin with, when I arrived at Diyarbakır, I met the male cousin of a friend of mine. As a woman who came alone to Diyarbakrr, I was taken from the station, driven to the guesthouse, and taken to the dinner. In all these times, I did not have a chance to get involved in the decisions he took and I remained passive. During the conversation, he asked me why I was in Diyarbakır and I briefly spoke of my research. When I finished, the reaction I got was: "Diyarbakır is no longer the former Diyarbakir. In the past, the locals of Diyarbakır had lived here, now it lets in lots of immigrants and has been disrupted." Then he asked me: "Do you know why these Kurds are giving birth to so many children?" The answer I received when I replied "No" was: "Because they think that the mountains [PKK] need men, and that is why they give birth to so many children."

In a geography that I did not know and where I was alone, it would be a tall order to continue the field research with someone from whom I was intellectually this much distant. Therefore, I thought that it would be better if I met with another friend's contacts who was referred me to. Glasius et al. argue that "to invest in 'warm contacts' is not only valuable because they can provide the researcher with contacts and 'analytical help,' but also for the researchers' own well-being" (Glasius et al. 2018, 93). Similarly, this new social circle not only made me notice the importance of personal relations while carrying out the research, but also helped me with accessing the interviewees, discussing my questionnaire and my observations both about the city and the interactions in the city. Accordingly, all this support facilitated my field research.

In the beginning, the fact that a non-Kurdish person was carrying out this research was not understandable for my participants. However, over time they came to believe in my sincerity and this enabled them to accept me. Thereby I felt that I was positioned outside the framework of the Turkish stereotype. Even sometimes, by referring to the cliché "I also have Kurdish friends,"[16] waggishly they said "She is Turkish but good." Since then, I found a channel through which I could share my thoughts and feelings that I could not talk about in my own environment. Being understood not only put my uneasiness and prejudices I had before the field research away, but also disburdened my sense of loneliness that I was feeling in my own social environment.

Yet, despite the fact that their support was undeniable, the attitudes of my own social environment increased my feeling of loneliness even more during the field research, particularly in Diyarbakır. First of all, my family was feeling uneasy because I was alone in the city. The sentence "we are worried about you" every time we talked caused me to be more distressed. Moreover, their perception of Diyarbakır and my research as "dangerous" led me to defend Diyarbakır and my research even more. Furthermore, although I had read the trauma stories of forcefully migrated before and felt ready for the field, I realized that this was not the case during my field research. As Glasius et al. (2018, 86) state when researchers "come upon hard stories unexpectedly," their impact on me was "much greater." The traumatic experiences I heard from the IDPs, such as a child witnessing their house being burnt down or a guerilla mother seeing the harm given to her child's corpse, started to affect me psychologically and when I could not cope, I felt that the need to share these with my immediate family. However, the reaction I got was the following: "They are lying, our soldiers do not do such things." This reaction did not only alienate me from my surroundings, but deepened my feelings of loneliness. What I thought I felt and defined as loneliness, yet I was not aware of, was probably the symptom of secondary trauma that researchers in conflict zones may experience (Wood 2006, 384). Trying to find a way, I remember asking some scholars that I thought are reliable, how they were able to cope with listening to traumas and resurrecting faded memories of interviewees in such research. But, I did not get a response that would satisfy my needs in that period of time. If I knew then what I know now, I would definitely prefer to get professional help to tackle my feelings.

HERSTORY OF THE FIELD

Another topic that has been discussed for a long time in the social sciences is the role of gender when conducting field research (Easterday et al. 1977; Gurney 1985; Kosygina 2005). Discussions can generally be grouped into two tendencies: While the first tendency is to argue that women and male researchers are not treated equally and that women researchers are at a disadvantage particularly in male-dominated social structures; the second one is to argue that because women are perceived as harmless and unthreatening in general, it is easier for women to access the interviewees (Ergun and Erdemir 2010, 30). To put my experience simply, being a woman researcher facilitated my field research. First of all, as a young woman coming from Ankara to a city, which I had never been to, conducting a research on Kurdish forced migration, I was indeed embraced and perceived as if I was in need of protection. Much as to define this attitude as sexist and discriminatory is unfair to a degree, it can be said that it is not completely independent of this perception and therefore of patriarchy (Easterday et al. 1977). Particularly during my research in Diyarbakır, representatives of NGOs or political parties, who helped me with arranging the interviews, drove me and picked me up for the interviews most of the time. Furthermore, I was persuaded of informing them when I needed something or had any trouble. Besides, as a young woman, especially in Diyarbakir, I had my share of the hospitality identified with the region. Considering the literature on the issue, it is stated that this "guest" perception, which is valid for Muslim societies, places the researcher in a position through which the tables are turned on power relations and the researcher accepts to comply with (Adams 1999, 341). Occasionally, I encountered similar situations during my fieldwork as well. However, it is important to note that this compliance was not perpetual. Bearing these points in mind, it seems more significant to assert that the "tactics" produced under volatile conditions are more decisive (Kalır 2006, 244) and that these conditions are mutually and continuously negotiated, rather than considering the positioning of researcher as a "guest" an absolute compliance or reversal of power relations.

Another point about gender roles was that young women, especially those living in Diyarbakir, negotiated my gender identity with various questions such as "How did your family allow you to come here alone?," or "Are you married?," and so forth. I explained them that I did not have much trouble with my family because they knew that I was conducting a research, but they were to some extent nervous because of common prejudices toward Diyarbakır. When I told that I was not married, they indicated that it would be a problem to do this work if I was already married. Afterward, some of the interviewees shared their dreams of being educated and working as a lawyer or teacher. In doing so, they associated the reasons for their dreams not being realized with patriarchal oppression and living conditions surrounding them, which connoted not only the conditions of conflict but to some extent the social class distinctions among us. At this point, I was perceived as a woman who carried through their unrealized dreams and in my opinion this positioned me as an outsider for these women.

WHO IS THIS "RESEARCHER"?

The answer to the question of who the researcher is, is very much related to how s/he is characterized by the institutions/organizations contacted or the people interviewed. First, in Diyarbakir, I was perceived as a researcher from the "West."[17] Indeed, this point reflected how I was personally perceived as well. In other words, I was considered as someone who came possibly with prejudices to listen to them for a study from the Western part of the country to the East. The word "someone" was associated with the words "teacher," "journalist," or "researcher." The fact that I had affiliation with the university played an important role especially in establishing the trust relationship. Despite the fact that representatives of NGOs or of other bodies accepted me as a graduate student, my role constantly varied for my interviewees. In fact, the role I was provided with not only led to an anticipation[18] that I could help them for their situation and in the difficulties they experienced, which is a common pattern of behavior in researches with refugees and IDPs (Pittaway, Bartolemei, and Hugman 2010, 232), but also brought about an indefinable feeling of responsibility and guilt. When I asked a young woman in Istanbul aged nineteen if she wanted to add something at the end of the interview, she expressed her expectation from me: "All I want from you, just give these [interviews, records] to your university, your teachers, your instructors. Let them listen to these very carefully. I don't know what they already do. . . . You can tell your own people, we tell them but they don't believe us."

Furthermore, the questions particularly asked by youngsters were signs of how my role was perceived and how the regional disparities stuck in their mind: "What do people in the West think about Kurds, about Diyarbakır?," "What do people living in the West think about the Kurdish issue?" Therefore, coming from a university in the West, I was perceived as having better conditions and was placed in a relatively superior position. At this point, the influence of the social class differences between us were at stake, but it was the role of "knowing researcher" attributed to me that played a more important part in the perceived difference in our positions. Accordingly, in some of the interviews this position prompted them to answer my questions as "You know better but . . . ." Yet, this was not a definite position and sometimes my interviewees denounced me for the fact that it was impossible for someone coming from the West for a short time to understand the Kurdish reality. Beyond all these flexible attributions, particularly in Istanbul, one question underlined others: How reliable was I? The answer was given by my interviewees themselves: Sometimes I was so unreliable that my interviewee asked for the voice recorder to be turned off when she was talking about her experiences of forced migration, and sometimes I was so trustworthy that a young, male interviewee shared with me how he would try to join the PKK.

CONCLUDING REMARKS

"The millions of displaced people . . . are nothing but refugees of an unacknowledged war. And we are condoning it by looking away. Why? Because we're told that it's being done for the sake of the greater common good. That it's being done in the name of progress, in the name of national interest. Therefore gladly, unquestioningly, almost gratefully, we believe what we're told. We believe that it benefits us to believe. Arundhati Roy" (Cited in Jongerden 2007, 93).

In this chapter, as a "Turkish" female researcher, I tried to self-reflexively depict my experiences when conducting research on the experiences of the most impoverished and marginalized citizens in Turkey, namely the internally displaced Kurds. As I mentioned, my given identities have been constantly questioned, invented, reproduced, given, and taken back from me during my field research. Thence, I sometimes became a typical example of the Turkish stereotype as it stick in my interviewees' mind and thus reinforced their prejudices, yet sometimes they embraced me by saying "She is Turkish but good." My identity, as a woman, was mostly stable both in Diyarbakır and Istanbul: I needed to be protected because I was actually "entrusted" to them. My female identity was questioned only in certain points, that I was still unmarried and conducting this research on my own. Furthermore, there were rare but remarkable occasions when my femininity was forgotten. When young, male interviewees spoke of how they were subjected to torture, how their houses were burnt down, and how their relatives were killed in front of their eyes, they did not care shedding tears in front of a woman. I did not feel uncomfortable with my interviewees' taking upper hand, except when I could not fulfill the requirements of my role as a guest throughout the fieldwork. I specifically tried to avoid the relationship between a searching subject and a searched object, and I included the data I gathered to the extent my interviewees allowed for it because my goal was just to understand and make these experiences visible.

For the majority of my own surroundings, I stayed as "one of them." Some of my acquaintances helped me to transcribe my interviews and grew more understanding with participants and me after listening to their horrendous stories. This intellectual alteration was a hope that alleviated the loneliness I was feeling. There were times during the field research, when I hit the bottom, which made me question the meaning of writing and my own role as a researcher. First, it was my supervisor who calmed me down and encouraged me to complete my research. Yet, until a short while ago the only thing that relieved my sense of guilt to some extent was that my interviewees thanked me for listening to them. In the midst of all this, it is worth mentioning that that sense of guilt was with me after the field. Eventually, I started thinking about moving to Diyarbakır to do more[19] than just a fieldwork with the guilt I felt. Fortunately, in 2010 I started to work as a project coordinator for an EU-funded project, which aimed at empowerment and employment of women with a particular attention to forcedly migrated women, at Diyarbakır

Metropolitan Municipality. However, this was totally a distinct experience since I was very much an outsider. Not all but most of the women's organizations that we, as the project team worked with for the project, pondered why a "Turk" from Ankara came to conduct the project while women in the region were unemployed. Moreover, there was no trust left for me in Diyarbakır. Women's organization not only put pressure on me to show them the project budget, but also I was accused of employing women under bad conditions since they were paid on minimum wage.

At this point, it seems important to remember what C. Wright Mills enunciates: "It is the political task of the social scientist . . . to translate personal troubles into public issues" (Mills 2000, 187). But more important is to lend an ear to Buroway. Criticizing Mills for his elitism (see Buroway 2008), Buroway argues that "the success of public sociology will not come from above but from below . . . when sociologists then carry it forward as a social movement beyond the academy" (Buroway 2005, 25). Agreeing with Buroway, in my view and experience, another remarkable point is that of whether the political atmosphere in the countries where social sciences are ignored allows researchers to do what he puts forth. In my opinion, the recurrence of Kurds' internal displacement was bygone and very unlikely when I conducted the field research. Nevertheless, just two years earlier this chapter was written, Turkish Kurdistan was razed to the ground for months, resulting in hundreds of thousands of Kurds forced to migrate, hundreds killed and thousands stuck in the middle of an armed conflict. This has made me question my role once more since neither me nor any other body could not do anything to prevent or stop another wave of internal displacement, although the long-term negative consequences of forced migration had already been experienced. In the last instance, I believe, it is important to remember that in every case that raison d'état is gloatingly at work, recurrence of the phenomenon researched will weigh on the social scientists' conscience, who undertake playing that political role.

NOTES

1. PKK is the abbreviation of Partiya Karkerên Kurdistanê (Kurdistan Workers' Party) and TSK of Türk Silahlı Kuvvetleri (Turkish Armed Forces). PKK was formed in late 1970s with an ideal of an independent Kurdish state. To that end, it launched an armed struggle against Turkish state in 1984. Its struggle was not independent from the former Kurdish rebellions for equal citizenship rights and to put an end to the exclusion of the Kurdish identity. Despite the announced ceasefires and declaration of PKK that they do not wish a separation from Turkey, the armed conflict continued for nearly forty years. PKK has been listed as a terrorist organization by Turkey, the European Union, and United States since several decades.

2. The provided number of internally displaced persons varies a great deal. The Parliament's Report (1997) claims that the number of internally displaced persons is 378,335. However, almost all of the nongovernmental organizations, both national and international, claim that the numbers provided by the state are considerably lower to reality. NRC Global IDP Project places the number of internally displaced persons in Turkey to 1 million; United Nations High Commission of Refugees to 2 million and Minority Rights Group International to 3 million and Göç-Der claims the number to be between 3, 5, and 4 million. Despite the fact that it is not possible to know the exact number of neither the internally displaced persons nor the evacuated settlements, the most accurate estimation seems to be provided in the study that was carried out by Hacettepe University Institute of Population Studies and submitted to the State Planning Organization According to this study (2006), the number is between 953,680 and 1,201,000.

3. Both the transformations taking place in the field of critical ethnography and increasing number and quality of studies show that gender, age, ethnic identity, class, and all existing identities and/or belonging not only have an effect upon the research process but also on the variability of the relations established in the field.

4. The terms "internal displacement" and "forced migration" are used interchangeably throughout this study.

5. Despite being generally referred to as "victims of forced migration" in Turkey, following international literature and terminology of the United Nations, this group in Turkey falls in the category of internally displaced persons, which is defined as: "Persons or groups of persons who have been forced or obliged to flee or to leave their homes or places of habitual residence, in particular as a result of or in order to avoid the effects of armed conflict, situations of generalized violence, violations of human rights or natural or human-made disasters, and who have not crossed an internationally recognized State border."United Nations Guiding Principles on Internal Displacement; available at: http://www.refworld.org/docid/3c3da07f7.html (Last access: 12.01.2018).

6. Yeşim Mutlu, *Turkey's Experience of Forced Migration and Social Integration: A Comparative Analysis of Diyarbakır and İstanbul*, unpublished Master thesis (Ankara: METU, 2009).

7. I have conducted the field research with the funding provided by Middle East Technical University Scientific Research Projects Coordination Center.

8. In 2009, DTP was closed on charges of "becoming the focus of terrorist activities."

9. CHP is generally cited as the founding party of modern Turkey. It is a Kemalist party and identifies itself as a social-democratic political party. Six Arrows in the party's logo represent Republicanism, nationalism, statism, populism, secularism, and reformism.

10. What is meant by this is that I would join PKK.

11. Erzincan is a province in the Eastern Anatolia region. It is not a province that is densely populated by Kurds and the vote rate for the pro-Kurdish parties is low, yet it is acknowledged to be included in Kurdistan by the Kurdish movement.

12. Çanakkale is a province located in the Northwestern part of Turkey. Considering the Gallipoli Campaign in World War I, it has a special place in Turkish history.

13. The word "patriotic" is an expression that civilians who support the Kurdish movement use widely to describe themselves and each other. Patriotic youth refers more to the student groups that support the Kurdish movement and that is organized around universities and/or associations.

14. Özgür Halk is a monthly published, political, theoretical, and cultural magazine that began its publication life in 1990. It is allegedly the legal media outlet of PKK. It suspended its publication activities due to a variety of reasons in 2010 and restarted again in 2014. Its employees have gone through severe processes ranging from kidnapping, detention, arrest, and murder. Several people are still under custody. Since the first day of its launch, the police have confiscated the magazine many times without any legal decision other than the closure and withdrawal orders. Repeatedly confronted with the decision to close the magazine, it has continued to broadcast for twenty-eight years.

15. What they made mention of is the books written by Abdullah Öcalan: *Özgür İnsan Savunması* (Defence of the Free Human Race 2003) and *Bir Halkı Savunmak* (Defending a Nation 2004). Bir Halkı Savunmak is also known as the pleading that Öcalan gave to the court after his arrest.

16. Some Turks use this expression when they want to emphasize that they do not discriminate against Kurds.

17. Here the word "West" denotes both to the geographical regions and accompanying regional disparities. Turkish Kurdistan is referred to as "East" both by Turks and Kurds. In contrast to "East," the usage of the word "West" changes both geographically and semantically. Nevertheless, most of the time "West" is connotative of more modern, European, educated, "white" and to some extent upper class. Accordingly, it is the opposite of more backward, traditional, Middle Eastern, uneducated, and lower class, that is the Kurdish "other."

18. What is meant here is that the people interviewed become hopeful that as a result of the interview their material and/or spiritual conditions would improve. In addition, they expected the researcher to be able to "help" them in this sense.

19. Tara Warden sincerely makes mention of this feeling of guilt in her article: Tara Warden, (2013) "Feet of Clay: Confronting Emotional Challenges in Ethnographic Experience," *Journal of Organizational Ethnography* 2 no. 2, 150–172. Working with and for sex workers in Guatemala, she writes on her experiences and elaborates on the issue of guilt and isolation particularly in relation to post-fieldwork process. Accentuating her perpetual isolation based upon "the insincerity of concern" of her family and friends, Tara Warden sends and email to her supervisors and writes "life here seems so easy, and yet I miss the important and strong connections I've left behind, being a part of something bigger, the struggle for positive change" (Warden 2013, 162). What I felt in my post-fieldwork process was almost the same; I was trying to convey what I heard from my interviewees to my friends and if we were drinking, mostly in tears. They were listening to me, I was participating in works of NGOs, seminars, conferences to share the findings of my research and plight of IDPs, but I was not contented with them.

BIBLIOGRAPHY

Adams, Laura L. 1999. "The Mascot Researcher: Identity, Power and Knowledge in Fieldwork." *Journal of Contemporary Ethnography* 28, no. 4: 331–363.

Alvesson, Mats and Dan Kärreman. 2011. *Qualitative Research and Theory Development*. London: Sage.

Baser, Bahar and Mari Toivanen. 2018. "Politicized and depoliticized ethnicities, power relations and temporality: İnsights to outsider research from comparative and transnational fieldwork." *Ethnic and Racial Studies* 41, no. 11: 2067–2084.

Bravo-Moreno, Ana. 2003. "Power Games between the Researcher and the Participant in the Social Inquiry."*The Qualitative Report* 8, no. 4: 624–639.

Buroway, Michael. 2005. "For Public Sociology." *American Sociological Review* 70 (February): 4–28.

Buroway, Michael. 2008. "Open Letter to C. Wright Mills." *Antipode* 40, no. 3: 365–375.

Buscher, Dale and Carolyn Makinson. 2006. "Protection of IDP Women, Children and Youth." *Forced Migration Review Special Issue - Putting Internally Displaced Persons on the Map: Achievements and Challenges*, December. http://www.fmreview.org/sites/fmr/files/FMRdownloads/en/FMRpdfs/BrookingsSpecial/full.pdf.

Castles, Stephen. 2003. "Towards a Sociology of Forced Migration and Social Transformation." *Sociology* 37, no. 1: 13–34.

De Andrade, Lelia L. 2000. "Negotiating from the Inside Constructing Racial and Ethnic Identity in Qualitative Research." *Journal of Contemporary Ethnography* 29, no. 3: 268–290.

Easterday, Lois, Diana Papademas, Laura Shorri, and Catherine Valentine. 1977. "The Making of a Female Researcher: Role problems in fieldwork." *Urban Life* 6, no. 3: 333–348.

Ergun, Ayça, and Aykan Erdemir. 2010. "Negotiating Insider and Outsider Identities in the Field: "Insider" in a Foreign Land, "Outsider" in One's Own Land." *Field Methods* 22, no. 1: 16–38.

Glasius, Marlies, Meta de Lange, Emanuela Dalmasso, Adele Del Sordi, Aofei Lv, Marcus Michaelsen, Jos Bartman, and Kris Ruijgrok. 2018. *Research, Ethics and Risk in the Authoritarian Field*, Palgrave Open Access.

Gunter, Michael M. 2011. "Turgut Özal and the Kurdish Question." In *Nationalisms and Politics in Turkey Political Islam, Kemalism and the Kurdish Issue,* edited by Marlies Cassier and Joost Jongerden, 85–100. London & New York: Routledge.

Gurney, Joan. 1985. "Not One of the Guys: The Female Researcher in a Male - Dominated Setting." *Qualitative Sociology* 8, no. 1: 42–62.

Jongerden, Joost. 2007. *The Settlement Issue in Turkey and the Kurds an Analysis of Spatial Policies, Modernity and War.* Leiden: Koninklijke Brill NV.

Kalır, Barak. 2006. "The Field of Work and the Work of Field: Conceptualizing an Anthropological Research Engagement." *Social Anthropology* 14, no. 2: 235–246.

Kosygina, Larisa. 2005. "Doing Gender in Research: Reflection on Experience in Field." *The Qualitative Report* 10, no. 1: 87–95.

Kvale, Steinar. 2007. *The Sage Qualitative Research Kit Doing Interviews.* London: Sage.

Lee, Raymond L., and Susan E. Ackerman. 1994. "Farewell to Ethnography? Global Embourgeoisement and the Disprivileging of the Narrative." *Critique of Anthropology* 14, no. 4: 339–354.

Machel, Graca. 1996. "The Impact of Armed Conflict on Children." *UNICEF.*

Mills, C. Wright. 2000. *The Sociological Imagination.* New York: Oxford University Press.

Mutlu, Yeşim. 2009. "Turkey's Experience of Forced Migration and Social Integration: A Comparative Analysis of Diyarbakır and İstanbul." MA diss., Middle East Technical University.

Pittaway, Eileen, Linda Bartolomei, and Richard Hugman. 2010. "'Stop Stealing Our Stories': The Ethics of Research with Vulnerable Groups." *Journal of Human Rights Practice* 2, no. 2: 229–251.

Sherif, Bahira. 2001. "The Ambiguity of Boundaries in the Fieldwork Experiences: Establishing Rapport and Negotiating Insider/Outsider Status." *Qualitative Inquiry* 7, no. 4: 436–447.

Taylor, Steven J. 1991. "Leaving the Field: Research, Relationships, and Responsibilities." In *Experiencing the Fieldwork,* edited by William B. Shaffir and Robert A. Stebbins, 238–247. Newbury Park: Sage.

Tedlock, Dennis. 1987. "Questions Concerning Dialogical Anthropology." *Journal of Anthropological Research-Critiques and Responses* 43, no. 4: 325–337.

United Nations Guiding Principles on Internal Displacement. http://www.refworld.org/docid/3c3da07f7.html.

Warden, Tara. 2013. "Feet of Clay: Confronting Emotional Challenges in Ethnographic Experience." *Journal of Organizational Ethnography* 2, no. 2: 150–172.

Wood, Elisabeth Jean. 2006. "The Ethical Challenges of Field Research in Conflict Zones." *Qualitative Sociology* 29, no. 3: 373–386.

Chapter 11

Straddling the Insider-Outsider Divide

Challenges of Turkish Identity as an Outsider Researcher in the Context of Kurdish-Turkish Conflict

Yasemin Gülsüm Acar and Özden Melis Uluğ

Within social psychology, fieldwork in conflict settings is still not commonplace, despite recent calls for more researchers to engage in fieldwork to understand conflict dynamics. However, as polarization and intergroup conflict seem to be on the rise on a global scale, the importance of reevaluating the levels of analysis that mainstream social psychology utilizes and the ways that it approaches these group-based conflicts has become more important than ever. Despite important strands of social psychological research focusing on issues such as intergroup conflict, conflict resolution, violence, civil disobedience, and peace building, the way that social psychology tackles these issues has remained generally the same; as a discipline, social psychology relies heavily on experimental methodology. While experimental methodology certainly has its place, even in these topics, we posit that the importance of context and nuance tend to become lost when research stays only in the lab.

The recent recognition, however, of the importance of nuanced, contextual work on conflict in social psychology has led some researchers to conduct more qualitative, field-based research (see, for example, Acar 2018; Alfadhli and Drury 2018; Uluğ and Acar 2018; Moss 2017; Uluğ, Odağ, Cohrs, and Holtz 2017). With this chapter, we wish to emphasize the importance of conducting fieldwork to the future of social psychological science by referring back to our own fieldwork on the Kurdish-Turkish conflict (see, for example, Acar 2018; Uluğ and Cohrs 2017a), while simultaneously acknowledging the challenges such research entails in the researcher-participant relationship.

We do so by focusing on our context as Turkish social psychologists researching the Kurdish question and the Kurdish region of Turkey (*Bakur*, Northern Kurdistan). We therefore self-label as "outsiders," referring to Voloder and Kirpitchenko's (2014) definition of insider researchers as those who have a perceived closeness and shared attributes to the reference community. We contest that there are varying levels of closeness to that community, and therefore varying levels of being "inside" or "outside."

In conjunction with the "outsider" position, we also attempt to address the way that this positionality and perceptions of power can influence the researcher-participant relationship and the way our research is conducted. We utilize the social identity (e.g., Tajfel and Turner 1979) and self-categorization (Turner 1982) approaches within social psychology to address the relationships between these constructs. In particular, we focus on how it influences our research as Turkish researchers with Kurdish participants and in the context of the Kurdish-Turkish conflict, and how it should be reflected in the new wave(s) of qualitative and/or mixed methods work in social psychology in general.

Below, we provide a background of the Kurdish-Turkish conflict and our research about the conflict, discuss how the social identity tradition can help us understand the insider/outside dilemma, as well as the ways that the dilemma interacts with various levels of identity and privilege. We will follow this with a discussion based on the perspectives of Kurdish participants.

THE KURDISH-TURKISH CONFLICT

After the foundation of the modern Republic of Turkey in 1923, the main ideology of the state, Kemalism (Kirişçi and Winrow 1997), denied non-Turkish identities and cultural expressions. This ideology aimed to homogenize the people in Turkey under the umbrella of "Turkishness" and left little room for other identities (Yavuz and Özcan 2006). Kurds revolted against the Turkish state eighteen times between 1923 and 1938; however, all the uprisings of the Kurdish movements were suppressed, and Kurdish language and expressions of identity were banned (Olson 1996). Kurds and Kurdish identity continued to be perceived as dangerous to the territorial integrity of Turkey, and while there were almost no uprisings between 1938 and 1984 (Heper 2008), the 1980 military coup and its aftermath were especially oppressive toward the Kurdish population.

Human rights violations against the Kurds, including torture and extrajudicial killings, followed the 1980 military coup period. The Junta Regime banned all political parties and oppressed the people in the east and southeast regions of Turkey, allowing the Kurdistan Workers' Party (PKK, *Partiya Karkerên Kurdistan*) to gain supporters (Barkey and Fuller 1998). After four years into the military regime and five years after its formation, the PKK announced its uprising and began its insurgency under the leadership of Abdullah Öcalan in 1984. Clashes continued until 1999, when Öcalan was captured in Kenya; he has remained imprisoned ever since. Though clashes and negotiations did not stop in 1999 and there were negotiations that took place prior, in 2013, the formal peace process started with the meetings of pro-Kurdish Peace and Development Party's (BDP, *Barış ve Demokrasi Partisi*) parliamentarians and Öcalan. The peace process continued until July of 2015, falling apart after the June 2015 parliamentary elections.

The conflict has predictably affected the relationship between Turks and Kurds. Though intergroup contact in terms of cross-group friendship is high among both Turks (e.g., 59.4 percent state they are close friends with a Kurd) and Kurds (e.g., 83.6 percent say they have a close Turkish friend; Seta and Pollmark 2009, 69–70); the level of outgroup trust (i.e., an attitudinal measure of trustworthiness of a particular outgroup; van der Linden, Hooghe, de Vroome, and van Laar 2017) is quite low among both Turks and Kurds (Seta and Pollmark 2009; see also Çelebi, Verkuyten, Köse, and Maliepaard 2014). One of the main reasons behind this low trust may be related to Turks' not acknowledging the political claims of Kurds. For example, one nationally representative survey conducted by KONDA (2011) indicates that 23.4 percent of Kurds reported that they could not express their ethnic identity freely, whereas among Turks it was only 3.2 percent. Although there is a high discrepancy between these two statistics, a substantial majority of Turks tend to see the Kurdish-Turkish conflict as a terrorism problem rather than as an identity problem for Kurds (see also Uluğ and Cohrs 2016), likely because the conflict is very much framed this way in public and political discourses (e.g., Uluğ and Cohrs 2017a).

Throughout this chapter, we will refer back to our own experiences conducting fieldwork on the Kurdish-Turkish conflict during the relatively calm period of the peace process (2011–2014). Acar's research described here will focus mainly on two large field studies: the first, on Kurdish Alevis' self-identification, perceptions of the state and political actors, and of the peace process (Yaman, Yükleyen, Köse, and Acar 2014), and the second on the role of the village guards[1] in the Kurdish-Turkish conflict (see Acar 2018). Uluğ's work here will focus on intergroup conflict in the Kurdish-Turkish conflict context with politicians (Uluğ and Cohrs 2017a), experts (Uluğ and Cohrs 2017b) and lay people from different ethnic backgrounds (Uluğ and Cohrs 2016, 2017c; Uluğ et al. 2017).

SOCIAL IDENTITY AND SELF-CATEGORIZATION

Social identity theory (e.g., Tajfel and Turner 1979; Turner, Hogg, Oakes, Reicher, and Wetherell 1987; also see Abrams and Hogg 2010; Hogg 2006) and the related self-categorization theory (Turner 1982, 1985, 1991; Turner et al. 1987) put forth the concept of social identity, which can be understood as the part of the self-concept derived from membership in social groups. Social identity is multiple and part of a complex system, rather than a single unit. Personal identity, which refers to those characteristics that make an individual unique, is distinct from social identity. Whereas personal identity defines "I" in terms of individuality and unique characteristics compared to others, social identity defines it in terms of "we," meaning members of a social category in relation to other social categories (Turner 1991, 1999). Constructs of religion, political ideology, nation, or gender cannot be properly understood outside of such traditions.

Turner (1982, 1991; Turner et al. 1987) suggests that self-categorization is the psychological basis for group behavior. When it comes to group behavior, we define ourselves according to the behavior of other group members. We evaluate ourselves based on the relevant identity in a particular context and perform the behavior that is expected of a person with that identity. Having a salient social identity tends to lead people to make comparisons with others, especially about the self along the basis of group membership and prototypicality. When dealing with comparisons within a group, individuals tend to focus on similarity and uniformity with other group members. When dealing with comparisons outside of the group, that is, with members of another group, comparisons are focused more on the differences between the groups, especially those that have a positive valence for the ingroup (Hogg 2006).

As intragroup comparisons tend to evaluate the self's degree of similarity with other group members, it follows that others' deviations from group prototypicality would be viewed quite negatively. Group members who are considered nonprototypical are generally not liked or trusted within the group (Hogg, Fielding, and Darley 2005). As such, they can sometimes be viewed as a threat to the integrity of group norms. Hogg, Fielding, and Darley (2005) argue that group members' reaction to deviants are based on whether the deviant is on the boundary with the outgroup, whether there is a threat to the group's valence or distinctiveness, and whether the deviant attributes deviance to the self or to the group.

Social categorization is essential to understanding deviance (Abrams, Marques, Brown, and Henson 2000). The extent to which individuals or groups view themselves as deviant, as well as how that deviance is understood or judged in varying social contexts, determines how one places oneself in any given situation. It is believed that social identity and how one views that identity in context (i.e., as "good" representatives of those identities) play an important role in how individuals engage with others in their community and with the government, as well as their views on contemporary (and historical) political issues. How one, for example, sees themselves in terms of their identity as a Kurd, citizen of Turkey, or as a member of the local community (or all of those things), and how "well" they feel they represent those ideas. It is in this vein that we take identity constructs in theory and apply them to our work in the field. While social identity perspectives discuss the ways identity plays a role in individual lives and communities, through our work, we attempt to give those discussions more weight.

Through our own work, we address these levels of identification and the way they impact not just the individual-level changes that occur with identity, but also the way identification at the individual-level impacts changes within and across groups. Through her work on conflict narratives, for example, Uluğ (2016) learns perspectives on the Kurdish-Turkish conflict from laypeople, providing information not just on how they view the conflict themselves, but the metaperceptions they carry about the conflict as well, which have the potential to influence interactions across ethnic lines.

MULTIPLE IDENTITIES AND NAVIGATING THE INSIDER-OUTSIDE LINE

We all have multiple identities. As different identities become salient in different contexts, when asked, "How do you identify?" most people would have to ask for some sort of qualifier. On what dimension, exactly, do we identify? Qualifiers are essential with a question like this, as clearly, people do not just identify as one thing or another; rather, we have a whole host of identifications at our disposal. Mother, sister, lawyer, Kurdish, Alevi, lesbian, all can be used to describe the same person. Many if not all of those identifications will be important for that person in determining how to answer the question of how one "identifies." In different contexts, one identification could be more important than the others, but all can coexist within the same person, providing a sense of self that is built upon the blocks of all those dimensions, whether similar or not (Roccas and Brewer 2002).

But if one person defines themselves along all of those categories, to what extent is that person representative of any one of them? Our perceptions of self and the degree to which we view ourselves as embodiments of the groups we are part of are intimately related to how many aspects of self we have, and how much we believe those selves overlap or are distinct. Social identity complexity (Roccas and Brewer 2002) is a construct based on the perceptions of the relationships between various social identities, and refers to the nature of the subjective representation of multiple ingroup identities, and reflects how much overlap exists between an individual's simultaneous group memberships.

Clearly, no individual is a representative of just one common-identity group. Memberships in crosscutting groups refer to situations in which "the constitution and meaning of different ingroups do not completely converge" (Roccas and Brewer 2002, 89). Simple self-concepts are represented in terms of a small number of self-aspects with overlapping features and attributes. In contrast, complex self-concepts consist of multiple aspects with independent features. In order to have a more complex social identity, the individual must accept the nature and variety of her or his nonoverlapping group memberships. That is, one must recognize the many group memberships one possesses and the degree to which they differ, or are distinct, from one another.

In their fieldwork with Kurdish Alevis, Acar and colleagues (2014) discuss how participants oftentimes struggled with multiple minority identifications, and the way that their identities would come in conflict with the majority (Turkish, Sunni) or even with one of their minority identities. This was even more profound in participants who not only saw themselves as Kurdish and Alevi, but also as leftists and women. The more identities the individual associated themselves with, the more they could see the ways those identities could potentially clash in various contexts.

Several factors come together to inform social identity complexity. Specifically, experiential, personal, and situational factors determine whether an individual has a complex or simple social identity (Brewer, Gonsalkorale, and van Dommelen 2013; Brewer and Pierce 2005). For example, living in a multicultural or relatively homogenous society can help determine complexity, as can an individual's values, openness to change, or tolerance for ambiguity.

In the same way that we understand the various, intersecting identities we have, we can also recognize that the insider-outsider division, as discussed in methodological literature on researcher positionality, is just as varied. While some previous work has seen the two positions as mutually exclusive (e.g., Olson 1977), others, including the authors, have stressed the importance of context (e.g., Acar and Uluğ 2016; Christensen and Dahl 1997) or the ability to be "multiple" insiders (e.g., Deutsch 1981). Much of the discussion of insider-outsider positionality has taken place outside of the social psychological tradition, and questions of the intersection and importance of identities such as gender, age, or education and their intersection with ethnicity or nationality can impact the way that researchers and participants negotiate their respective positions (Voloder and Kirpitchenko 2014). But as mentioned with social identity complexity above, a number of factors can determine the extent to which a person recognizes the importance or relevance of their multiple identities, including contextual and personal factors. Recognizing these factors and the relationship between complexity and being an insider and an outsider can help determine in what situations a researcher can reach out to participants based on a particular identity, or if it is better to recognize one's position as wholly outside according to the participant.

One situation this is especially important is in a conflict context. The relevance of intersecting identities can be questioned here; in an ethnic conflict, for example, ethnicity may trump education as an important factor in terms of level of identification and perceived closeness or perception of the researcher as being an insider. Other factors, such as gender, which are subject to deep and long-standing systemic inequalities, may not be so easily dismissed (see, for example, Giles and Hyndman 2004). However, it is again important to stress that this can depend on the contextual and personal factors that influence the participant.

In either case, the importance, relevance, and position of these various intersecting identities cannot be understated. Levels of identification can be made salient in recruiting or finding participants, while others might be muted in order to maintain contact with the participants. Contextual and temporal cues can also be relevant in helping the researcher decide when and how these identities are brought to the forefront. There may be certain times or places where a relevant intersecting identity may be discussed or utilized, and others where it could be construed as inappropriate. One instance, for example, from Acar's (2018) work on the village guard system involved an interview with a Kurdish Yezidi[2] (*Êzidî* in Kurdish) participant. The participant oftentimes referred to Yezidis and Kurds as separate identities, sometimes referring to himself as a Yezidi and others as Kurds, other times referring to himself as a Kurd when discussing his relationship to the Turkish government. A research assistant, who himself identifies as Kurdish, interrupted the participant to tell him those identities were overlapping, and that he could be both Kurdish and Yezidi at once. The participant became a bit withdrawn after his exchange, and chose not to discuss this particular issue further. Researchers should be clear, in these situations, that there is no one way to identify, that it is not their role to "police" identities, and to "display not only who they are, but also who they are not" (Nowicka and Cieslik 2013, 7). Below, we further discuss the potentially intersecting identities discussed above, as well as the relevance and privilege those identities entail when finding and working with participants.

PRIVILEGE AND INTERSECTIONALITY

As discussed earlier, accessing people's viewpoints in intergroup conflict contexts may be quite challenging (e.g., Lundy and McGovern 2006). Both researchers' and participants' identities play an important role in this process. An individual's identity—in our case, both researcher's and participant's ethnic identity—influences the way they experience the world. However, as both researchers and participants have multiple identities, we believe approaching the identity dynamics in intergroup conflict contexts as only *singular identities* (e.g., Turkish vs. Kurdish identities) is problematic (see also Bloom 1998). Rather, we argue that both researchers and participants having multiple identities shapes the research in general and the data collection process in particular. In our own experiences as researchers, our some privileged, yet intersecting identities, including ethnicity, gender, age as well as our education level and class have had a huge impact on our interactions with Kurdish participants.

Identifying as female researchers has been beneficial for us, especially in male-dominated settings such as gatherings in public (see, for example, Gurney 2003; Reeves 2010), despite the barriers that can be created between Turkish researchers and Kurdish participants. Making gender salient in such contexts better enables us to connect with [Kurdish] female participants in a more personal and subjective way (see Coffey 1999). In the simplest of ways, being female is likely to grant more access to female participants in the context of the Kurdish-Turkish conflict. In a focus group she conducted with four male and four female participants (see Uluğ et al. 2017), Uluğ asked participants about the impact of the Kurdish-Turkish conflict on Kurdish participants' everyday lives. Male participants talked about various outcomes of the conflict, but female participants remained silent. When the focus group ended, the female participants invited her to another room in the house to drink tea together. They then started talking about other outcomes of the Kurdish-Turkish conflict from their own perspectives, including harassment and abuse by the state police. They did not want to share this information while male participants were present.

In addition to gender, the age of a researcher (e.g., being perceived as young, and therefore, inexperienced) shapes the interaction between researchers and participants. One of the common challenges we have faced as young female academics conducting fieldwork is the paternalistic dynamics that come about when the participant is an older male (see, for example, Easterday, Papademas, Schorr, and Valentine 1977). It is still quite common for younger, female researchers to be referred to as "young lady," or to not be taken seriously (Moss et al. 2018). In line with this, older male participants have been more likely to approach our research or areas of expertise in a patronizing way (see, for example, Solnit 2015, for a discussion on mansplaining) or suggest we conduct research in a manner they deem more appropriate. Though one could certainly contest that, in a situation where ethnic identity is salient and can influence who is in a better situation to "know" the subject, previous research on paternalism (e.g., Christensen and Jensen 2012; Eagly, Diekman, Johannesen-Schmidt, and Koenig 2004; Rudman and Glick 2008; Windsong 2016) indicates that this particular type of interaction is likely to occur even across other status boundaries.

In addition to the importance of age in the researcher-participant relationship, we believe the researcher's status, construed here through education and class, is also crucial to how participants engage with the researcher in a given context. In many contexts, being educated (e.g., having a doctorate) may create a hierarchical relationship between the researcher and the participant (see also Elwood and Martin 2000). Uluğ experienced this during data collection in Diyarbakır (*Amed*), where, even though participants talked about their personal stories related to the conflict, some qualified their own experiences with statements such as "of course, you know better than us, you're an expert," or "I'm sure you already know what I mean, you're an educated person."

However, we believe this is not a unidirectional relationship: the researcher's education level may also shape the way they approach participants. Recent studies indicate that educated people might hold more negative attitudes toward less educated people than toward highly educated people (see Kuppens, Spears, Manstead, Spruyt, and Easterbrook 2018 for a discussion on educationism). These results highlighted less educated people face subtle, yet pervasive bias, one that the researchers may unconsciously utilize, especially given the context and the perception that the researcher-participant relationship may be inherently hierarchical (see Mills, Bonner, and Francis 2006). In a context such as Turkey, where status is quite palpable in social relations, it is important for the researchers to be aware not just of our own potential biases, but of the subtle cues we may inadvertently give off.

Closely linked to education, another status marker that influences research relationships is class (see Ortbals and Rincker 2009). Despite efforts to avoid it, there have been instances in our past work where class status has become a salient part of the interaction with participants. Some researchers (see, for example, Falconer-Al-Hindi 1997; Oberhauser 1997) argue that conducting interviews in participants' homes may be a crucial strategy in order to disrupt power hierarchies between researchers and participants, even while not totally erasing those differences. We have also sometimes followed this strategy. In Acar's (2018) research on the village guard system, most participants chose to be interviewed at home. She describes a fairly similar routine in every home: the researchers would first be invited for a meal and then tea, and maybe some fruit or nuts. Only after everyone had eaten and typical pleasantries were out of the way would research be discussed. The only difference between homes of varying socioeconomic status would be the amount or type of food at each meal. In a household where the family income was higher, some kind of meat and a larger variety of food would be served. In others, where maybe the family had a lower income, meat would be replaced with eggs. In one home the most they could offer was fresh bread and tea. In any case, because of the culture of hospitality, the researchers were a guest in that person's home, and the participant was the host, which would shake up the stricter hierarchy that is typical for researcher and participant.

PERSPECTIVES OF KURDISH PARTICIPANTS

While we, as researchers, have an awareness of our role in the researcher-participant relationship, especially when that relationship is hinged on insider-outsider relationships, we must also recognize that it is feedback from participants that can influence how we continue conducting research in the context of the Kurdish-Turkish conflict. Anecdotal interactions with Kurdish participants in our previous studies (e.g., Acar 2018; Uluğ and Cohrs 2016, 2017a, 2017b, 2017c, 2017d) led us as Turkish researchers to some important questions that we attempted to address through the theoretical discussions above: Which identities matter more when discussing the Kurdish issue with Kurdish respondents as Turkish researchers? What factors matter to Kurdish participants in the *performance* of research as a Turkish academic? In order to briefly discuss these questions, we have drawn on our experiences during our fieldwork in the Kurdish region of Turkey. Below we address the different recurring themes that our discussions with the Kurdish participants brought about.

When asking Kurds about their perspectives on Turkish researchers conducting research on the Kurdish issue, one important factor was the (intersecting) identities and perspectives of Turkish researchers (e.g., political affiliation or ideology, seeing the conflict from an identity perspective for Kurds). Some stated that the way the Turkish researcher approached the Kurdish-Turkish conflict and whether or not they shared certain values with the Turkish researcher (e.g., shared ideology) were important in agreeing to contribute to their research. Some participants stated that it depended on the researcher's political views (e.g., the party they voted for or their political ideology), with some stating explicitly that they would have to share a political perspective. Others spoke a bit more broadly about views on "freedom and justice" as an important qualifier for their participation; one participant stated that "rather than identity, their perspective on [social] class is important." If they felt they could identify with the researcher's political views and identities beyond ethnicity, then they would be more comfortable participating in the research.

Others felt that the very fact the researchers were Turks was reason enough not to participate in their research. One person stated that though it would not prevent them from participating in the research, it would certainly cause them concern:

> I would know that we don't speak the same language. I would doubt that the [Turkish] researcher understands everything I say. But my decision wouldn't be negative or positive just because the researcher is Turkish, it's just that I would be worried. We know Turkish [language]; this is mainly all we have in common.

Another perspective focused on the low level of intergroup trust between Kurds and Turks. Some participants argued that Turkish researchers would not be able to get truthful responses from Kurdish participants (see, for example, Lundy and McGovern 2006 on conducting research in Northern Ireland). The main reason behind this barrier between a Turkish researcher and a Kurdish participant was the researcher's own ethnic identity (i.e., belonging to a group that has suppressed their own for years):

> No, it doesn't affect me, but [I'm sure] it would affect many people's [decision to participate in research conducted by Turkish researchers]. In my opinion, it is naïve to expect very sincere and frank answers from the Kurdish people under these circumstances, of being suppressed by Turks for years.

On the other hand, some people stated that participating in research conducted by a Turkish researcher meant that their voices would be heard from a different population, and maybe at a larger scale, than if they participated in research conducted by other Kurds:

> A researcher whose ethnic background is Turkish conducting a study [on the Kurdish issue] would positively affect my decision [to participate in that research]. As I believe that the [Kurdish] problem is actually a "Turkish problem," it would be easier for the problem to be publicized.

As can be seen in the above example, some of the Kurdish participants see giving an interview to a Turkish researcher as an opportunity to become more visible in the public (see Watters and Biernacki 1989). In other words, participating in research conducted by a Turkish researcher also makes it possible for Kurdish participants to make their voices heard.

It is not surprising that perspectives on Turkish researchers are, of course, quite varied. While an intersecting identity can be useful in engaging with Kurdish participants, it is not enough to ensure Kurdish participants' willingness to work with a Turkish researcher. More than any other issue, trust was discussed as the most important motivating factor for willingness to work with Turkish researchers (see also Lundy and McGovern 2006; Norman 2009). If researchers who have different identities than participants have a way to "vouch" for their sincerity on the issue, their ability to reach participants has the potential to be much higher (see also Moss et al. 2018).

Overall, we believe our own experiences in the field are closely linked to the discussions in the literature on social identity and social categorization (Tajfel and Turner 1979; Turner 1982). As mentioned above, we take identity constructs in theory and apply them to our work in the field. We argue that some identities may be a double-edged sword: some may make it harder to be taken seriously by participants (e.g., being female) or to get truthful responses (e.g., being Turkish), but they may also pave the way for reluctant respondents to give an interview for different reasons (see also Moss et al. 2018). Last, we emphasize that the researcher-participant relationship may be inherently hierarchical, and therefore, there is a need to acknowledge our own privileges as researchers (see Mills et al. 2006). More importantly, we underline the role of intersecting identities when interacting with participants that can influence how we continue conducting research in the context of the Kurdish-Turkish conflict. We believe being a Turkish researcher when interacting with Kurdish participants may bring with it particular challenges due to intersecting identities (being "in" and "out" at the same time; Deutsch 1981; Roccas and Brewer 2002), the need to build trustful relationships (Norman 2009) and making it possible for Kurdish participants to have a voice (Watters and Biernacki 1989).

CONCLUSION

Throughout this chapter, we have discussed the relevance of a social psychological perspective in the insider-outsider debate, especially as social psychologists begin to engage more in fieldwork in conflict contexts. We have used a social identity perspective (e.g., Tajfel and Turner 1979) to help shape and contextualize the way we understand what it means to be an insider and outsider, as well as the role in particular of Turkish researchers working on the Kurdish-Turkish conflict. Through this chapter, we have tried to present different perspectives and the importance of intersecting identities (the idea of being "in" and "out" at the same time; Deutsch 1981; Roccas and Brewer 2002) as a means to contextualize interactions with participants.

Through this chapter, we as Turkish researchers have reflected on our own positionality and privilege in relation to the Kurdish-Turkish conflict. In addition to Turkish identity, we also discussed gender, age, education, and class as other potential identities/factors that may influence researcher-participant relations. We also felt it important to share the perspectives of (potential) Kurdish participants as they reflect on the possible issues they feel could arise when Turkish researchers attempt to take on the Kurdish-Turkish conflict.

We recognize that, as Turkish researchers ourselves, we have faced firsthand these particular challenges, and recognize the precariousness of our position in researching this context. While there is always space for future research and more voices on these issues, we hope our discussion of our experiences in the field and the theoretical constructs that shape those experiences can bring greater attention to identity, intersectionality, and issues of privilege when conducting fieldwork in social psychology.

NOTES

1. The village guard system was created and funded by the Turkish State in the mid-1980s to act as a local militia in Eastern and Southeastern Turkey against the PKK. The guards have the right to carry arms and kill in the name of the State, and are informally granted immunity to exercise violence and settle private affairs (Balta and Akça 2013). Since its inception, the system has remained extremely problematic, and its abolition has been a continued point of discussion, though the necessary steps for disarmament have never been taken.

2. Predominantly ethnically Kurdish religious minority who have long been persecuted for their beliefs.

BIBLIOGRAPHY

Abrams, Dominic, and Michael Hogg. 2010. "Social identity and self-categorization." In *The SAGE Handbook of Prejudice, Stereotyping and Discrimination,* edited by John F. Dovidio, Hewstone Miles, Peter Glick, and Victoria Esses, 179–94. London: SAGE Publications.

Abrams, Dominic, Jose M. Marques, Nicola J. Bown, and Michelle Henson. 2000. "Pro-norm and anti-norm deviance within and between groups." *Journal of Personality and Social Psychology* 78, no. 5: 906–12.

Acar, Yasemin Gülsüm. 2018. "Village guards in the Turkish-Kurdish conflict: Approaching identification, intergroup relations, and resolution." Manuscript submitted for publication.

Acar, Yasemin Gülsüm, and Özden Melis Uluğ. 2016. "Examining prejudice reduction through solidarity and togetherness experiences among Gezi Park activists in Turkey." *Journal of Social and Political Psychology* 4, no. 5: 166–79.

Alfadhli, Khalifah, and John Drury. 2018. "The role of shared social identity in mutual support among refugees of conflict: An ethnographic study of Syrian refugees in Jordan." Manuscript submitted for publication.

Balta, Evren, and İsmet Akça. 2013. "Askerler, köylüler ve paramiliter güçler: Türkiye'de köy koruculuğu sistemi [Soldiers, villagers, and paramilitary powers: Turkey's village guard system]." *Toplum ve Bilim* 126: 7–35.

Barkey, Henry J., and Graham E. Fuller. 1998. *Turkey's Kurdish question.* Boston: Rowman and Littlefield.

Bloom, Leslie Rebecca. 1998. *Under the sign of hope: Feminist methodology and narrative interpretation.* New York: State University of New York Press.

Brewer, Marilynn B., and Kathleen P. Pierce. 2005. "Social identity complexity and outgroup tolerance." *Personality and Social Psychology Bulletin* 31: 428–37.

Brewer, Marilynn. B., Karen Gonsalkorale, and Andrea van Dommelen. 2013. "Social identity complexity: Comparing majority and minority ethnic group members in a multicultural society." *Group Processes and Intergroup Relations* 16: 529–44.

Çelebi, Elif, Maykel Verkuyten, Talha Köse, and Mieke Maliepaard. 2014. "Outgroup trust and conflict understandings: The perspective of Turks and Kurds in Turkey." *International Journal of Intercultural Relations* 40: 64–75.

Christensen, Ann-Dorte, and Sune Qvotrup Jensen. 2012. "Doing intersectional analysis: Methodological implications for qualitative research." *NORA – Nordic Journal of Feminist and Gender Research* 20: 109–25.

Christensen, Donna Hendrickson, and Carla M. Dahl. 1997. "Rethinking research dichotomies." *Family and Consumer Sciences Research Journal* 25: 269–85.

Coffey, Amanda. 1999. *The ethnographic self: Fieldwork and the representation of identity.* London: Sage.

Deutsch, Cynthia P. 1981. "The behavioral scientists: Insider and outsider." *Journal of Social Issues* 37: 172–91.

Eagly, Alice H., Mary C. Johannesen-Schmidt, Amanda B. Diekman, and Anne M. Koenig. 2004. "Gender gaps in sociopolitical attitudes: A social psychological analysis." *Journal of Personality and Social Psychology* 87: 796–816.

Easterday, Lois, Diana Papademas, Laura Schorr, and Catherine Valentine. 1977. "The making of a female researcher: Role problems in field work." *Urban Life* 6, no. 3: 333–48.

Elwood, Sarah A., and Deborah G. Martin. 2000. "'Placing' interviews: Location and scales of power in qualitative research." *The Professional Geographer* 52, no. 4: 649–57.

Falconer-Al-Hindi, Karen. 1997. "Feminist critical realism: A method for gender and work studies in geography." In *Thresholds in feminist geography*, edited by John Paul Jones, Heidi J. Nast, and Susan M. Roberts, 145–64. Lanham: Rowman and Littlefield Publishers.

Giles, Wenona, and Jennifer Hyndman. 2004. *Sites of violence: Gender and conflict zones.* Berkeley/Los Angeles: University of California Press.

Gurney, Joan Neff. 2003. "Female researchers in male-dominated settings: Implications for short-term versus long-term research." In *Qualitative approaches to criminal justice: Perspectives from the field*, edited by Mark Pogrebin, 377–82. London: Sage.

Heper, Metin. 2008. *Devlet ve Kürtler* [The state and the Kurds]. İstanbul: Doğan Kitap.

Hogg, Michael A. 2006. "Social identity theory." In *Contemporary social psychological theories*, edited by Peter J. Burke, 111–36. Palo Alto: Stanford University Press.

Hogg, Michael A., Kelly S. Fielding, and Darley, John. 2005. "Fringe dwellers: Processes of deviance and marginalization in groups." In *The social psychology of inclusion and exclusion,* edited by Dominic Abrams, Michael A. Hogg, and Jose M. Marques, 191–210. New York: Psychology Press.

Kirişçi, Kemal, and Gareth M. Winrow. 1997. *The Kurdish question and Turkey: An example of a trans-state ethnic conflict.* London and Portland: Frank Cass.

Kuppens, Toon, Russell Spears, Antony S. R. Manstead, Bram Spruyt, and Matthew J. Easterbrook. 2018. "Educationism and the irony of meritocracy: Negative attitudes of higher educated people towards the less educated." *Journal of Experimental Social Psychology* 76: 429–47.

Lundy, Patricia, and Mark McGovern. 2006. "Participation, truth and partiality: Participatory action research, community-based truth-telling and post-conflict transition in Northern Ireland." *Sociology* 40: 71–88.

Mills, Jane, Ann Bonner, and Karen Francis. 2006. "Adopting a constructivist approach to grounded theory: Implications for research design." *International Journal of Nursing Practice* 12, no. 1: 8–13.

Moss, Sigrun Marie. 2017. "Identity hierarchy within the Sudanese superordinate identity: Political leadership promoting and demoting subordinate groups." *Political Psychology* 38: 925–42.

Moss, Sigrun Marie, Özden Melis Uluğ, and Yasemin Gülsüm Acar. 2018. "Doing research in conflict contexts: Practical and ethical challenges for researchers when conducting fieldwork." *Peace and Conflict: Journal of Peace Psychology.* Advance online publication. http://dx.doi.org/10.1037/pac0000334

Norman, Julie M. 2009. "Got trust? The challenge of gaining access in conflict zones." In *Surviving field research: Working in violent and difficult situations,* edited by Chandra Lekha Sriram, John C. King, Julie A. Mertus, Olga Martin-Ortega, and Johanna Herman, 71–90. London: Routledge.

Nowicka, Magdalena, and Anna Cieslik. 2013. "Beyond methodological nationalism in insider research with migrants." *Migration Studies* 2: 1–15.

Oberhauser, Ann M. 1997. "The home as "field": Households and homework in rural Appalachia." In *Thresholds in feminist geography,* edited by John Paul Jones, Heidi J. Nast, and Susan M. Roberts, 165–82. Lanham: Rowman and Littlefield Publishers.

Olson, David. 1977. "Insiders' and outsiders'" views of relationships: Research studies." In *Close relationships: Perspectives on the meaning of intimacy,* edited by George Klaus Levinger, and Harold L. Raush, 115–35. Amherst: University of Massachusetts Press.

Olson, Robert. 1996. *The Kurdish nationalist movement in the 1990s: Its impact on Turkey and the Middle East.* Lexington: The University Press of Kentucky.

Ortbals, Candice D., and Meg E. Rincker. 2009. "Fieldwork, identities, and intersectionality: Negotiating gender, race, class, religion, nationality, and age in the research field abroad: Editors' introduction." *PS: Political Science and Politics* 42, no. 2: 287–90.

Reeves, Carla L. 2010. "A difficult negotiation: Fieldwork relations with gatekeepers." *Qualitative Research* 10, no. 3: 315–31.

Roccas, Sonia, and Marilynn B. Brewer. 2002. "Social identity complexity." *Personality and Social Psychology Review* 6, 88–106.

Rudman, Laurie A., and Peter Glick. 2008. *The social psychology of gender: How power and intimacy shape gender relations*. New York: The Guilford Press.

SETA and POLLMARK Research Report. 2009, October. "Public perception of the Kurdish question in Turkey." At http://www.setadc.org/reports/281-research-re port-qpublic-perception-of-the-kurdish-question-in-turkeyq-by-seta-a-pollmark.

Solnit, Rebecca. 2014. *Men explain things to me*. Chicago: Haymarket Books.

Tajfel, Henri, and John C. Turner. 1979. "An integrative theory of intergroup conflict." In *The social psychology of intergroup relations*, edited by William G. Austin and Stephen Worchel, 33–47. Monterey: Brooks-Cole.

Turner, John C. 1982. "Towards a cognitive redefinition of the social group." In *Social identity and intergroup relations*, edited by Henri Tajfel, 15–40. Cambridge: Cambridge University Press.

Turner, John C. 1985. "Social categorization and the self-concept: A social cognitive theory of group behaviour." In *Advances in group processes*, edited by Edward J. Lawler, 77–122. Greenwich: JAI Press.

Turner, John C. 1991. *Social influence*. Milton Keynes: Open University Press.

Turner, John C. 1999. "Some current issues in research on social identity and self-categorization theories." In *Social identity*, edited by Bertjan Doosje, Naomi Ellemers and Russell Spears, 6–34. Oxford: Blackwell Publishing.

Turner, John C., Michael A. Hogg, Penelope J. Oakes, Stephen D. Reicher, and Margaret S. Wetherell. 1987. *Rediscovering the social group: A self-categorization theory*. Oxford: Blackwell Publishing.

Uluğ, Özden Melis. 2016. "A Q methodological investigation of the Kurdish conflict frames among parliamentarians, experts and lay people in Turkey." PhD diss., Jacobs University Bremen.

Uluğ, Özden Melis, and J. Christopher Cohrs. 2016. "An exploration of lay people's Kurdish conflict frames in Turkey." *Peace and Conflict: Journal of Peace Psychology* 22, no. 2: 109–19.

Uluğ, Özden Melis, and J. Christopher Cohrs. 2017a. "'Who will resolve this conflict if the politicians don't?': Understandings of the Kurdish conflict among members of parliament in Turkey." *International Journal of Conflict Management* 28, no. 2: 245–66.

Uluğ, Özden Melis, and J. Christopher Cohrs. 2017b. "How do experts differ from politicians in understanding a conflict? A comparison of Track I and Track II actors." *Conflict Resolution Quarterly* 35, no. 2: 147–72.

Uluğ, Özden Melis, and J. Christopher Cohrs. 2017c. "Examining the ethos of conflict by exploring lay people's representations of the Kurdish conflict in Turkey." *Conflict Management and Peace Science*, Advance online publication. https://doi.org/10.1177/0738894216674969

Uluğ, Özden Melis, and J. Christopher Cohrs. 2017d. "'If we become friends, maybe I can change my perspective': Intergroup contact, endorsement of conflict narratives and peace-related attitudes in Turkey." *Peace and Conflict: Journal of Peace Psychology* 23, no. 3: 278–87.

Uluğ, Özden Melis, and Yasemin Gülsüm Acar. 2018. "What happens after the protests? Understanding protest outcomes through multi-level social change." *Peace and Conflict: Journal of Peace Psychology* 24, no. 1: 44–53.

Uluğ, Özden Melis, Özen Odağ, J. Christopher Cohrs, and Peter Holtz. 2017. "Understanding the Kurdish conflict through the eyes of Kurdish and Turkish lay people: Do ethnicity and region make a difference?" *International Journal of Conflict Management* 28, no. 4: 483–508.

van der Linden, Meta, Marc Hooghe, Thomas de Vroome, and Colette Van Laar. 2017. "Extending trust to immigrants: Generalized trust, cross-group friendship and anti-immigrant sentiments in 21 European societies." *PloS ONE* 12, no. 5: e0177369.

Voloder, Lejla, and Liudmila Kirpitchenko. 2014. *Insider research on migration and mobility*. Farnam: Ashgate Publishing.

Watters, John K., and Patrick Biernacki. 1989. "Targeted sampling: Options for the study of hidden populations." *Social Problems* 36, no. 4: 416–30.

Windsong, Elena Ariel. 2018. "Incorporating intersectionality into research design: An example using qualitative interviews." *International Journal of Social Research Methodology* 21: 135–47.

Yaman, Ali, Ahmet Yükleyen, Talha Köse, and Yasemin Gülsüm Acar. 2014. Kürt Alevileri ve Çözüm Süreci [Kurdish Alevis and the Peace Process]. *Süreç Analiz*.

Yavuz, M. Hakan, and Nihat Ali Özcan. 2006. "The Kurdish question and Turkey's justice and development party." *Middle East Policy* 8: 1–7.

Part IV

ESSAYS ON FIELD EXPERIENCES

Chapter 12

Beyond the Insider-Outsider Dichotomy

Conducting Ethnographic Fieldwork as a Kurdish Returnee in Iraqi Kurdistan

Lana Askari

CONVERSATIONAL FAILURES

"I'm not coming," the voice turned silent. "Are you held up by traffic? I'm sure we can manage to start a bit later, I just need to explain to them." His voice cut me off, "I am not coming. Frankly, I do not think that you have given me the respect I deserve as head of a university department." I blanked, "Excuse me? I don't follow?" I was standing in the middle of the library at the Kurdish Heritage Institute in Silêmanî together with a large group of German and American students, journalists, professors, and researchers. It was eight months since I had started my fieldwork, and I finally had started feeling somewhat comfortable as an anthropologist and Kurdish returnee in the city. Having made some contacts at the institute before, a friend of mine asked me to organize a visit and lecture there for her foreign visitors. She was working for a travel company that organized political excursions in the Middle East, and this was the first trip they had organized in the Kurdistan Region of Iraq (KRI). Having just arrived at the airport a couple of hours earlier, Silêmanî was the start of the group's Kurdish adventure and they were eager to absorb anything they could get their hands on. Luckily then, they were not paying any attention to me as the book sections on the different parts of Kurdistan were generating more interest.

"Just a moment professor," I walked outside to the balcony to get more privacy. "Maybe this is not how they do it in the West, but here I am used to a certain level of respect *Lana ghan* (Miss Lana)." I rolled my eyes and held the phone at a distance from my ear as he continued in the same tone.

It probably looked as if I was trying to get reception on my phone, the way I was pacing up and down. When he finished I replied, "My apologies, but I don't understand why you should think so, I didn't have any intention to not be respectful and am genuinely awaiting your presence." I was confused, had I missed something in our previous phone conversations? "I am running late from teaching, and it would take me too long to get there anyway," he said. I thought maybe he did not have access to a car, or worse, that the past months where public salaries had not been paid out by the government meant he could not afford gas or a car. "Do you need us to send someone to pick you up?" I said. "If you cannot make it that would be a shame, everyone here is waiting for you, but if you really don't want to come that's something different." "No, it's not that. I did not like your tone in our previous phone conversation," he said. I waited to reply. "Your interpretation is really not what I intended," my voice was trembling by now, "Maybe something was misunderstood because we are talking by phone," I said. I started getting very annoyed, had I really been that disrespectful? Did I not know by now how to negotiate the subtle formalities of Kurdish speech?

A week earlier I had found the professor's contact through my aunt, who had called up several other people to find someone who could give a lecture on the history of Silêmanî. I had called the professor to see if he would be able to give this lecture in English and if he was available next week. He had agreed to come and had even called me the morning of the lecture to confirm the time of his arrival. Trying to distance myself from insecurities, I continued to simple respond in what I thought would have a neutral tone, "I have 20 *gharaghi* (foreigners) waiting for you at the institute. But if you do not want to come anymore, I can let them know the lecture is cancelled." "I'll be there in 20 minutes," he replied, and our conversation ended.

The professor arrived shortly after and came in with his child son. I had told my contact at the institute about my conversation and confusion about the contact with the professor. As always sweet and gentle in his approach, our institute guide showed the professor in and introduced us with an air so far away from conflict that the rest of the interactions went smoothly. It was only when we went up to the lecture room that the professor asked me, when previously he had committed to giving his lecture in English, to have me translate his talk into English for the crowd. Put on the spot I obliged, and for the next hour our minds were filled with modern stories of Kurdish history. Reflecting on the whole incident later on, I passed my initial annoyance. Why the professor had seemed eager to come before and changed his mind only a couple of hours later seemed strange. Perhaps he did have money issues, maybe he had another appointment he wanted to go to, or a lunch invitation. Perhaps he had to pick his son from school, maybe he had felt insecure about his English, or perhaps I had indeed sounded very harsh over the phone. Either way, I would never really know the exact reason. What I did know was that in that moment I felt that I had failed in fieldwork, or at least at holding up expected social conversation skills, which were necessary to ethnographic research.

Feelings of frustration, awkwardness, slamming doors, embarrassment, or inaptness are of course part and parcel of the fieldwork experience, moments that later hopefully illuminate certain aspects of the field site or a society. You learn by failure, as underlying structures of society emerge in these moments of disruption. Following Turner's (1969) structure and anti-structure ideas, ritual is seen as cultural performances of a processual nature where social drama in social life reveals social structure in action. That is to say, following moments that arrest the social process by breaking a norma-tive structure, breached relations are examined and finally the "crisis" of this breach are addressed (Turner 1975, 1–3). In my case, the personal reaction and advice I received in the phone call set me straight. As a young woman from the Kurdish diaspora I had engaged in conversational tone that was not fit for my position, I had performed wrongly. The professor, an older man of certain social status had to make this clear by setting straight my position in society. Thus, in conversations such as the one I had had, the normative power and gender dynamics of the city were revealed.

This chapter seeks to explore outsider-insider research and the impact of gendered positionality during fieldwork conducted in Iraqi Kurdistan, a de facto state faced with an economic crisis and political instability. Since the "reflexive turn" became an integral part of the discipline of anthropology in the 1980s, fieldwork reflections have helped to understand the intersubjective premises on which ethnographers build their analysis. Based on long-term fieldwork conducted in the city of Silêmanî (2015–2016), I, as a Kurdish ethnographer from the diaspora, aim to explore how one negotiates the differ-ent identities ascribed to them in the field. Following Stoller's (1989) under-standing that anthropologists have to allow themselves to be transformed by the encounters in the field, I argue that instead of an insider-outsider duality, fieldwork is crafted through shifting daily interactions and understandings of identity. Thus, existing partly within the social structure, yet at times outside of it, this shifting relationality shapes the possibilities and limits of the field and sets off a process of self-formation, which is integral to the ethnographic production of knowledge.

LOCATING THE FIELD SITE IN TIMES OF CRISIS

While one can never anticipate what will happen during fieldwork, I did not anticipate such a sudden change in my field site compared to my visit to Iraqi

Kurdistan in 2014. While the past decade was filled with building up the country and gaining more political autonomy, the first months of my fieldwork started a period of "crisis." Having reworked my original research proposal, during the course of my twelve-month fieldwork I set out to research how people in Kurdistan imagine and plan their future in times of uncertainty.

A war and conflict-ridden region, Iraqi Kurdistan today is a federal region in Iraq, under the ruling body of the Kurdish Regional Government (KRG). Although existing since the early 1990s, the KRG attained greater autonomy and significance post-2003 that brought a decade of stability, incoming foreign investment and oil wealth. The KRG is run by a two-party coalition of the Kurdistan Democratic Party (KDP) and Patriotic Union of Kurdistan (PUK), but was challenged in the last years by the opposition party Gorran. While latest estimations of the population in Iraqi Kurdistan account for about 5.6 million of Iraq's 39 million population, in the past years there has been an in- and out-flux of over 3 million refugees from Syria and internally displaced people (IDP) from other parts of Iraq, increasing the population in the Kurdish region to an estimation between 8 and 9 million.[1] In recent years, Iraq has been unstable as terrorism and clashes between different groups continue to divide the country. Unlike other parts of the country, the Kurdish region in the North has been relatively secure since the fall of the Ba'th regime in 2003. It was considered an economically prosperous "safe haven," attracting other groups in Iraq to migrate to work in the North. In the past decade, foreign investment had redeveloped the cityscape in Iraqi Kurdistan and new hotels, compounds, and shopping malls were built, changing the urban and rural landscape. When the presence of *DAESH*, the Islamic State (IS), became imminent in Iraq and neared the Kurdish border in 2014, the KRG military forces, the Peshmerga, entered into battle against IS with support of Western powers. In the following year public salaries were delayed in pay due to the unrest between the Iraqi government in Baghdad and the KRG, the falling oil prices, incoming Syrian refugees and Iraqi IDP's, and corruptive governmental practices that had finally resulted into what was then talked of as the *qairani aburi* (economic crisis). It was against this backdrop that my fieldwork in Iraqi Kurdistan started in September 2015.

The city of Silêmanî (Sulaimani), where my field site was located, is placed in the Western part of Iraqi Kurdistan, making it the North-Western part of Iraq, close to the Iranian border. With about 1.5 million inhabitants, it is the second largest city in the region after the capital Hewlêr (Erbil). Silêmanî has distinguished itself as the "cultural" city in the region and has preserved a more liberal political character compared to the conservative governmental capital that has received international appeal. In addition to a war that was being fought on the border areas, the stop in public salary pay trickled down into the wider economy, halting work in construction, schools, universities, and public offices from running. Moreover, the KRG parliament stopped convening after the head of parliament, a member of the Gorran party, was denied access to Hewlêr by the KDP in October 2015. This event followed a political outbreak between the regional party strongholds, Silêmanî, and Hewlêr. All these events meant that a shift in daily life routine happened during my stay, the bazaar and city center became emptier than usual, working hours lessened, and uncertainty progressed as the economy and political scene destabilized further. In 2016, economic reforms and austerity measures were put into place after the World Bank and the International Monetary Fund stepped in with loans and reform plans for the KRG budget.[2] Qubad Talabani, deputy prime minister of the KRG, referred to these reforms as "trimming the fat."[3] The recent independence vote in 2017, and the following measures that Baghdad has taken in the past months, have only furthered the economic and political instability. The prolonging of the "crisis" and halt in public salary payment, which was met by protests throughout my fieldwork, have lasted until the present day leading to violent police action that reached its highest point in March 2018.[4]

My ethnographic research was focused on people's understanding of their current predicament and how this affected their future imaginations and plans through a body of research strategies, including participant observation, (expert) interviews, walking and driving tours, document and (social) media discourse analysis and the use of documentary film, both as a visual method and output. Particularly, I worked as a research affiliate at a university, as well as an assistant at an urban planning and architecture company to see how future plans were shaped and enacted on. Through these places, family contacts, and more through meeting people at informal occasions, the field site opened up for me over time. The changes in the city did not feel as if life had stopped or that people were merely waiting for things to get back to "normal" just because construction sites had been abandoned or that public offices were limited their opening hours. Rather, the many changes in governmentality were changing people's perceptions as governmental misinformation and lack of information resulted into popular speculating that the 1990s were returning, a time of hardship between the two main political parties, KDP and PUK. While the mood in the city was low, this also meant that people had time on their hands to express their worries and talk to me, a gifted ethnographic horse that an anthropologist could not look in the mouth.

REFLECTING ON FIELDWORK PROCESSES

Long-term ethnographic fieldwork is thought of as a transformative period in an anthropologist's life. As one leaves for an extended period of time to study people, we are dependent on the goodwill and cooperation of those we want to work with. Ethnographic fieldwork as a personal and intimate constitution can be understood as a matter of "participating in a culture of craftsmanship" (Marcus 2009, 3), rather than a strict set of methods and techniques learned beforehand (Ibid., 9). These set of practices undoubtedly shape the fieldwork and ethnography that comes out from it. Predicated on the discipline's colonial history, reflexivity acknowledges the epistemological and political forces that create the ethnographer's writing, revealing unspoken rules and analytical connections that kept the ethnographer at a distance from the observed and researched "other" while in the field.

The "reflexive turn" in anthropology then pointed out to an important paradigm shift within the discipline in the 1980s. Before, the anthropologist was never presented within the ethnographic writing, giving the impression of the researcher as ontologically separate from his/her informants. The anthropologist was merely thought of as a researcher collecting and analyzing social facts. Undoubtedly, this shift was influenced by feminist and postcolonial scholarship, which in the period of the 1980s and 1990s also brought reflections on these issues to the forefront of academia (Kanafani and Sawaf 2017). At the same time with the discipline's literary turn, marked partly by the iconic book *Writing Culture* (Clifford and Marcus 1986), which argued to experiment with writing style and understanding ethnographic texts as texts, reflexivity and anthropology at home became a new part of anthropology.

Since then, reflections have become integral to ethnographies, as to reveal the conditions of their production (Marcus 2009; Collins and Gallinat 2010, 2–5). With fieldwork being conducted in Western societies more and more, anthropologists became more aware of ethnography's subjective nature and changed ideas about insider and outsider as a stable category. Anthropology at home pushed anthropologist to rethink how straightforward conducting fieldwork within his or her own group was when "no one is simply at home" (Strathern 1987). Moreover, if no group can be thought of as homogeneous, how can we think ourselves as "native" to any group then? Narayan (1993) has discussed the insider-outsider and native anthropologist as a problematic stable category and pushed away from the paradigm emphasizing a dichotomy. What is considered an "authentic" insider is questionable in her opinion, as each anthropologist has shifting identifications and certain factors, such as gender, age, class, education, and race, can offset this cultural identity we consider as insider or outsider. Identities are multivocal and both insider and outsider anthropologists can exhibit different "cards" one can play, or are observed by informants at different times. Instead of emphasizing understanding of "insider" or "native," Narayan argues that there should be "a focus on the quality of relations with the people we seek to represent" and how knowledge is situated in fieldwork and negotiated as part of an ongoing process (1993, 672, 682). In the following paragraphs I will discuss how this negotiated practice was tangible during my fieldwork as a returnee from the Kurdish diaspora.

(RE)LEARNING HOW TO BE KURDISH

As part of the Kurdish diaspora in Europe, my visits to Iraqi Kurdistan had been limited to short family visits every few years. My fieldwork period was the first time I would be staying in Silêmanî for more than three weeks. More importantly, in the year previous to my fieldwork, my parents had decided to leave Europe and return to live in Silêmanî. Having left Iraq in the early 1990s as part of a larger Kurdish exodus, my parents settled in the Netherlands where they continued to live for twenty years. With new political and economic possibilities starting to build up after 2003, many diaspora Kurds attempted to return to Iraqi Kurdistan. After I had left the Netherlands to pursue my studies abroad, my parents decided that with the economic opportunities that existed there, they would return to Silêmanî to be with their near family, despite the political and economic unrest that followed in the years after.

Notions of identity and diaspora as political categories have been long questioned in anthropology, considering a more "fluid" nature of their understanding through intersectional theory needed to study these new "diaspora spaces" (Brah 2005), and emphasizing the "in between" spaces that create binaries of emigration and immigration (Markowitz and Stefansson 2004). Kurdish diaspora studies have also focused on these transnational movements and networks, political mobilization, imagination, and belonging (van Bruinessen 2000; Østergaard-Nielsen 2001; Alinia et al., 2014; Galip 2015). In addition, diasporas have also been involved in becoming actors of peace-building in post-conflict regions (Faist 2007).

Kurdish non-state actors have a long history of collective lobbying in the West. However, the de facto state of Iraqi Kurdistan has introduced new possibilities for Kurdish diaspora and returnees to engage politically and economically in their homeland. While new implications of circular mobility that affect the social, political, and economic landscape in the home country exist (Emanuelsson 2008), reintegration into the Kurdish workspace and equal career opportunities remain questionable. Studies have pointed out to the complex relations between returnees and stayees in post-conflict areas such as in Bosnia-Herzegovina, and also the formation of returnees' groups and behaviors toward guilt and privileges created by migration (Stefansson 2006).

In the Iraqi Kurdish case, Paasche (2016) discusses the ethical implications of operating within an environment of corruptive practices for Kurdish returnees' reintegration. Leading from interviews conducted with returnees, he argues that they experience the unequal job opportunities, political party nepotism, slow bureaucratic system and lack of the rule of law as detrimental to their life (career) plans and the restrictions in career opportunities for them within the KRG region. Here, returnees are often met with disdain by the stayees, who blame the returnees for their feeling of superiority because of experiences from abroad. On the other hand, returnees often feel excluded out of the social structure as they struggle with the right actions to secure bureaucratic needs through own networks and the moral implications of corruptive (*gandali*) practices that have become widespread in the last decade (Ibid.). As an informant once told me, "In this country, you have to be *gandal* (corrupt) to survive." Thus, returns are never clear-cut as returnees enter a renegotiation of normative frameworks upon their return (Askari 2015). Many Kurds continue to live transnational lives between Europe and Kurdistan as different priorities and perspectives about return divide family members (Emanuelsson 2008). Furthermore, while return was motivated by an active investment in the social, political, and economic upbuilding in the context of nation-state building, the current economic and political landscape and mismatch in expectations of homecomings have also influenced a rereturn to host countries (Baser and Toivanen 2018).

As part of the Kurdish returnee community, my fieldwork move then became somewhat of a "homecoming," even if I had never actually lived in Iraqi Kurdistan. Narayan has put forward that "in some ways the study of one's own society involves an inverse process from the study of an alien one" (1993, 678). It was a peculiar thing, living with my parents again after many years of living independently across different European countries. Living on my own as a young woman in Silêmanî, where most of my family lives, would not have been appreciated, as a researcher friend of mine from another city experienced more than several times. Therefore, trying to avoid raised eyebrows, as the old school anthropologist would enter fieldwork by living with a local "native" family, I also had to learn again how to behave as a daughter in my parent's house.

Sometimes, it was indeed an inverse of the actions I already knew and understood, such as serving tea to guests and making sure what to serve in the right order, reflecting gender and age relations. For other interactions, such as the opening vignette tells, I had to learn about these structures by receiving a social education throughout the fieldwork. Inevitably, being back into a state of adolescence reflects the liminal state of being an anthropologist; participating in society, but also standing outside of it and observing it. By performing daily life rituals and conversations, I started to participate and understand better the particularities of being a young person in Silêmanî.

BECOMING A KURDISH ANOMALY

Anthropological fieldwork can be seen as a process of (ethical) self-formation (Kondo 1990; Lambeck 2015): through your relations and encounters with people you shape different selves in the field. In *Crafting Selves*, Dorinne Kondo reflects on her experience of conducting fieldwork in Japan as an American-Japanese woman (1990). As she looked physically "Japanese," but lacked a particular cultural competence that was expected of her by others, people's response to her were to make her as Japanese as possible to conform her to an ascribed identity. Kondo shares that she participated in this performance of what was expected of her, until one day she looked up and did not realize that the typical Japanese woman she was seeing was actually her own reflection in a mirror. Thus, adhering to the performative bodily habitus of movement, speech, and dress, she was shocked to realize that investing in one identity (Japanese) meant that she was losing other parts of her American identity to the extent that she did not recognize herself anymore. Kondo used this negotiated understanding of the shifting and shaping self to shape her research on how identity and selves are crafted in Japan. Seeing this as a creative process that implies forms of agency, working and enacting out identity in the plural, in ethnography the researcher partly becomes his or her own tool, shaping up different types of strategies and ending up with different results.

As I grew up in Europe as part of the Kurdish diaspora, my particularity was too that physically I looked "Kurdish," but since I was not raised there I did not possess the required behavior that was expected. In my phone conversation, I felt I had failed at performing a certain type of "Kurdishness." Furthermore, people in Silêmanî became confused about my identity as they could not place me quite as local. Something was off in my behavior and manner of speaking, which at times left me feeling incompetent. I recall the look of two office clerks at the Silêmanî municipality's media office when I failed to give them my full name as they were filling out a film permit I had requested. After asking for my surname repeatedly, I kept on repeating the same name as they kept on looking at me as if I had just come from outer space. The room we were in had no other people working there, but I still felt mortified because of the confusion. Finally, the man asked me what my father's name was and I finally understood my mistake. In Iraq, last names are registered as your father and grandfather's first name. Since I also had an additional family surname, which I used in Europe, it took me a couple of minutes to realize what they had been asking for. Feeling somewhat stupid for not having realized this earlier, I progressed to give them my "correct" last name. Throughout my fieldwork I felt that this change in last name gave me somewhat of a different identity, a different name to go with my "fieldwork self."

This type of confusion about my identity continued throughout the field when people tried to stabilize my confusing identity. Walking through the market sometimes led to questions about my background, upon which I would answer "from here." Rarely, sellers would say or ask if I had been a returnee. More than often, they asked me if I was from Rojhelat, the Eastern part or Iranian part of Kurdistan, because I sounded from Rojhelat, they said. I started to think about this. I had learned Kurdish through my parents and grandfather, who had left the country two decades ago. Perhaps the strangeness of my language that was shaped in an old-fashioned way did not fit my performance of a young *Suli* (Silêmanî) woman. Undoubtedly, there is some interaction between Iraqi and Iranian Kurds, in terms of trade, work migration, and previous cross-border migration due to war. However, instead of placing me as part of the diaspora, to make sense of me, I had to be labeled as an "other." Not the type of Kurdish from there locally, but an imagined proximity to it.

As Kondo (1990) reflects, foreigners trying to learn the local language are met with praise as they advance in their skills. However, as part of the diaspora or inhabiting the required physical appearance, your language failures are experienced as negative by people. Growing up, I had always been praised by others for my Kurdish language skills in the West. However, learning that I was not quite native enough during fieldwork, I remember as a confronting learning curve. This was likewise with other local skills, such as navigating the city. As I was new to the city and learning to drive in a chaotic and hilly Middle Eastern setting, I had to ask for directions. Not comprehending that I had never lived in Silêmanî before, people's answers where often made with a surprise, "You don't know where the so and so cafe is?" Thus, being an insider-outsider entails a constant negotiation of the field. Different aspects of one's identity are placed to the forefront by daily interactions with people, shaping the ethnographer's understanding of the self and their relationality to others.

SHAPING METHODOLOGY
THROUGHOUT FIELDWORK

Critique on reflexivity argues that too much relativism would be a move away from anthropological generalization, only creating a language of elite uniqueness. Other criticism, like Donna Haraway (1988), opt for "situated knowledge." As ethnographies are based on the experiences of particular individuals they become situated knowledge (Abu-Lughod 1991), here the ethnographer can make his/her identity and their relation to others explicit and create openness about the complexities of lived interaction (Jackson 1989; Stoller 1989). This idea also reaffirms the discipline's goal; if we understand ourselves better, we can understand others better too (Collins and Gallinat 2010). Furthermore, Herzfeld (2005) has argued that good fieldwork is made of "cultural intimacy"; one's competence in culture that creates social intimacy with informants. This interplay creates a type of research of both the "other" and the ethnographer himself (Marcus 2009, 24). The key challenge is then "How to make the phenomenological intimacies of fieldwork speak to larger theoretical empirical engagements with systems, institutions, networks and global processes?" (Ibid., 11). As ethnographic material is based on a set of relationships, the modes of performance in the field create a "radically different field" for each anthropologist. Undoubtedly, the trick of the ethnographer is to shape the messiness of fieldwork into a situated knowledge that is also of comparative value to others.

As an American Indian anthropologist, Narayan (1993) felt that during her fieldwork in India different parts of her identity became more important than others at different times. Indeed, I was partly able to maneuver my fieldwork site easily because I was Kurdish, spoke the language and had family contacts. My fellow "Western" researcher friends perhaps had a harder time coming to the understanding of certain structures or unspoken gender rules in society. On the other hand, they were often received with more hospitality as they were "foreign guests" who had no one else helping them. Gaining access to certain places or interviews could go faster when the *gharaghi* card was played. When I requested a copy of Kurdish historical book through a literary center, I was put in place by the director as them having done a great favor to me. However, when I helped a foreign middle-aged male researcher to find a particular text, he was received amicably, particularly by men.

In ethnographic research, daily interactions and participant observation shape one's perception of the field. Through this the anthropologist can begin to understand the context and society they are researching. My particular positionality as a returnee meant that sometimes my relation to interlocutors was easy as I was accepted as Kurdish. At other times, my being of the diaspora in Europe involved tensions with the stayees, as I was understood not to exhibit "proper" manners. After some time, I started to clearly state when I introduced myself or at the start of an interview, that I was a returnee from Europe and new to the city in order to avoid confusion during questions. It also enabled me to use this card to ask for more detailed answers or explanations throughout conversations, such as "I am not familiar with the context here," or "I did not grow up in the city, could you explain this to me again." In addition, conducting research with returnees was easier for me. A shared background made approaching them easier and holding interviews without much challenge, as we could discuss and share similar experiences.

While all these aspects were part of my experience, the most difficult was to negotiate access that was available to me through family connections, as often they conflicted with my position as a young woman from the diaspora. At the beginning of my fieldwork I was reaching out to the department in charge of municipality planning, without much success. When I got a contact through an uncle, I was able to have a few initial interviews with some of the planners. However, I realized quickly through their distant answers and reluctance to share certain documents or information with me that my presence was not welcomed. After pressing for an interview with the head of the department, I was told to come back the next morning. Arriving at the municipality the next day, the gates were closed and I got the point. Having encountered the same secrecy surrounding governmental documents before, I realized that I could simply not access certain documents, or information, which in some cases were indeed outdated, nonexistent or part of a continuation of institutionalized secrecy from the dictatorial Ba'th regime. They probably did not want some doctoral student from abroad snooping around, and unless I had another contact (*wasta*) that could force my presence, I would not have any access to more information.

Feeling stuck after months of fieldwork, I realized that the self that I was shaping brought me closer to the lifeworlds of young people. At the beginning I felt that because the youth were not protesting on the street, or rebelling against the older generation, they simply did not care about politics. It was with time that I started understanding this differently and shifted my field site to youth events, centers, and trips that opened up the myriad of ways in which Kurdish youth negotiate their identity and generational divides about uncertain futures in a precarious context. Becoming more "Kurdish" over time shaped me and my understanding of how local young people also deal with generational, gender and political tensions. I found it easy to converse with anyone between the ages of fifteen and thirty because my background or gender did not restrict me in these interactions, the spaces in which we interacted, namely cafe's and youth centers, were partially lifted from the many normative frameworks that existed outside them. Furthermore, this younger generation was much more attuned to globalized and cosmopolitan ideas and actions, such as the use of social media to post and vlog about issues of gender equality. More importantly, my positionality meant that I was part of this youth imaginary, our different imagination of future horizons helped me understand the field beyond initial understandings of apolitical attitudes and a region that was stuck in a crisis.

CONCLUSION

Fieldwork relations and the multiplicity of identities surfacing at different times are never straightforward and are constantly negotiated within the field, making ethnography an intimate and personal endeavor. My position vis-à-vis the social structure as a Kurdish returnee was then slightly outside of these structures, but inside it at other times. Because of this fluctuating force, I became inserted into the field in different ways because of my body, performance, and my family ties. Being a "Kurdish" anomaly, looking Kurdish, but not performing as a local Kurd, made my fieldwork an unstable space of negotiation multiple identities while at the same time undergoing a social education. Positionality shapes your field with possibilities, but also limits them at the same time, setting off an ongoing process of coming to terms with one's different selves.

In conclusion, my fieldwork experience brought me closer to the generational divide I was experiencing myself and how local Kurdish youth were negotiating these relations in their current context of precarity. Following phenomenological ideas on intersubjective understanding of gaining knowledge about people, my positionality thus led me to shift my methodological approach. Focusing on what emerged from me and my interlocutors' relationship and perception of each other, and our future imaginations for life in Kurdistan, illuminated my understanding of how people there enact agency in times of uncertainty. Understanding how people navigate life under precarity, that is, how current contexts are shaped by globalization, neoliberal restructuring, and technological development, as well as daily mundane rituals, tells us how the future enacts on the present. This is where I place the comparative value of my fieldwork in Iraqi Kurdistan in respect to the anthropological endeavor to make sense of what it means to be human.

NOTES

1. See also http://refugeesinternational.org/where-we-work/middle-east/iraqhttp://iomiraq.net/issues-focus/iraq-idp-crisishttp://www.krso.net/Default.aspx?page=article&id=1680&l=1http://www.worldometers.info/world-population/iraq-population/

2. World Bank. 2016. The Kurdistan Region of Iraq - Reforming the Economy for Shared Prosperity and Protecting the Vulnerable (Vol. 2): Main report (English). Washington, D.C.: World Bank Group.

3. My own translation from attending Mr. Talabani's speech during the Silêmanî Forum in March 2016.

4. See also https://www.hrw.org/news/2018/04/15/kurdistan-region-iraq-protesters-beaten-journalists-detained

BIBLIOGRAPHY

Abu-Lughod, Lila. 1991. "Writing Against Culture." In *Recapturing Anthropology: Working in the Present,* edited by Richard G. Fox, 137–162. Santa Fe: School of American Research Press.

Alinia, Minoo, Östen Wahlbeck, Barzoo Eliassi, and Khalid Khayati. 2014. "The Kurdish Diaspora: Transnational Ties, Home, and Politics of Belonging." *Nordic Journal of Migration Research* 4, no. 2: 53–56.

Askari, Lana. 2015. "Filming Family and Negotiating Return in Making Haraka Baraka: Movement is a Blessing." *Kurdish Studies* 3, no. 2 (November): 192–208.

Baser, Bahar, and Mari Toivanen. 2018. "Diasporic Homecomings to the Kurdistan Region of Iraq: Pre-and Post-Return Experiences Shaping Motivations to Re-Return." *Ethnicities*, 0, no. 0: 1–24.

Brah, Avtar. 2005. *Cartographies of diaspora: Contesting identities.* Routledge. London and New York: Routledge.

van Bruinessen, Martin. 2000b. *Kurdish Ethno-Nationalism versus Nation-Building States: Collected Articles.* Istanbul: The Isis Press.

Collins, Peter, and Anselma Gallinat. 2010. "The Ethnographic Self as Resource." In *The Ethnographic Self as Resource: Writing Memory and Experience into Ethnography*, edited by Peter Collins, and Anselma Gallinat, 228–245. New York: Berghahn Books.

Emanuelsson, Ann-Catrin. 2008. "Shall We Return, Stay or Circulate-Political Changes in Kurdistan and Transnational Dynamics in Kurdish Refugee Families in Sweden." *Journal of Migration & Refugee Issues* 4: 134.

Faist, Thomas. 2007. "Transnationalism and Development(s): Towards a North-South Perspective." *COMCAD working paper* no. 16, Bielefeld: Center on Migration, Citizenship and Development.

Galip, Özlem Belcim. 2015. *Imagining Kurdistan: Identity, Culture and Society.* London: IB Tauris.

Haraway, Donna. 1988. "Situated Knowledges: The Science Question in Feminism and the Privilege of Partial Perspective." *Feminist Studies* 14, no. 3: 575–599.

Herzfeld, Michael. 2005. *Cultural Intimacy: Social Poetics in the Nation-State.* New York: Routledge.

Jackson, Michael. 1989. *Paths toward a Clearing: Radical Empiricism and Ethnographic Inquiry.* African Systems of Thought. Bloomington: Indiana University Press.

Kanafani, Samar and Zina Sawaf. 2017. "Being, Doing and Knowing in the Field: Reflections on Ethnographic Practice in the Arab Region." *Contemporary Levant* 2, no. 1: 3–11.

Kondo, Dorinne K. 1990. *Crafting Selves: Power Gender, and Discourses of Identity in a Japanese Workplace.* Chicago: University of Chicago Press.

Lambek, Michael Joshua. 2015. "Living as if it mattered". In *Four Lectures on Ethics: Anthropological Perspectives*, edited by Lambek, Michael Joshua, Veena Das, Didier Fassin, and Webb Keane, 2015. Chicago: Hau Books.

Markowitz, Fran, and Anders H. Stefansson. 2004. *Homecomings: Unsettling Paths of Return.* London: Lexington Books.

Marcus, George E. 2009. "Introduction." In *Fieldwork Is Not What It Used to Be: Learning Anthropology's Method in a Time of Transition,* edited by James D. Faubion, and George E. Marcus. Ithaca: Cornell University Press.

Marcus, George, and Clifford, James. 1986. *Writing Culture. The Poetics and Politics of Ethnography.* Berkeley: University of California Press.

Narayan, Kirin. 1993. "How Native Is a 'Native' Anthropologist?" *American Anthropologist* 95, no. 3: 671–686.

Østergaard-Nielsen, Eva Kristine. 2001. "Transnational Political Practices and the Receiving State: Turks and Kurds in Germany and the Netherlands." *Global Networks* 1, no. 3: 261–282.

Paasche, Erlend. 2016. "The Role of Corruption in Reintegration: Experiences of Iraqi Kurds upon Return from Europe." *Journal of Ethnic and Migration Studies* 42, no. 7: 1076–1093.

Stefansson, Anders H. 2006. "Homes in the Making: Property Restitution, Refugee Return, and Senses of Belonging in a Post-War Bosnian Town." *International Migration* 44, no. 3: 115–139.

Strathern, Marilyn. 1987. "The Limits of Auto-Anthropology." In *Anthropology at Home*, edited by Anthony Jackson, 16–37. London, New York: Tavistock Publications.

Stoller, Paul. 1989. *The Taste of Ethnographic Things: The Senses in Anthropology.* Philadelphia: University of Pennsylvania Press.

Turner, Victor. 1969. "Liminality and Communitas." In *The Ritual Process: Structure and Anti-Structure*, edited by Victor Turner, Roger D. Abrahams, and Alfred Harris, 94–113, 125–130. Chicago: Aldine Publishing.

Turner, Victor Witter. 1975. *Dramas, Fields, and Metaphors: Symbolic Action in Human Society.* Ithaca: Cornell University Press.

Chapter 13

Embedded Research and Political Violence

Kurdish Studies in Conflict Areas

Thomas Schmidinger

Fieldwork in a region like Kurdistan means fieldwork in a contested and politically complex territory. Not only political scientists, but also researchers interested in culture, language, or music could be confronted with aspects and results of political conflict and violence. Most parts of Kurdistan were and continue to be, regions of political crisis, including transnational conflicts and civil war. Thus, in many cases, research in Kurdistan also means research in crisis areas.

In this chapter, I will provide some thoughts about field work in such crisis and war zones. Having done fieldwork mainly in the Syrian and Iraqi part of Kurdistan, for many years, these considerations are personal comments based on my own fieldwork experiences reflected in the literature. Social science and especially political science requisites fieldwork in weak states and armed conflict zones. However, such research is institutionally and practically difficult and necessitates careful preparation. Researchers must also consider the ethical aspects of field work in conflict zones. Finally, fieldwork in crisis zones necessitates more self-reflection about the scientific results brought back from the field. This chapter is an invitation to such a self-reflection on research in crisis zones.

STUDYING VIOLENCE

In their book *Fieldwork Under Fire*, cultural anthropologists Antonius Robben and Carolyn Nordstrom (1995) argue that these first encounters with violence "might be misinterpreted as culture shock. The tensions experienced by most of us can be better qualified as existential shock. This shock can be felt as much in our own familiar social circle as in another culture. It is a disorientation about the boundaries between life and death, which appear erratic rather than discrete" (Robben and Nordstrom 1995, 13). Even if the focus of the research is not violence but rather culture, language, or something else, researchers carrying out research in Kurdistan are likely to be confronted with violence, especially if the research is done in a conflict zone, such as Syria and Turkey and some parts of Iraqi Kurdistan. This violence is not only something that can be observed but also something that can be experienced. Not only intellectuals from the region who did research about the Kurds like Pınar Selek or İsmail Beşikçi became victims of state repression. There are several international researchers and journalists, like Finnish sociologist Kristiina Koivunen, French Journalist Loup Bureau, or Dutch Journalist Frederike Geerdink who were detained and/or deported from Turkey due to their research on Kurdish issues during last decades.

Since most Europeans and North Americans today did not grow up during periods of war in their own countries (*in contrast to most of their grandparents*), for many European or North American researchers, fieldwork in Kurdistan could be their first encounter with war and an existential form of violence. In fact, from my own experience and that of my colleagues, I have to say that nobody knows exactly how they will react to their first experience of violence. Neither do I think that it is really possible to prepare yourself for your first encounter with violence. The only thing that is certain is that this first encounter will change you and it is, after all, an irreversible experience. If you are not willing to make a sacrifice for this experience, then it might be smarter to stay away from research in conflict zones, this means stay away from fieldwork in Kurdistan.

Encounters with violence can be direct or indirect but sometimes the indirect encounters can touch you more than the violence that you witness directly. People function very differently when confronted directly with violence. For instance, while running away under fire from border guards during an illegal border crossing, I realized that physically and mentally I can work very well in such situations. I also had no problems photographing mass graves and documenting the bones of victims of the genocide committed by the so-called Islamic State against the Yazidis of Sinjar (Shingal) in 2014. However, I had a complete breakdown after interviewing survivors of that same genocide two years later in the Internally Displaced Persons (IDPs) camps in Iraqi Kurdistan. It was unexpected, because I did not see any physical violence there. The situation was not at all dangerous for me, but these people's intense personal stories, together with their complete lack of hope, brought me close to a psychological breakdown. I had faced more direct encounters with violence three years before in Syria, but then I had also seen some hope and optimism in the people I was working with. What I could hardly stand was the genocide survivors' despair; they felt completely abandoned by the international community and forgotten by the world.

After a few days of doing one interview after the other, I realized that I simply could not continue any longer. I became physically ill and had to return to a hotel in Dohuk, Iraqi Kurdistan, where I literally slept for two days. These conversations with survivors in the IDP-Camp at Xanke in Iraqi Kurdistan changed my perception of violence and my own experience of violence more than any other difficult situation in my fieldwork in Kurdistan. I sometimes still dream about the stories and the people who told them to me and whenever people have to flee from similar militias, as in March 2018 in Efrîn in Kurdish region in Syria, I am reminded of the stories and pictures of those Yazidi survivors of the genocide in 2014. Not only during the daytime but also at night. I would not say that I was traumatized by the research, because I listened to my body which told me clearly that I had had enough, and only continued my research later on, but I was at least, very close to it and that fieldwork definitely had more consequences for me as a person, than any other fieldwork I have done.

Deep first encounters with violence cannot be predicted. You never know in advance when and how violence will touch you. You only have the opportunity to deal with it in some way afterward. Supervision or other institutional support is very rare in the scientific community concerning this. You may at least have the chance to speak with colleagues about your fieldwork. It also helps to talk about what this means for you, yourself! This not only helps your own psyche but also your reflection as a researcher, to reflect upon your own role in the research setting and your perception of what you saw, heard, or experienced. In cases when universities and research projects do not offer supervision, we still have the chance to meet with colleagues for a beer and talk about it. It is important that we admit to ourselves that research about, or at least in a setting of, violence is something that affects us not only intellectually as a researcher, but also goes much further. It can affect our psyche and our body and these effects of violence on the researcher's body and psyche can also affect our research.

We are not neutral observers. We are not merely researchers in our interactions with human beings, we are also human beings ourselves. Reflection on our own emotional attachment and our own involvement in the social setting, which we are conducting research, is necessary not only for our own mental well-being but also for our research. I cannot offer a final recipe for dealing with these questions, but I think it is necessary to keep these reflections in mind and to take enough time to step back from the field and reflect about your own role and involvement in the research setting and your own reaction to experiences of violence.

The other side of what Robben and Nordstrom called an "existential shock" (Robben and Nordstrom 1995, 13) is the normalization of violence or what Linda Green, a social anthropologist working with victims of the civil war in Guatemala, called the "routinization of terror" (Green 1995, 108). In fact many people get used to violence surprisingly quickly. I discovered that during own fieldwork in different parts of the Middle East; dealing with armed men and even seeing human remains in mass graves becomes surprisingly normalized. For me, it even became too normalized sometimes. I had to remind myself that I was in a war zone and that I should not become too adventurous if I wanted to survive and report my research. The same phenomenon can be observed among people who have to live under such circumstances for a longer period than the researcher. However, that does not mean that such a normalization of violence would not have any long-term consequences. Green argues that

> "one cannot live in a constant state of alertness, and so the chaos one feels becomes infused throughout the body. It surfaces frequently in dreams and chronic illness. Sometimes in the mornings my neighbours and friends would speak of their fears during the night, of being unable to sleep or being awakened by footsteps or voices, of nightmares of recurring death and violence" (Green 1995, 109).

Green admits that after six months of research in a Guatemalan Mayan village, she too "started to experience night-time hysteria, dreams of death, disappearances and torture" (Green 1995, 109).

This might not be the same for everybody. It might not only depend on the duration and intensity of the fieldwork but also on the researcher's personality. I did not experience those intense dreams and fears. However, I did have such nightmares after carrying out research with survivors of the genocide committed by the so-called Islamic State (ISIS), against the Yazidi in Sinjar and these nightmares reappeared suddenly when the Yazidis in Efrîn were attacked not by ISIS but by similar groups, in March 2018. Therefore, it seems that these pictures are stored somewhere in my psyche and can be triggered by similar events. As long as nightmares or other psychological consequences of the routinization of terror only reappear occasionally and do not strongly disrupt your normal life, they might be a price worth paying for your research. However, if they start to influence your daily life, it might be necessary to search for professional help.

REVOLUTIONARY VIOLENCE AS FUN?

It might be a taboo subject not to be discussed in public, but violence, especially revolutionary violence, can be attractive to researchers. French author

Jean Genet, who visited Palestine, and Sabra and Shatila in Lebanon two days after the massacre of Palestinian and Lebanese Shiites by Christian militias supported by Israel in 1982, admitted that "it was for fun as much as anything, that I'd accepted the invitation to spend a few days with the Palestinians." He finally stayed two years and claimed that he was "neither afraid nor surprised but amused to be there" (Genet 1989, 9). He was fascinated by the Palestinian movement's revolutionary spirit, like that of many other leftists in the 1970s, when Palestinian guerrilla movements became a much-admired inspiration for radical left-wingers from Europe, the Americas, and even Japan (Andrews 2018, 83).

Revolutionary movements and revolutionary situations attract not only novelists and playwrights like Genet, but also researchers. Especially for left-wing "romantics," revolutionary situations, such as Syria in 2011–2012, are attractive. If we are honest with ourselves, some living in politically stable Western democratic societies can have an adventurous desire to visit or in some cases even participate in armed struggles and revolutions. Some colleagues might even find it fascinating to be confronted with revolutionary violence. I was attracted not so much by the violence but the revolutionary hope, and this attraction was deeply romantic. I must admit that one of the moments during fieldwork in Rojava (Syrian Kurdistan) which had the greatest impression on me was a moment when I was sitting with people from revolutionary youth groups in a very small, dark room above the market of the town of Amûdê, in January 2013. An old member of the Communist Party was teaching them to play the Oud, the Middle Eastern stringed instrument used by Arabs, Kurds, and Iranians likewise. At the back of the room, pictures of Khalid Bakdash and other veterans of Syrian communist movements, made it clear that we were sitting in a communist environment. As there was electricity for only one hour a day, the whole town was completely dark. Only a candle lightened the small room above the shops of Amûdê´s bazaar. Hassan Draieî, the old communist teacher, played Kurdish versions of Bella Ciao and Katyusha with his students and they spoke of their dreams for a future of Syria and Kurdistan. Such moments make a deep impression and are part of the "fun" when conducting research in conflict regions.

While defending the lives of civilians against invaders, as was the case in the Yazidis' struggle against the so-called Islamic State in 2014, is definitely not a revolutionary struggle and a much more horrifying experience than revolutionary violence, the latter can create a hopeful, optimistic, and even party-like atmosphere. The cultural anthropologist, Ted Swedenburg, argued in support of Jean Genet's reflections about his attraction for Palestinian fighters, that "if we admitted that struggles sometimes exude a party atmosphere and exert a magnetic pull, the heroism sometimes associated with our dangerous ethnography would be diminished" (Swedenburg 2004, 412). Having conducted a lot of research about Palestinian armed movements,

Swedenburg confesses that he was "enamoured of the Palestinian revolution, ensnared by its charms and dangerous allure."

So, when talking about dangerous ethnography, I must admit that there is the appeal, the thrills inherent in projects for social change. I feel extraordinarily lucky to have tasted something of the joys of insurrection, the—if I may détourn Durkheim's phrase—collective effervescence of revolt (Swedenburg 2004, 413). Admitting your own attraction to revolutionary processes, including revolutionary violence, might not only help to deglorify your own work and your own position as a researcher in conflict areas; instead, it could also help to reflect your own position as a researcher and the problem of closeness and distance to the people, political groups, and finally also to armed movements. After all, working in conflict areas and studying violence also means being, to a certain degree, an embedded researcher.

EMBEDDED RESEARCH?

Many parts of Kurdistan are war zones. Some of these regions are only accessible with special permission from different states or Kurdish militias. Some areas of conflict are only open to conduct field research with security staff, which means that you often travel with armed militias or are at least accompanied by members of political parties and movements with close contacts to armed militias. Researchers are escorted either by Kurdish political or military actors, and they must deal with states which tend to be anti-Kurdish and thus not research-friendly in Kurdish areas or with Kurdish para-states that have de facto control of the research territories. As a result of such situations, much of the research in Kurdistan's conflict regions is completed using some kind of approach of embedded research. Like embedded journalists also scientific researchers can be escorted by armed forces and might depend on locals who play a similar role than fixer for journalists.

Like journalists, scientists sometimes depend on the support and safety provided by different armed forces. Because of this dependency and contact, researchers often adopt the guardians' narratives whereas the narratives of rival political parties or other ethnic and religious minorities are largely ignored. In Kurdish studies, that means that many researchers voluntarily or involuntarily adopt the role of being an advocate for a certain political current or party in the Kurdish movement. Many books and scientific articles written about Kurdistan bear the name of fellow travelers from the main Kurdish political movements, either the Kurdistan Workers Party (PKK) whose allies dominate Kurdish politics in Turkey and Syria, the Democratic Party of Kurdistan (PDK) of Barzani—the ruling party of Iraqi Kurdistan and the

PKK's strongest rival—or the Patriotic Union of Kurdistan (PUK) with its stronghold in the region around Silêmanî (Iraqi Kurdistan), and thus run into danger of (re)producing propaganda instead of research.

In this chapter, I am not proposing an objectivist approach and complete abstinence from all political judgments in social science. All kinds of social science are influenced by researchers' ideologies, values, and beliefs. Rather than acting as a completely objective outsider, I suggest that we need to reveal and reflect upon our own positions and values instead of hiding them. They must be identified as such and should not be hidden and dressed up as completely neutral and objective facts. And as social scientists, we should at least listen to different and often rival actors and include their voices in our scientific works.

As we all know, not only Kurdish and non-Kurdish actors but also rival Kurdish parties, often tell different narratives. Nevertheless, there are some researchers in Kurdish studies who tend to depend on their relationship to a single Kurdish party, specifically: There are researchers in Kurdish studies who tend to depend on the PKK and its front organizations and there are other researchers who tend to depend on the PDK and the institutions of the Kurdistan Regional Government (KRG) in Northern Iraq. There are even research institutions, universities, and think tanks which obviously belong to one of these big political currents. However, serious research needs at least some level of independence from political parties and funders, and it needs to be attentive to different narratives.

From a practical point of view, I can see certain possible traps which could arise from this kind of "embedded research":

1. People tend to be grateful to people who care for and protect them. This is perfectly natural. However, researchers must keep in mind that this gratitude can impair one's critical thinking. A lack of distance to the people protecting the researcher often results from this gratitude.
2. In a fractionalized political situation, like that in different parts of Kurdistan, the relationship to one fraction of the Kurdish political movement could result in neglecting other perspectives, which are also present in Kurdish society and Kurdish political life.
3. The Kurdish guerrilla movements' armed struggle might also willingly, or in most cases unwillingly, function as a projection surface for European or American researchers' "revolutionary dreams." Just as Latin American guerrilla movements or anti-colonial armed groups played an important role for left-wing social scientists from the 1950s to the 1970s, especially the PKK and their sister movements in Rojava[1] became a focus of Western leftists' revolutionary dreams. This seems to be understandable to a certain extent, given the feminist and socialist positions of PYD

(Democratic Union Party), YPG (People's Defence Units), and YPJ (Women's Defence Units), the ruling political party and armed militias in Syrian Kurdistan. However, using such movements as projection surface for one's own political dreams and desires, one can hinder the understanding of local power dynamics and structures in the society. It can result in a cheap translation of Western political ideas toward the Middle East and an ignorance of the regional framework of political organization.

4. If the researcher's contact to Kurdish society and politics is mainly through a certain political party or militia, this could lead to an over-politicized perspective of Kurdish society. Kurdish, as any other society, also includes people who are not ideologically and politically inclined, who are not involved in any party or nationalist activities, or people for whom references other than Kurdish policies are important, including for instance religious, tribal, or other collective identities. There is a danger in ignoring these other categories, which might be downplayed in the different variations of nationalist discourses but that are nevertheless important for many people and thus important to account for in social scientific research as well.

I do not intend to offer a recipe for dealing with these problems that would suit every case study. However, the basic foundation of all research in conflict regions, where you are depending on some kind of "embedded research," is to be aware of these problems and to reexamine your own work from the perspective of critical self-reflection. This starts with the simple question: Why am I interested in this particular topic? Why am I interested in that region? If the motivation is only to find a revolutionary utopia, then you would do better to work for your revolution, wherever you are. If you want to understand the political dynamics within the region or want to study the consequences of these political dynamics on the societies, this might be a better starting point for research in Kurdistan. Sometimes colleagues need to be reminded of the simple fact that scientific research must be a process with an open outcome. Being surprised is one of the pleasures of research and we can only enjoy that pleasure if we accept that things might be different in the end, contrary to our expectations at the beginning. Movements might be more pragmatic than what our "revolutionary dreams" make us think. Information might be mixed with propaganda and voices within the Kurdish society might be more ambiguous than what we originally thought.

Even in war situations that are characterized by an enemy-friend dichotomy, realities on the ground can be more often characterized by shades of grey than black and white. The fear of such complicated shades of grey can result in ignorance of the relevant parts of Kurdish society and their perspectives. To give just one example: Kurdish studies tend to ignore the religious-conservative part of Kurdish societies and the role played by Muslim madāris ("madrasas") in preserving Kurdish culture and language. Apart from Mehmet Kurt's important work (Kurt 2017), very little has been published about Kurdish political Islam. The Barzani family's religious background and the role of the Naqshibandi tariqa are often ignored by many Kurdish studies scholars, who try to portray the Kurdish movement entirely secular. This even extends to a German research center at Erfurt University, dropping the *Mullah* from the name *Mullah Mustafa Barzani* and simply calling itself the *Mustafa-Barzani-Arbeitsstelle für Kurdische Studien*. Even in research about the Kurdish diaspora, most scholars focus on the secular and nationalist parts of the Kurdish diasporas and ignore those Kurds who are organized in conservative Muslim associations. This is not necessarily a result of ignorance, but rather of the fact, that scholars of Kurdish studies in Western universities tend to have easier access toward secular nationalist movements than to conservative or Islamist movements. Nevertheless, ignoring this conservative part of the Kurdish population means to misjudge the political situation as a whole.

The fact that many scholars in Kurdish studies neglect the religious-conservative part of Kurdish society is only one example of the ignorance that we often tend to develop. We are sometimes trapped by the desire to have a clear picture with a dichotomy which we assume from warlike situations and which also makes it difficult to see the divisions and different interests within Kurdish societies clearly. Another example would be that there has been hardly any research about the Kurdish groups who collaborated with national governments against Kurdish uprisings, like the *korucu*[2] in Turkey or the groups that collaborated with Saddam Hussein's regime in Iraq, the so-called *cahsh*.[3]

These examples just give a hint of the gaps that exist in the field of Kurdish studies. To remedy the situation, it would help to be conscious which topics the Kurdish political movements wish to emphasize and to also search for aspects that are hidden or more present in divergent, but nevertheless Kurdish, narratives. This one-sidedness becomes an even bigger problem in the field, when we are in a situation of armed conflict. Nevertheless, we have to bear in mind that the narratives of actors other than the people we might be in contact with most of the time, might also be relevant for our research.

While doing fieldwork in crisis regions, I kept asking myself: To what extent do I adopt the perspective of the people who accompany me? To what extent do I neglect other perspectives? Does my research put other people in danger? Do I only talk with certain political activists or do I also include a focus on the daily lives of people who are just trying to survive under the given conditions? Are the perspectives of women, people of all kinds of minorities (religious, ethnic, sexual minorities, people with special needs, etc.) included, or do I only speak with heterosexual, elderly men from the dominant religious background? My answers to these questions were never completely satisfactory. However, by asking myself them, I managed to open up new perspectives in my research.

I will give you an example from my own fieldwork in Sinjar (Şingal). When doing fieldwork on Sinjar mountain after 2014, it was essential for me to talk not only with one of the different militias there; I focused on the civilian population, but I also did interviews and visited the regions controlled by rival militias like the Peshmerga of PDK, as well as the fighters of Haydar Şeşo's Hêza Parastina Êzîdxan (HPÊ) and the YPG/HPG-affiliate Yekîneyên Berxwedana Şingalê (YBŞ).[4] Nevertheless, I did not consider that that research was complete until I finally also made it to the territories controlled by the pro-Bagdhad Êzîdî Popular Mobilization Forces (PMF), who took over southern Sinjar in spring 2017.

Or another example from Syrian Kurdistan: When I did my research for my book about Rojava (Schmidinger 2018), I traveled to the Syrian part of Kurdistan several times. To get a more balanced and accurate picture of what was going on, I made sure that I did not only travel with one Kurdish party, but with different opponents of the Kurdish political spectrum. In contrast to most of the researchers who have visited Rojava in recent years, I did not only rely on the dominant Democratic Union Party (PYD) and the People's Protection Units (YPG). While I did arrange some of my research trips with the PYD and their allies, I also did one trip with some of their stout opponents from the Kurdish National Council in Syria (ENKS), who supported Barzani and completely rejected the PYD's rule and their system. In addition to the trips with PYD and ENKS activists, I also once went on a kind of diplomatic mission, where I tried to help negotiate in a conflict between the owner of a hospital in Kobanê and the local leadership of the PYD administration. This journey was organized mainly through personal connections with relatives of Kurdish friends from Syria and allowed me to add some meetings with relatives of friends who had no political involvement. These different perspectives enabled me to get to know multiple perspectives on the situation in Rojava. As I did not depend on only one Kurdish party, I got access to different political actors, including the groups who oppose the present system in Rojava. And finally, I was also able to get some perspectives from ordinary people, who told me about their everyday struggles and not about their ideological perspectives on Kurdish politics.

CROSSING CONFLICT LINES

In addition, I also tried to meet people from "the other side" when I traveled with the support of the PYD. This was possible, but difficult. It was not that the PYD would have prevented me from meeting their opponents but some members of the ENKS parties who oppose the rule of PYD and were threatened by their forces did not want the PYD to know that I had met with them. I still do not want to go into detail about how I finally managed it but after all, I have to mention that crossing conflict lines is one of the biggest difficulties when researching in conflict zones.

This not only includes political conflict lines between Kurdish groups, but also between armed opponents in civil wars. I can still remember waiting for hours on the border of Azaz, the Syrian border next to the Turkish border crossing of Öncüpınar near Kilis in February 2015 and drinking liters of tea with different Ahrar ash-Sham, Liwat al-Tawhid, and Jabhat al-Nusra[5] commanders, who were all present in Azaz at that time, to negotiate our onward journey to Efrîn. Negotiating with armed commanders in the field requires a lot of patience and resilience. In such situations, I never took a "no" for an absolute no, but started long discussions, including conversations about Austria, my family, and my counterpart's family. If you manage to build personal connections, it can be a first step to changing a "no" into a "perhaps." A self-confident and respectful style of communication is always the basis of such negotiations. One way to succeed is to build personal connections with your counterpart. If you talk about family, bring some small presents from home and if you are able to drink a lot of sweet tea with a lot of people, this might help.

However, field research in war zones can also fail and caution is always advisable. Of course, research in crisis zones is always dangerous to a certain extent, but I always tried to minimize the risks as much as possible. Normally we gain no further information for our research by risking our lives directly on the frontlines or by doing things that are more likely to lead to a researcher's death than to a new book. Therefore, I had to learn the art of failure. As a passionate mountaineer coming from the Alps, I know that sometimes you have to step back or return even if you can see the peak of a mountain. Something that seems to be possible one day, can be completely impossible another day because conditions can change. The same goes with research in conflict areas. Sometimes it is advisable to step back and try things later and in another way. As the weather conditions in the mountains can change on a daily basis, so do also security conditions in conflict areas. The weather forecast can be as important for the mountaineer as the local news can be for the researcher in conflict areas. Therefore, it is important to follow news and to talk with locals about local conditions. This information is important for a permanent risk management. Such a risk management means that at every point of a research it is necessary to rethink if something is not too dangerous. After all, at every point of the research anything can be stopped if it seems too risky for the moment being.

Although I can be quite persistent when negotiating with different militias and revolutionaries to find my way through frontlines, I also had to learn that sometimes ways that I thought could work or that might have worked at a different time, do not work at the moment you need them to. My research about Rojava included illegal border crossing by night with Kurdish smugglers, but it also included ending one such attempt, when I realized, that the people I was trying to cross the border with, had failed a few days before and even lost one of their colleagues. I do not want to go into detail about that, but I did return empty-handed twice, without crossing the border from Turkey to Rojava. I had to learn that responsible research in war zones also means risk management and that includes the possibility of failing sometimes.

INSTITUTIONAL DIFFICULTIES AND
FREELANCE RESEARCH

To understand war, you must also know what war looks like in the field. However, that does not necessarily mean that you understand the big picture afterward and vice versa. A war can appear very different in different regions and war zones. Or as peace and conflict scholar, Carolyn Nordstrom, writes: "To understand a war is not the same thing as understanding a war in the town X and among the people who populate it. In the same way that a body cannot be understood by a finger, a war cannot be understood by a single locale" (Nordstrom 1995, 139). We ultimately need to see war from different perspectives: the big picture from abroad and the local pictures in different regions, towns, conflict zones. This means that we need fieldwork and fieldwork is an essential element, but if we want to understand why local and regional actors act the way they do, we also need time and reflection to connect the results from the field with the bigger geostrategic picture of the region.

One of the major problems faced by many colleagues with stronger institutional affiliations, like full-time employment at universities or research institutes, is the fact that their institutions do not allow them to do any "risky" fieldwork. Colleagues with full-time positions at universities or research institutions are often confronted with the problem that their institutions no longer allow them to go to conflict regions. Increasingly universities are finding it too risky for their scholars to visit conflict regions and do research there. Of course, it is more dangerous to do fieldwork in regions where crisis prevails and in civil war zones, than for example, diaspora communities in Europe. Nevertheless, if social anthropologists, political scientists, or sociologists no longer go into the field, we lose a lot.

Most of my research in Kurdistan could be only done because I am not a full-time employee of a university. Most of my fieldwork is funded by projects with very limited institutional backing and done on my own risk. Nevertheless, I do think that this fieldwork is important.

BECOMING A TERRORIST?

Finally, doing research with Kurdish political movements also includes doing research with armed groups that are considered to be "terrorists" by some states, including some Western states.[6] I have always insisted strongly that academic freedom also includes contact with real or imagined "terrorists." In my research about Jihadism, another field in which I do research, I also had contact with ISIS-fighters and other people who are more readily considered terrorists. In some European states, this has become a legal problem in recent years, because even contacting terrorists can make you appear suspicious in the eyes of some prosecutors.

This problem does not only exist in Kurdish studies. Basque anthropologist Joseba Zulaika, who conducted research about ETA, emphasized that "any ethnographer of subjects labelled 'terrorist' may ipso facto become liable to charges of contamination by merely having transgressed the taboo of never talking to them, even if they are neighbours with whom one has to deal on a daily basis"(Zulaika 1995, 216). This is an even bigger problem in Kurdish studies than it is for people who specifically research armed underground organizations, because movements which are considered as "terrorist" by some states in the region rule certain parts of Kurdistan. Moreover, some of Kurdistan's main political actors are considered "terrorists" by some of the states in the region, in particular the PKK and its front organizations, which are listed as terrorist organizations by Turkey and its allies.

If you carry out research in Rojava, in Sinjar, or in Qandil, the hotspots of activities of the PKK and its sister organizations, you must be prepared for the possibility that you could be denounced as a sympathizer of terrorists or even a terrorist yourself, by Turkish officials or lobby organizations, especially if you also do some outreach. For example, I recently faced public denouncement by high-ranking Turkish politicians in Turkish newspapers, interventions by Turkish officials, and AKP-lobbyists against lectures at universities and public insults on social media calling me a "Zionist top terrorist," and with other offensive statements. Besides describing critiques of Turkish policies as "terrorism," the other tactic of AKP-lobby organizations in Europe is to denounce them as "Islamophobic." Hundreds of Facebook accounts denounced me of being a PKK-member after I criticized Turkey's invasion in Efrîn on Austrian television. There is not a lot that you can do against such things and the situation might get even worse with the increasing authoritarianism of the Erdoğan government. The Turkish secret service and lobby organizations of the ruling Justice and Development Party (AKP) in the country also have a wide presence in Europe. For them, every picture you take of any armed fighter or even pictures of pictures of Abdullah Öcalan, the jailed Kurdish leader, can be used to prove that you are a "terrorist."

CONCLUSION

Kurdish studies take place in a very sensitive political environment. Everybody who starts to get involved with it has to realize that s/he is researching in a controversial field. There is hardly anything you can research in Kurdistan that is "unpolitical." For us as researchers, the only way to deal with it is to do honest and high-quality research. This means that we should neither become a mouthpiece for any political party, nor should we fear power and steer away from politically sensitive topics. The fun thing about working on Kurdistan is therefore that you still have the chance to fight for academic freedom and your research is relevant.

It can even be said that if everybody likes your research, something is wrong. Research in Kurdish studies should shed light on existing power dynamics and should reflect on how material is collected in the field. This means also to reflect about different layers of power (state, para-states, dominant and less dominant political parties, ethno-religious groups, etc.) and their influence on the access of material. As pointed out earlier, research should take into account more diverse narratives and voices—within and outside Kurdish society. Thus, Kurdish studies should also produce research that is challenged, not only by the Kurds' enemies, but also debated in Kurdish circles. Kurdish studies must be controversial! Only such works will enrich the debate.

NOTES

1. Western Kurdistan = Syrian Kurdistan. Since 2012 supporters of the PKK-sister-party PYD established a de facto autonomous region in Rojava. They established a kind of council-democracy with a strong participation of women. However, this political structure is not recognized by their Kurdish rivals with political connections to Barzanis PDK in Iraq. Their armed forces played an important role in the struggle against the jihadists of the so-called Islamic State.

2. Village guards: Kurdish armed counter-guerilla who work with the Turkish state against the guerilla of the PKK.

3. Cahşh (cehş) is a pejorative word for the Kurdish collaborators of Saddam Husseins regime. Literally it means "young donkeys" and it is widely used in Iraqi Kurdistan for the different Kurdish militias working with the Baathist regime against the Peshmerga.

4. After the Sinjar (Şingal)-Region was recaptured from ISIS by different militias, these different militias were in control of different parts of the region until the Iraqi army took over most of the region in October 2017. However, until today a pro-PKK force led by local Êzîdî (Yekîneyên Berxwedana Şingalê, YBŞ) still controls the northwest of the region.

5. Ahrar ash-Sham, Liwat al-Tawhid, and Jabhat al-Nusra are different Islamist militias who controlled Azaz in 2015. Jabhat al-Nusra was still a part of al-Qaida back then. Liwat al-Tawhid was close to the Muslim Brotherhood and Ahrar ash-Sham was a politically salaftist group closely linked to jihadism, however, with a regional focus on Syria and not with a global focus like al-Qaida or ISIS.

6. The PKK is still mentioned in the list of persons, groups, and entities involved in terrorist acts and subject to restrictive measures of the European Union, set down in common position 2001/931/CFSP. While some EU states do not actively oppress the PKK, others like Germany are very active in closing down associations with PKK affiliations and even repress the use of any symbol of the PKK. Even more, Germany even criminalizes the use of symbols of the Syrian-Kurdish YPG and YPJ although they are not considered as terrorist organizations by the common position of the European Union. Like the European Union, the United States also considers the PKK as a terrorist organization. The United States even listed the Iraqi Kurdistan Democratic Party (KDP) and the Patriotic Union of Kurdistan (PUK) as terrorist organizations under the Patriot Act between 2001 and 2015—although it had a military alliance with them already since 2003.

BIBLIOGRAPHY

Andrews, William. 2018. *Die Japanische Rote Armee Fraktion*. Wien: Bahoe Books.

Genet, Jean. 1989. *Prisoner of Love*. London: Picador, 9.

Green, Linda. 1995. "Living in a State of Fear." In *Fieldwork under Fire. Contemporary Studies of Violence and Survival,* edited by Carolyn Nordstrom and Antonius C. G. M Robben, 105–127. Berkeley/Los Angeles/London: University of California Press.

Kurt, Mehmet. 2017. *Kurdish Hizbullah in Turkey: Islamism, Violence and the State*. London: Pluto Press.

Nordstrom, Carolyn. 1995. "War on the Front Lines." In *Fieldwork under Fire. Contemporary Studies of Violence and Survival,* edited by Carolyn Nordstrom and Antonius C. G. M Robben, 129–154. Berkeley/Los Angeles/London: University of California Press.

Robben, Antonius C. G., and Nordstrom, Carolyn. 1995. "The Anthropology and Ethnography of Violence and Sociopolitical Conflict." In *Fieldwork under Fire. Contemporary Studies of Violence and Survival,* edited by Carolyn Nordstrom and

Antonius C. G. M Robben, 1–23. Berkeley/Los Angeles/London: University of California Press.

Schmidinger, Thomas. 2018. *Rojava: Revolution, War and the Future of Syria´s Kurds*. London: Pluto Press.

Swedenburg, Ted. 2004. "With Genet in the Palestinian Field." In *Violence in War and Peace: An Anthology,* edited by Nancy Scheper-Hughes and Philippe Bourgois, 25–40. Malden, MA/Oxford/Carlton: Blackwell Publishing.

Zulaika, Joseba. 1995. "The Antropologist as Terrorist." In *Fieldwork under Fire: Contemporary Studies of Violence and Survival,* edited by Carolyn Nordstrom and Antonius C. G. M Robben, 205–222. Berkeley/Los Angeles/London: University of California Press.*Thomas Schmidinger*

Conclusion

Reflections on Research: Challenges and Opportunities

Begum Zorlu and Yasin Duman

This edited volume was set off to contribute to the reflexivist turn in qualitative research methods and Kurdish studies by exploring under what preconditions and circumstances knowledge production takes place (Baser and Toivanen 2018; Day 2012; Neumann and Neumann 2015; Sultana 2007). At a contentious time that is dominated by armed conflict, civil resistance and repression, there is an urgent need to enhance the debate on ontology, epistemology, methodology, and the related issues, such as researcher positionality. The contributors of this book aid this effort by portraying sincere, critical, and illuminating accounts of their own research processes, which elucidate the tasks both the researcher and the researched face. All of the chapters in the volume elaborate on the practical and ethical dimensions of the research and underline the power structures that shape available knowledge. Therefore, we believe that this volume will be beneficial not only for researchers and students in Kurdish studies, but also for any qualitative researcher who is engaged with these debates.

The dynamics of each research project are different. Therefore, as McAreavey and Das (2013, 216) emphasize, research processes cannot be standardized as the field is full of uncertainties and varying dynamics. However, different research practices expand one's horizons about their positionality and how one can tackle the challenges of the field. The researcher, consequently, should perform fieldwork with what McAreavey and Das (2013, 215) label "phronesis" (*practical wisdom*), to "exercise critical judgement" and "employ site-specific strategies," to undertake the challenges that emerge in the field. The experiences shared in this volume contribute to understanding how this practical wisdom can be employed.

In this concluding chapter, we elaborate on the sections of the book with an emphasis on the literature on qualitative methods under three interrelated headlines: the importance and dynamics of positionality, the external and systemic challenges of studying the studied phenomenon, and the opportunities-constraints of fieldwork. Positionality is the most significant issue that all authors considered to be of paramount importance, due to its impact on the research, through generating credible results, and grasping the path of responsibility. Therefore, we aim to explain the notions of trust, location, time, and "communionship" in research processes, to grasp the complex account of the changing positions and the dynamics that alter those standpoints. Second, as knowledge production is tied to external and historically patterned forms of power, unpacking, and creating awareness of these structures is crucial (Foucault 2002). Some chapters of the book tackled these visible and invisible structures that shape the scope of the research and underlined how embracing an essentialist perspective can hamper the research. Thus, in this section, we emphasize the notion of "epistemological injustice," the impact of authoritarian rule and the institutional constraints that affect the research process. Lastly, in order to enhance the dialogue on fieldwork experiences, we present the opportunities and constraints that can emerge in the field. By reflecting on the chapters of the book, we discuss the impact of the polarized nature of inquiry, the role of the gatekeepers, and strategies to enhance the formulation and conduct of the research.

THE IMPORTANCE AND DYNAMICS
OF POSITIONALITY

A strong relation exists between a researcher's (multiple) positionalities and his/her research (Mason-Bish 2018; Ryan 2015). Positionality can be termed as the experiences of one's "previous life," which actively shape the identity of the researcher and motivate him or her to choose a subject, formulate research questions, find a way to access the research field, define the dynamics of the fieldwork and lastly, impact the conclusions of the research (Day 2012; McAreavey and Das 2013; Sultana 2007). While researchers' positionality can be attributed to more static characteristics like gender, age, ethnicity, and social class (Chacko 2004; Sultana 2007), dynamic characteristics, like political views, also determine the relationship between the researcher and the researched.

The literature mainly divides these position(s) of the researcher as "insider" or "outsider" to mark how they relate to the researched group but also to underline the power structures that are evident in the research (Chacko 2004, 58). As Voloder (2014, 3) underlines, while insiderness has been praised for how it equates to easy access to the field, the advantages of being an outsider can materialize by providing neutrality. This is because the insider position has been questioned for its "academic authority." Yet, these two positions are degrees of distance (Voloder 2014), not challenges that should be overcome, but reflected upon (Bucerius 2011; Mikecz 2012). As Baser and Toivanen (2018, 2069) underline, there can be "moments of insiderness and outsiderness" that carry the potential to change dynamics of research, and the character of a researcher at any time. This can also be defined as a form of closeness or remoteness from the interviewee, which depends not only on the "previous life" of the researcher, but multiple dynamics. As Mickez (2012, 491) emphasizes, a researcher's knowledgeability decreases the "status imbalance" between the researcher and researched, as it enhances the conduct of a "meaningful and informed conversation."

This book's authors and editors moved away from this duality and are in consensus that positionality is not static, and that there is no clear-cut answer as to who would count as an insider or an outsider. As Arpacık (115) has stated in this volume, the phenomenon of insiderness or outsiderness are not "purely historical, cultural constructs," but they are also "political, situational, and imposed." Therefore, for Arpacık (110) while insiderness can occur "as moments of proximity," outsiderness can come about in "moments of distance that transpire in dialogue." In the same way, O'Connor and Çelik (140) argue in this volume that their positionality becomes important "differently at specific times and places" and is dependent on the researchers' behavior in the field.

As Acar and Uluğ embark upon in this volume, we usually have multiple identities and even though one part of our identity can be in conflict with the researched in the field, the other may be consonant. Positionality, driving from these contentious identities, shapes the field with possibilities, but also limits them at the same time. Askari (215) states in her chapter that being aware of positionality sets of, "an ongoing process of coming to terms with one's different selves." She stresses that as a diaspora returnee to Kurdistan, she has been labeled as an "other" and that "confusion" about her identity continued in her research process. Her chapter, in this sense, is of critical importance for comprehending the dynamics of this duality, as she clearly showed that insiderness is not based on static characteristics like ethnicity.

One important theme that comes along with positionality is building trust with the researched community. Gaining one's trust can be a lengthy endeavor that is in relation with dynamics that the researcher can and cannot control. McAreavey and Das (2013) underline that "identifying commonalities" with the researched contributes to building trust. As social statuses do not solely account for positionality, there is an evident quest by the researched group to "attribut[e] identities" to the researcher (Baser and Toivanen 2018, 2075). We saw an effort to affiliate the researcher to a position in many of the chapters in this volume. As Casier underlined in this volume, even though she could have been labeled as an evident outsider, members of the researched community aimed to bound her with the notion of solidarity as the interviewees viewed her ethnicity as facing similar restrictions. However, as Schäfers (79–80) stated in her chapter, a resourceful outsider could take the role of a promoter which can provide benefits for the researched group. The researched community also can frame the research as an arena where their voices can be heard and expect the researcher to promote their "cause." Schäfers's and Casier's chapters elaborated on this issue by underlining that this also bore a danger as there can be the rise of expectations by the researched or an aim to instrumentalize the position of the researcher.

The expectations that the research process generates and how it affects the dynamics of the researcher and the researched is crucial on the arena of trust. First, the interviewed group might be disappointed if they do not see an outcome that the research brings and lose trust in the researcher. In order to avoid these possibly false expectations the researcher must be transparent and earnest about the possible implications, impact, and scope of the research. This can also aid balancing the power relationship. Positionality, therefore, is crucial for the sake of the research as it can build trust with the interviewee. Therefore, a reflexivist approach can contribute to overcoming the hierarchy between the researcher and it sets a tone for the researcher (Chacko 2004, 52). What Chacko (2004, 52) names as "active measures" of openness about the research agenda can help to "equalize the balance of power" between the scholar and the researched.

On the other hand, the location of the interview and the concept of time are crucial to grasp the relationship between the researcher and the researched. Given how individuals affix meaning to spaces where an interview occurs is significant for the unfolding execution of the research. If one feels an affinity or sense of belonging to a space, they can be more welcoming to interviewers and feel more comfortable. As Mutlu (171) puts it "conducting research in a place that belonged to them (the interviewed) gave them a self-confidence and therefore the power originating from being in their own places." One crucial parallelism between chapters was how Mutlu and Alpman experienced similar negative encounters in urban metropolises, which were spaces that did not belong to their interviewees. As their accounts demonstrated, it was more difficult to establish trust with the interviewees, and there was a constant, pervasive questioning and suspicion that emerged from some of the interviewees. Yet, from their reflections it was evident that the distrust was not due to the faults of the researcher, but to the external problem of state policies of oppression. This was also stated previously by Bahar Baser (Baser and Toivanen 2018), who stressed that she felt the burden of the "sins of the Turkish state" in her reflection as a Turkish researcher on the Kurdish issue. Alpman (94) has similarly stated in this volume that "the insecurity toward the state was reflected on [him]" and he was unable to convince some of the interviewees at some points of the research. It is also difficult to be questioned or being blamed by the interviewees constantly; however, the researcher should become resilient to such questionings to continue the research. This resilience can produce "critical moments" (Baser and Toivanen 2018) during which bonds and trust can be formed, especially in case of multiple interviews with same participants (Oakley 1981, 56). The reoccurring encounters can transform this perception over time.

EXTERNAL AND SYSTEMIC CHALLENGES THAT THE RESEARCHER AND THE RESEARCHED FACE

The quest to provide a reflexive account comes from disabling epistemological problems that can drive from the subjectivity of the researcher (Day 2012, 63) or through power relations. Apart from the decisions the researcher makes, there are structural constraints in research processes, in our case, studying the Kurdish regions and population. In this volume, Arpacık (106) underlines that these barriers are contributions to a dreadful "epistemological injustice" and as categorizations are shaped by the status quo and the lack of alternative framing, which creates the danger of making the minoritized groups more vulnerable. It also contributes to the state becoming the sole "controlling body for the knowledge production" (Arpacık 106) which limits the scope of research.

The fact that Kurds are a "stateless people" has also shaped knowledge production as they do not have the resources of a state which oversees processes of knowledge production. Winrow's chapter in this volume argued that approaching Kurdish studies from the angle of a reflexive and transnational or global history in turn requires being mindful of how Kurds have been constructed and represented in various imperial and national archives. It echoed the postcolonial insight (Sultana 2007) that scholars need to approach archives as ethnographic sites rather than neutral repositories of information. Explaining how a dearth of recorded information on certain topics may eliminate the use of archival research altogether, it suggested that researchers use multiple archives to gain a more complete picture of history and by subjecting archives and how they are used, to critique in order to advance emancipatory and critical research. Likewise, Arpacık (116) underlined that the researcher should bear in mind the "systemic challenges that are imposed on a certain people or region" and suggested that they should refrain from knowledge production that "legitimize nation states, its boundaries, and its ontology."

This reflexive turn is also followed by Jongerden (31) in this volume, as he states that inquiries that elaborate on fixed identities (re) produce essentialization of place in academia. Therefore, in order to understand the daily lives of people we study, he suggested that we should not reify them and instead should seek to explain their conduct with dynamic concepts. Similarly, Eccarius-Kelly and Alpman stated in their chapters than the researchers must be cautious not to reproduce discrimination systems internalized by the society and not to reproduce such essentialist approach (see also Nowicka and Cieslik 2014). Therefore, Eccarius-Kelly (4) suggested that the researcher must conduct critical ethnography which she defined as "going beyond practices of replication and affirmation of historically and politically normalized power structures," abandoning strict neutrality and focusing on "the perpetuation of inequalities and injustices."

Lastly, one crucial debate is on the formal institutions, mainly universities in which our research is conducted. The limitations start quite early on as many students in political and social sciences or international students are exposed to these ethical considerations during their bachelor's studies. During postgraduate and doctorate studies, most of these institutions expect a linear research process that follows the sequence of determining a research question, reviewing the relevant literature and methodology, going to the field and reporting. However, the research process is often not linear, but cyclical or repetitive, depending on how and when one acquires results. The researcher might even change their question when confronted with ontological challenges and arising issues. Also, in order to conduct fieldwork, universities tend to ask for an approval from ethics committees (McAreavey and Das 2013). As McAreavey and Das (2013, 114) state, these often take the form of static and one-off discussions about ethics that are not at all preparatory as "moral decisions made by researchers in the field . . . are central to the research process." On the other hand, the barriers of institutions, in the form of ethic forms, as Schmidinger underlined in his chapter, restrict the arena of maneuver of the researcher and shape the way in which the research can be conducted.

THE LIMITATIONS AND THE
OPPORTUNITIES OF THE FIELD

As the researcher has the superiority of discursive framing of the interviewee, the relationship can be perceived as a hegemonic-hierarchical one. However, the field both has its merits and challenges and there is a relationship of mutual dependency between the researcher and the researched. In this manner, Ezzy (2010, 164) states that in a good research neither the interviewer nor the interviewee dominates each other. We appreciate a process of acquiring knowledge to which both the interviewer and interviewee contribute, which Ezzy (2010, 168) calls, "communion rather than conquest."

In this sense, the encounters and dynamics of the field both shape the interviewer and the interviewee. For example, as Sirnate underlines, in some contexts, the fact that a woman is the researcher "could be defiance" (2014, 401). The literature and some of the texts in this volume show that while there can be challenges for women who are not expected to do research in such contexts, this can also contribute to the changing perceptions of that given society. Therefore, the research process becomes not solely a "conquest" where the researcher tries to grab the most beneficial information for his or her research but thinking in a holistic way becomes a "communion" that integrates the members of the interviewed community.

Sirnate (2014, 398) states that the field is a "constantly evolving, dynamic, and unpredictable universe." One of the main questions of research processes is how to enter the field and how to maintain access as a researcher. The fieldwork required by research includes multiple actors (which can be clashing with each other) and constant negotiation on the researchers' presence and conduct. Researchers usually enter the field with people or groups known as the gatekeepers, who introduce and acquaint potential interviewees. The gatekeepers possess influence as "they have the power to deny access to the researcher and they may also influence whether individuals opt in and out of a process" (Ruth and Das 2011, 116). Ruth and Das (2011, 122) underline how this brings about "active engagement" with gatekeepers, which the researcher must maintain through the fieldwork. Yet, as Bucerius (2011) underlines, gatekeepers can have their own agenda which can bring about arbitrary restrictions and pressures. Likewise, during the research, the researcher is dependent on the interviewee and, especially in conflict zones, the scale of dependency increases, as Schmidinger underlined in his chapter. To survive and conduct research in the field, researches have to adjust to the structures and have to find reliable gatekeepers.

On the other hand, the researcher is responsible of both protecting him and herself and the interviewees. In this volume, some of the authors reflected on choosing to anonymize the participants and not using recordable data on their interviews due to security reasons. Mahmod underlined that even though she was conducting research with online communities, she used pseudonyms to ensure anonymity. Alternatively, Casier discussed how recording interviews could have frightened the researched groups, led to self-censorship, and also externally be used to harm them. Also, O'Connor and Çelik (page number) chose to not record their interviews and found that it provided a form of "enhanced intimacy" with the interviewees. They also underlined that they enhanced their questions through time by "leaving the 'sensitive topics' to a further period," by choosing not to ask "why questions" and by being more creative about the questions they posed during their interactions.

Lastly, while one has to take into consideration these kinds of active engagements of protection that are mostly related to authoritarian research environments (Malthaner 2014), authoritarian rule is crucially important in polarizing the political sphere, which the researchers are not excluded from. This polarization can dominate the field and push the researcher to make explicit their loyalties and choose one object of allegiance over another. There can be division points that the researcher is not aware of and the researcher may also be pushed by the environment to "choose sides." This was visible in Schäfers chapter, which demonstrated how the divisions in the field play out to affect the trust between the interviewer and the interviewee. As these tensions determine further access to the field along with maintaining relationships with the interviewees, the researcher must be careful to balance the impact of polarization during his or her study.

PROMISING NEW VISTAS TO EXPLORE

This edited volume set off as an effort to reject the fixed perceptions of positionality and investigate the dynamic processes of knowledge production. Therefore, it has demonstrated that the boundaries of being an insider or an outsider are fluid and the distinction is on a "dynamic continuum" (Mikecz 2012, 483) that is negotiated in the process of the research.

The research process can occur in a way that challenges all the expectations of the researcher. Therefore, he or she should be equipped to grapple both ethical and practical considerations before and after the research. The researcher should also not forget that they too possess emotional investments (Ezzy 2010) and sentiments. Emotions can be hard to reveal, yet they are usually a part of the research and the researcher should listen to his or her intuition and judge whether to halt or withdraw from the process. Similarly, a researcher has a huge burden on their shoulders, as they bear responsibility for research participants. Therefore, entering "dangerous fields" is not solely about protecting yourself from emotional or physical dangers, but also protecting your interviewees from various types of dangers that could come in the form of state repression or emotional unease. This is "the burden" of the researcher as there are no uniform rules on the ethics and the responsibility that research requires.

Fieldwork is an arena of learning. In order to conduct a fruitful interview, we argue that the researcher should actively engage in equating the relationship with the interviewee. This does not mean that the researcher must be approving or disapproving the statements of the interviewee but creating a shared space based on trust and openness. The interviewer must also back up the interviewing process with statements on the rationale and possible scope of impact of the research as the interaction can create over-expectations for the interviewees.

Apart from all its "dangers" and challenges researchers have been and still are conducting exceptional research both on the field and through the use of various resources. The "dangerousness" of the field does not solely come from conducting research in conflict zones, but also in form of challenging the state-promoted perspectives. We agree with Arpacık's notion of "epistemological injustice" as this "dangerousness" makes the groups more vulnerable and puts pressure on knowledge production. It also normalizes the pressures and persecutions as the researcher is responsible for entering dangerous fields. Therefore, as a take away point, we wish to remind that in historical and discursive research or fieldwork, as Alpman (90) states, the researcher who is "the owner of the point of view" should be aware of his or her social privileges. As the chapters in this book demonstrate, self-reflection and responsibility, therefore, should continue throughout all stages of the research. However, as Maxey (1999, 206) argued, we can never know all the implications of our research and actions, or "how they will be perceived, interpreted and consumed." Yet, this does not decrease our responsibilities as the researcher. By discussing our experiences in the field, we can enhance the debate and learn from similar processes of knowledge production, circulation, and its uses.

BIBLIOGRAPHY

Baser, Bahar and Mari Toivanen. 2018. "Politicized and depoliticized ethnicities, power relations and temporality: Insights to outsider research from comparative and transnational fieldwork." *Ethnic and Racial Studies* 41, no. 11: 2067–2084.

Chacko, Elizabeth. 2004. "Positionality and Praxis: Fieldwork Experiences in Rural India." *Singapore Journal of Tropical Geography* 25, no. 1: 51–63.

Day, Suzanne. 2012. "A Reflexive Lens: Exploring Dilemmas of Qualitative Methodology through the Concept of Reflexivity." *Qualitative Sociology Review* 8, no. 1: 60–85.

Ezzy, Douglas. 2010. "Qualitative Interviewing as an Embodied Emotional Performance." *Qualitative Inquiry* 16, no. 3: 163–170.

Foucault, Michel. 2002. *The Archaeology of Knowledge.* London: Routledge.

Malthaner, Stefan. 2014. "Fieldwork in the Context of Violent Conflict and Authoritarian Regimes." In *Methodological Practices in Social Movement Research*, edited by Donatella Della Porta, 173–195. Oxford: Oxford University Press.

Mason-Bish, Hannah. 2018. "The Elite Delusion: Reflexivity, Identity and Positionality in Qualitative Research." *Qualitative Research*, 1–14. https://doi.org/10.1177/1468794118770078

Maxey, Ian. 1999. "Beyond boundaries? Activism, Academia, Reflexivity and Research." *Area* 31, no. 3: 199–208.

McAreavey, Ruth, and Chaitali Das. 2013. "A Delicate Balancing Act: Negotiating with Gatekeepers for Ethical Research When Researching Minority Communities." *International Journal of Qualitative Methods* 12, no. 1: 113–131.

Mikecz, Robert. 2012. "Interviewing Elites: Addressing Methodological Issues." *Qualitative Inquiry* 18, no. 6: 482–493.

Neumann, Cecilie Basberg, and Iver B. Neumann. 2015. "Uses of the Self: Two Ways of Thinking about Scholarly Situatedness and Method." *Millennium: Journal of International Studies* 43, no. 3: 798–819.

Nowicka, Magdalena, and Anna Cieslik. 2014. "Beyond Methodological Nationalism in Insider Research with Migrants." *Migration Studies* 2, no. 1: 1–15.

Oakley, Ann. 1981. "Interviewing Women: A Contradiction in Terms." In *Doing Feminist Research*, edited by Helen Roberts, 30–61. Boston and Kegan Paul: Routledge.

Ryan, Louise. 2015. "'Inside' and 'Outside' What or Where? Researching Migration through Multi-Positionalities." *Forum: Qualitative Social Research* 16, no. 2. http://dx.doi.org/10.17169/fqs-16.2.2333

Sirnate, Vasundhara. 2014. "Positionality, Personal Insecurity, and Female Empathy in Security Studies Research." *American Political Science Association* 47, no. 2: 398–401.

Sultana, Farhana. 2007. "Reflexivity, Positionality and Participatory Ethics: Negotiating Fieldwork Dilemmas in International Research." *ACME: An International E-Journal for Critical Geographies* 6, no. 3: 374–385.

Voloder, Lejla. 2014. "Introduction: Insiderness in Migration and Mobility Research, Conceptual Considerations." In *Insider Research on Migration and Mobility: International Perspectives on Researcher Positioning*, edited by Lejla Voloder and Liudmila Kirpitchenko, 1–17. London: Routledge.

Index

About the Contributors

Yasemin Gülsüm Acar received her PhD from Claremont Graduate University in 2015, where she specialized in social identity and identity politicization through collective action. Yasemin's research interests include social activism and identity constructs in Turkey, political protest and its consequences, political solidarity, politicization and social identity, and intergroup relations/conflict.

Polat S. Alpman was born in Istanbul, Turkey, in the neighborhood of Kocamustafapaşa. He holds a master's degree and a doctorate in sociology from Ankara University. Alpman, in addition to several book chapters and articles, published his book titled *Esmer Yakalılar: Kent, Sınıf, Kimlik ve Kürt Emeği* (Esmer Collar: Urban, Class, Identity and Kurdish Labor) with İletişim Publishing in 2016. He currently works at Yalova University as an assistant professor.

Demet Arpacık is a doctoral student in the Language, Context, and Culture strand of Urban Education department at the Graduate Center of the City University of New York. She received her M.Ed. in Educational Leadership and Administration from Boston College in 2013. She is currently a Graduate Teaching Fellow at the Educational Foundations department at Hunter College and Middle and Secondary Education department at Lehman College, New York.

Lana Askari is a PhD candidate in Social Anthropology with Visual Media at the Granada Centre for Visual Anthropology, University of Manchester. Trained in anthropology (MPhil Social Anthropology, University of Cambridge) and documentary filmmaking (MA Visual Anthropology, University of Manchester), her research focuses on migration, future imaginations, and the anthropology of planning and infrastructure with a focus on the region of Iraqi Kurdistan.

Bahar Baser is a senior research fellow at the Centre for Trust, Peace and Social Relations (CTPSR). She is also an associate research fellow at the Security Institute for Governance and Leadership in Africa (SIGLA), Stellenbosch University, South Africa. She will be a senior visiting fellow at the Kroc Institute for International Peace Studies, University of Notre Dame between January and June 2019. Baser completed a PhD in Social and Political Sciences at the European University Institute in Florence, Italy.

Marlies Casier is a visiting professor at the Ghent University, Department of Conflict and Development Studies. She holds a master's in Moral Philosophy and a master's in Conflict and Development from the Ghent University. Her PhD was awarded the "Jaarprijs Politicologie 2012" by the Dutch Political Science Association.

Semih Celik obtained his PhD degree in 2017 from the European University Institute, Department of History and Civilization. He worked at the Center on Social Movement Studies (COSMOS), Scuola Normale Superiore in 2017 as a visiting scholar on the contemporary refugee "crisis" in Turkey. He is currently employed as a postdoctoral research fellow at Koc University, Department of History.

Yasin Duman is a PhD student at Center for Trust Peace and Social Relations, Coventry University. He studied BA Psychology at Boğaziçi University and MA Conflict Analysis and Resolution program at Sabancı University, Turkey.

Vera Eccarius-Kelly is a professor of Comparative Politics at Siena College in Albany, NY, with a specialization on Kurdish and Central American Studies. Her research interests focus on diaspora Kurdish political mobilization and revolutionary movements in indigenous and ethnic minority communities. She completed her Ph.D. at the Fletcher School of Law and Diplomacy at Tufts University in Boston in 2002. She serves as the chair of the Scholars at Risk Initiative at Siena College.

Joost Jongerden is associate professor at Rural Sociology, Wageningen University, the Netherlands and project professor at the Asian Platform for Global Sustainability & Transcultural Studies at Kyoto University in Japan. He is also editor of Kurdish Studies. His research centres around the question how people create and maintain a liveable life under conditions of precarity. This research interest has expressed itself in two interrelated research tracks, one focusing on the ways in which people develop alternatives for market induced insecurities, the other how people develop alternatives for state induced insecurities. This he refers to as self-organized practices or 'Do-It-Yourself-Development.'

Jowan Mahmod has a PhD in Media and Communications from Goldsmiths University of London, United Kingdom. She is the author of *Kurdish Diaspora Online: From Imagined Community to Managing Communities* (2016, Palgrave Macmillan). Between 2013 and 2015 she was settled in the Kurdistan Region of Iraq conducting fieldwork on Kurdish repatriation and diaspora as social capital, exploring how lost refugees can turn into national resources.

Yeşim Mutlu studied sociology in the Middle East Technical University (METU) and graduated in 2006. She received her master's degree in sociology from METU in 2009 with her thesis "Turkey's Experience of Forced Migration after 1980s and Social Integration: A Comparative Analysis of Diyarbakır and İstanbul." In 2015, she was awarded a research grant by Raoul Wallenberg Institute, Turkey, and conducted the research on Syrian children's risk of statelessness in Turkey. In 2016, she received a grant from The Center for Gender Studies at Koç University and worked on a research project focusing on women's and LGBTI's perception of safety and security and their coping strategies with the spiral of violence in Turkey. With the article based on this research findings, she won Dicle Koğacıoğlu Article Award by Sabancı University Gender and Women's Studies Center of Excellence.

Francis O'Connor is a senior researcher at the Peace Research Institute Frankfurt since June 2017. He was part of the PRIME consortium working on Lone Actor Radicalization at the University of Aarhus from 2016 to 2017. He obtained his PhD from the Department of Social and Political Sciences at the European University Institute in 2014; his thesis analyzed the relationship between the PKK and its support networks.

Thomas Schmidinger is a political scientist as well as a social and cultural anthropologist. He has a lecturing position at the Vienna University's Institute for Political Science and at the Universities of Applied Sciences Vorarlberg and Upper Austria and is affiliated researcher of the Institute for the Sociology of Law and Criminology. Schmidinger is Secretary General of the Austrian Association for Kurdish Studies and coeditor of the Vienna Kurdish Studies Yearbook.

Marlene Schäfers is a social anthropologist and currently FWO [PEGA-SUS]² Marie Skłodowska-Curie Fellow at the Department for Conflict and Development Studies at Ghent University, Belgium. She obtained a PhD from the University of Cambridge in 2015 with a dissertation investigating the struggles for voice and audibility on the part of Kurdish women in Turkey.

Mari Toivanen currently works as a Postdoctoral Researcher in an Academy of Finland project, at the Swedish School of Social Science, University of Helsinki. Her research interests include migration-related phenomena that focus on migrant generations, political activism, diaspora politics as well as on identity, belonging and home. She holds a PhD in Social Sciences from the University of Turku and is an affiliated member of the School for Advanced Studies in Social Sciences (EHESS) in Paris. She wishes to thank the Academy of Finland (project: 287667) for the funding that made the work with this book possible.

Özden Melis Uluğ received her PhD in Psychology from Jacobs University Bremen, Germany, in 2016. She holds a BSc major in Psychology and a BA minor in Studies in Politics from Middle East Technical University in Turkey. She received her MSc in Political Psychology with distinction from Queen's University Belfast in Northern Ireland in 2011.

Marc Sinan Winrow is a PhD candidate in International Relations at the London School of Economics and Political Science. He completed his undergraduate degree in the University of Cambridge, and also holds an MSc in the Theory and History of International Relations from the LSE. His research interests include historical sociology, intellectual history, and political theory, including international political sociology, with a focus on the connection between the global and the local.

Begum Zorlu is a PhD candidate in the Department of International Politics at City, University of London. She holds an MSc in Democracy and Comparative Politics from University College London and an MA in Conflict Analysis and Resolution from Sabanci University. Her research focuses on social movements with a focus on the role of the political opposition and comparative peace processes.

www.ingramcontent.com/pod-product-compliance
Lightning Source LLC
Chambersburg PA
CBHW022304280326
41932CB00010B/978